Atul's CURRIES of the WORLD

ATUL KOCHHAR

A.

First published in Great Britain in 2013 by Absolute Press, an imprint of Bloomsbury Publishing Plc

Reprinted 2014.

Absolute Press
Scarborough House
29 James Street West
Bath BA1 2BT

Phone 44 (0) 1225 316013
Fax 44 (0) 1225 445836
E-mail office@absolutepress.co.uk
Website www.absolutepress.co.uk

Publisher Jon Croft
Commissioning Editor Meg Avent
Art Direction and Design
Matt Inwood
Editor Imogen Fortes
Assistant Editors
Norma MacMillan and
Gillian Haslam
Indexer Zoe Ross
Photography Mike Cooper
Food Styling Atul Kochhar

ISBN: 9781906650797

Printed and bound in China by South China Printing Company, Dongguan, Guangdong

A catalogue record of this book is available from the British Library.

Bloomsbury Publishing Plc
50 Bedford Square
London WC1B 3DP
www.bloomsbury.com

Bloomsbury is a trademark of Bloomsbury Publishing Plc.

A note about the text
This book is set in Minion and Helvetica Neue. Minion was created by Robert Slimbach, inspired by fonts of the late Renaissance. Helvetica was designed in 1957 by Max Miedinger of the Swiss-based Haas foundry. In the early 1980s, Linotype redrew the entire Helvetica family. The result was Helvetica Neue.

I would like to dedicate this book to
my mother, Mrs. S. Kochhar.
Throughout my journey, my father
was my inspiration; my mother has
been my strength.

She was my teacher at school
and my mother at home – but more
importantly, a very good friend who
I could talk to in all my hours of need.
Her strong will has given me and my
siblings a strength and belief that we
can achieve anything that we desire.
My journey from home to here has
had lots of doses of encouragement
from her – words, such as:

'Success without struggle
is absolutely useless';
'Believe in yourself and people
will believe in you';
'Failure is a very important feeling
to be able to enjoy success'.

All of these have had a deep impact on
my formative years. I hope that I can
pass my mother's values on to my own
children and guide them as she has
guided me through life – as a brilliant
parent and as an amazing friend.
Thank you for being there when
I need you most. Mom! I love you!

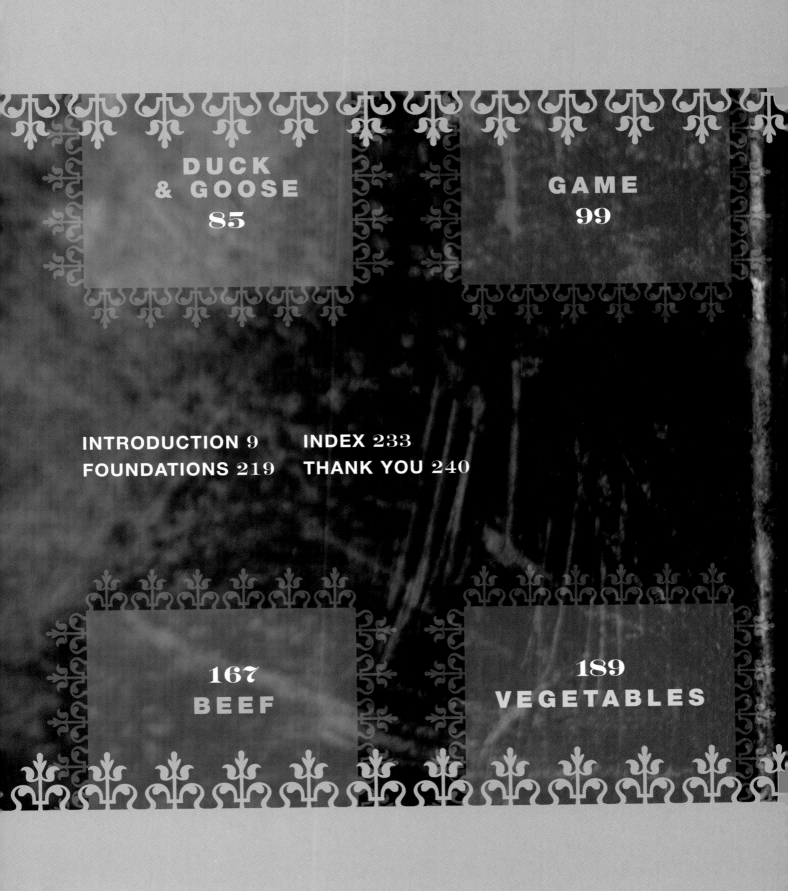

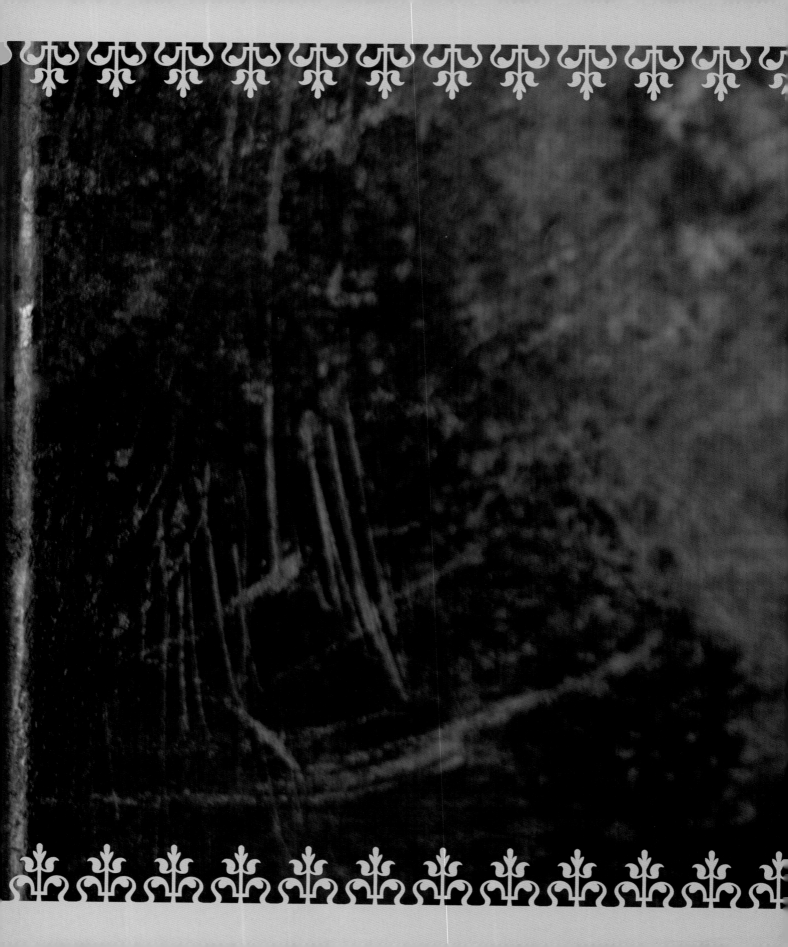

INTRODUCTION

> It is now widely acknowledged that a chicken tikka masala trounces good old fish and chips and steak and kidney pie as the winner of Britain's favourite dish.

But aside from knowing that the dish sits alongside an Indian repertoire and is generally found in a curry house, have any of us ever stopped to think about the origins of the dish and why we have developed such a love of spiced food in this country? Where does our relationship with the 'curry' come from and why is knocking up a Thai green curry so different to sitting down to an Indonesian korma (see pages 77 and 147), a Caribbean goat curry (see page 128), a South African bunny chow (see page 131) or a Malaysian rendang (see page 67) – all at their base 'curry' dishes? This book aims to answer all these questions but above all to share with you my recipes for this wonderful dish and its countless interpretations.

Even the very meaning of the word 'curry' causes confusion and is often misinterpreted. In the UK, the use of the term appears to date from the mid-seventeenth century, around the time of the spice trade, when British merchants first encountered spiced food on their travels to Asia and adopted the word to denote any type of savoury dish that was prepared using spices. In India, a curry refers to something more specific: it is a spiced dish with a sauce or 'gravy' or 'masala' base. Other spiced food would never be referred to as curry. Yet to confine it to such a simplistic definition would be a misrepresentation of the complexities of the dish. For a 'curry' is part of an Indian cuisine that has been influenced by over 5,000 years of a rich and diverse history, involving interaction with many different cultures and religions. The Indian ability to adopt and adapt has meant that the cuisine has changed accordingly and has been enriched by the ingredients and eating habits of these exchanges; but it has also meant that other cultures and nations have borrowed from Indian customs, the result of which has been the creation of curry dishes of their own. The modern-day 'curry' is thus a global term to describe the culmination of this past and now includes manifold varieties across the world.

You will find that throughout the book I have often referred to the Indian subcontinent, rather than just to India, by which I mean the entire historical region prior to the Partition of India and Independence in 1947 (modern-day India, Pakistan, Bangladesh and Sri Lanka). From a culinary perspective this is how it needs to be considered as much of the traits and influences I describe pre-date today's frontiers. Similarly, within the subcontinent it is common to distinguish between the North and South in terms of their styles of cuisine, while also acknowledging that within that there are innumerable variations according to region, religion and culture. Very broadly speaking, the commonly used spices are perhaps the biggest distinguishing factor. In the North, favoured spices include coriander, cumin, turmeric, chilli powder, cardamom, cloves, cinnamon and fennel – warming, colourful spices that bring visual vibrancy as much as heat and flavour. In the South, curry leaves, tamarind, fenugreek, chilli and peppercorns dominate giving rise to some of India's spiciest dishes. Northern Indians tend to prepare their whole spice mixes (*khada garam masala*) and add it to the pan at the beginning of cooking then layer the other elements of the dish around it, while in southern India, the spices may be added towards the end of cooking as spice powders (or *podi*) sometimes being fried in oil separately (known as a 'tarka' in the North) and simply poured over the dish right at the end. Naturally, the styles of cuisine are influenced by the geography and produce of the regions. Southern Indian food leans heavily towards seafood – so it is that Goans enjoy fabulous coconut-laden fish curries; and while northern Indians favour unleavened breads as their main starch (this region is home to the tandoor oven and thus to tandoori naan and roti, and parathas), no southern Indian meal would be complete without rice. Rice is the base around which the meal is built and only one curry should be tasted with each mouthful of rice in order to appreciate the individual spicing of each dish.

> Trade and colonisation
> have played a huge
> part in the evolution
> of the curry.

The use of native spices on the Indian subcontinent can be traced as far back as pre-historic times yet it is really once the trade of spices began that we can start to see some of the culinary divisions and variations emerge and the birth of the styles of regional cuisine we can distinguish today.

The early sixteenth century saw the establishment of the Mughal, or Mughlai, dynasty across the northern Indian subcontinent. The Mughlai emperors were muslims of Mangol origin and brought with them the customs and spices of their Arabic heritage. Mughlai kitchens employed an elaborate and rich style of cooking and the food was heavily spiced. Mughlai cuisine is distinguishable by its abundant use of ground spices and often the sauces can be creamy and luxurious. The court sat in the north of India so many of the characteristics of Mughlai cooking are today associated with the northern regions, in particular Utter Pradesh.

A period of European association began towards the end of the sixteenth century as the race to dominate and control the lucrative spice routes was fought out among the Portuguese, Dutch, French and British. It was in fact the Portuguese who introduced the chilli pepper to Asia, and other European trade introduced ingredients such as vinegar, garlic and potatoes. A colonial presence in Asia duly followed and in 1858 the British crown established its rule over most, though not all, of the Indian subcontinent. The reign of the British Raj is the longest in imperial history, lasting from 1858 to the Partition of India in 1947 and from a culinary perspective too its impact on both Indian and British cuisine was vast. Indian cooks took British techniques and ingredients and amalgamated them with their own to create an Anglo-Indian cuisine. Soups were flavoured with spices, giving rise to dishes such as mulligatawny; roast meats were baked in whole spices; condiments such as chutneys proliferated; and although its origins are less certain, kedgeree does certainly date from this time. Mixed marriages between British traders and natives also led to the adoption of European cooking techniques, such as baking, and it is said that some Britains abroad ate curry for breakfast, lunch and dinner. At the same time, Anglo-Indian cuisine was also finding its feet in the UK as British women tried to replicate Indian dishes and condiments that their husbands had enjoyed on the subcontinent. London enjoyed the opening of its first dedicated Indian restaurant in 1809, said to be popular with colonial returnees, and the popularity of Indian food grew steadily over the nineteenth century.

Meanwhile, the boundaries of the British Empire were being extended across the globe. Britain needed manpower and they turned to India to provide them with the workforce they needed to clear the land and build infrastructure. With these mass migrations India's cuisine, heritage and culture reached countries where it is now deeply embedded. In the 1800s indentured labourers were sent to the West Indies to work on the sugar plantations; and to South Africa and East Africa. They brought with them their Indian customs, but adapted them in line with the local produce. Thus curry, particularly the ubiquitous 'goat curry', is now characteristic across the Caribbean, but its components and style is a strong reflection of the local geography. Allspice is a fundamental seasoning in Caribbean curry powders as is their native Scotch bonnet chilli in their curry recipes.

In East African countries such as Kenya, Uganda, Zambia and Malawi, the style of curry varies according to the curry powder used, but a common feature to East African curries is the love of the chilli.

The British were not the only colonisers to settle in South Africa and influence the cuisine there. During the nineteenth century the Dutch brought in indentured labourers from Sumatra, who later became known as Cape Malays. Like the Indian community in Durban (see page 131), they brought with them their traditions and heritage, which gave rise to the 'Cape Malay' or 'Cape Dutch' cuisine. It is a very distinctive style of South African cooking notable in its use of eastern spices, particularly turmeric, cloves and nutmeg. The most famous example of Cape Malay cuisine is the 'bobotie' and I'd urge you to try my recipe for it on page 127; I fell in love with the comforting baked lamb dish the first time I tried it and haven't looked back.

Buddhist monks are said to have taken spiced dishes into other parts of southeast Asia as early as the seventh century, and subsequent trading and migration has also infiltrated the region with Indian cuisine. A glance at the recipes in this book reveals that Thailand, Cambodia, Laos, Vietnam, Malaysia, Indonesia, Singapore, Burma and Japan have all borrowed techniques, ingredients or spices from India and all have interpreted and developed curry dishes of their own.

Thai curries tend to start from a paste made from chillies, garlic, onions and shrimp paste (*kapi*). They are extremely aromatic dishes that use plenty of fresh herbs and other local ingredients such as ginger, galangal and lemongrass and the heat is generated through the use of chilli rather than ground spices. And as with many countries in this part of the world, the abundance of coconuts means coconut milk is often a fundamental ingredient, providing a cooling balance to the heat from the chillies.

Cambodia, Laos and Vietnam sit so close to Thailand that many people make the mistake of assuming their curry dishes are the same as Thai versions. But while the produce and aromatics used across the whole southeast Asian region are inevitably similar owing to their climate and geography, each country has its own unique way of constructing their curry dishes and while the differences may at first seem subtle, each country places different emphasis on the levels of sweet, sour and spicy notes and there are notable favoured ingredients. Similarly, each has had its own historical influences to contend with. Thus, while it would be unheard of to encounter baguette in Thailand, the French colonial presence is evident today in Cambodia and Vietnam, where French baguette is still a popular accompaniment to curry (see also page 50).

As the home of the 'Spice Islands' – Maluku – Indonesia's contribution to spiced dishes, particularly the curry, both in its own cuisine and abroad, has been significant. Spices such as nutmeg and cloves are native to Indonesia and it later became one of the world's biggest producers of black pepper. Indian merchants involved in the spice trade took the curry to Malaysian and Indonesian shores but the characteristics of the dish there generally bear greater resemblance to South Indian cuisine than North and also rely more heavily on its local produce and spices. Both Malay and Indonesian curries are rich in coconut, curry leaves and chillies, however that is

about as general as I dare be because within these countries there is great variety among the styles of cuisine, and wide-ranging variations on a single dish. The 'rendang', perhaps the most famous example of a curry that features in both Malaysian and Indonesian cuisine, is also perhaps the most controversial. In this book alone I have included four different recipes for a rendang (see pages 67, 180, 186 and 211) as its interpretation, ingredients and cooking method are so different depending on where you are and who is cooking it for you. You will discover as you experiment with the recipes that both Indonesian and Malaysian curries rely more heavily on pastes rather than powders, but there are nevertheless several Malay curry powders (see pages 220–227).

Burmese food is an intriguing mix of cultures, cuisines and influences. Burma has borrowed extensively from many of its neighbours, not just India, and while rich, colourful curries are now an important part of a meal, they are only a component and will sit alongside salads, soups, noodle dishes and other condiments. Meat is considered quite a luxury so the meat element may only be small, and as a rice-producing country, rice is an essential part of a meal but a Burmese meal is also always balanced: rich, oily curries are partnered with plain soups and stronger-flavoured soups accompany mild curries.

The Gulf countries' abundance of native spices and other tradable produce such as silks and cottons meant that they were hugely influential players throughout the spice trade and trade with the Indian subcontinent and subsequent influence on the cuisine to both India and the Gulf countries was significant. The tandoor oven, now a fundamental part of northern Indian cuisine, originally came from Iran, though there they are made from iron, rather than clay as they are traditionally in India; and the use of nuts and dried fruits, which is commonplace in Middle Eastern cuisine and now in northern Indian too, can also be said to result from the Mughal Persian influence. In return, the Gulf countries have enjoyed taking classic Indian dishes, such as the korma and curries, and adapting them to their own tastes (see the recipes on pages 25, 64, 74). They have also developed their own spice powder, baharat, which forms the basis of their curry recipes.

Finally, in 1947, British rule in the subcontinent came to its end and independence was granted to India. But as independence approached, violence erupted among different religious communities and India was in the end split into India, Pakistan, Sri Lanka and Bangladesh; each country taking with it a piece of its phenomenal culinary history. But although Britain's formal ties with its colony came to an end, India's gift to our food history has simply gone from strength to strength. The concept of the 'curry house' pioneered in the nineteenth century grew in popularity throughout the 1950s and 60s, mainly thanks to the large Bengali community who came to work in the UK.

And after 1971, when Bangladesh was created, there was a huge influx of Bangladeshis who came to work in the catering trade and it is in fact Bangladeshi families who own the lion's share of our curry houses today. Indeed, curry has became so interwoven in our national fabric that not only do we now find curries on pub menus, as sandwich fillings and even as pizza toppings, we have also created our own curry dishes – the 'balti' is a completely British invention (see page 171) as is the beloved chicken tikka masala (see my recipe on page 73).

> This collection of curry recipes is the culmination of my experiences with this wonderful dish.

I grew up in India where I was lucky enough to live and study in different parts of the country so I have been exposed to all kinds of different Indian curries. But I've also been living in the UK for over 20 years so am very familiar with the British 'curry house' and its offerings. And in my work as a chef, I've had the good fortune to travel, sampling food from all over the world. I think this global selection reflects just how wide-ranging our 'national dish' can be and I hope you will enjoy experimenting with the flavours and culinary styles as much as I've enjoyed writing, learning about and above all cooking them!

Finally, a general note on the use of spice and on how to serve curry. Like many other foods in your storecupboard – spices do not have an indefinite shelf life! They deteriorate over time and do lose their flavour so it's a good idea to try to buy them in small quantities and replenish as necessary; that way you keep them as fresh as possible.

You will find that many of the recipes in the book require the use of a specific spice powder or paste that I've created. These mixes are a vital element of each dish and are what help give each one its individual character and flavour. So while some of the lists of basic curry powder ingredients may seem long, once made up they are easy to store and you will have them to hand for when you want to cook each recipe. Mixes such as the Garam Masala (see page 223) are used in many recipes so if you are cooking curry fairly regularly it is one you will be using repeatedly. The quantities and combinations used to create each powder is a carefully constructed, delicate balance to ensure that no spice overwhelms and that the spices that give heat are offset with spices that cool. The different combinations of spices used in various parts of the world is an intriguing maze that will unravel slowly as you experiment your way through the recipes. For every 'masala' known to us in the East – there is a different spice combination from the other side of the world that would amaze us. The way cumin is used by Indians is totally different to the way Moroccans or North Africans would use it in their cuisine, for example. And of course, curry powders change according to the cook's tastes so there are countless variations. These are my versions and I feel that they represent the essential elements of the recipe.

For many Indians and nations that eat a lot of curries, the curry is often just one part of a meal. Generally a starch forms the basis of the meal and there are other vegetable and condiment dishes served alongside it. You may not always have the time or inclination to prepare the different elements so these recipes have all been devised to be sufficient as a main course if simply served with rice, bread or a steamed vegetable, as wished. I have provided some serving suggestions, based on the starch the curry might be particularly suited to being accompanied by, but of course the choice is yours.

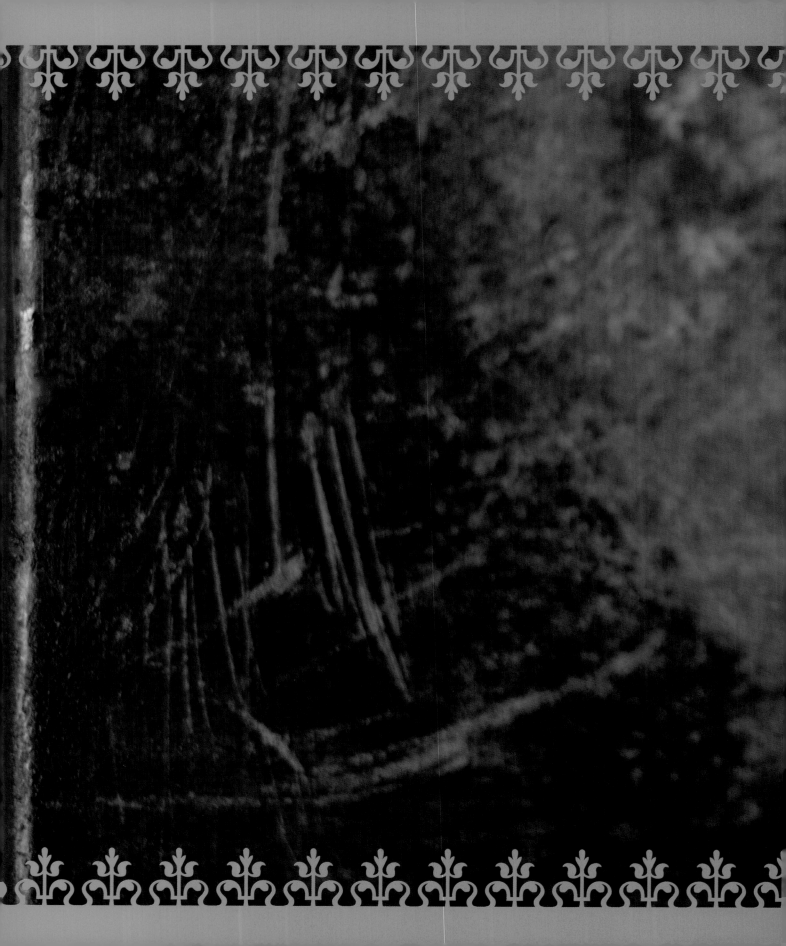

FISH

AMOK

Amok is often considered to be the national dish of Cambodia and certainly it features on most restaurant menus throughout the country. Traditionally it is made with fish and a slightly bitter, citrus-flavoured leafy green called morinda, or noni leaves. Swiss chard, kale and pak choi are good substitutes for the green and you could also add shellfish, as I've done here, or substitute another protein, such as chicken or tofu.

SERVES 4

3 tablespoons vegetable oil
2 tablespoons Kroeung (Cambodian Spice Paste; see page 224)
400g sea bass fillets, cut into small 4cm pieces
150g raw prawns, peeled,
cleaned and deveined
400g Swiss chard, kale or pak choi leaves, shredded
500ml coconut milk
100g ready-cooked mussels
1 tablespoon palm sugar
4 tablespoons fish sauce

Heat the oil in a wok and sauté the spice paste until lightly browned. Add the fish, prawns and leaves. Sauté for 1–2 minutes, then add the coconut milk, mussels, sugar and fish sauce. Bring to the boil and simmer until the seafood is cooked, about 2–3 minutes. Serve immediately with jasmine rice.

BAKED FISH CURRY

PALLU CURRY

Pallu is a tropical type of oily fish, heavily prevalent in Bengali cooking and in the Sindh region of Pakistan. Black or sea bream would be a good substitute.

SERVES 4

6 tablespoons vegetable oil
3 onions, chopped
2 teaspoons red chilli powder
1 tablespoon ground coriander
1/4 teaspoon ground turmeric
4 tablespoons Tamarind
Water (see page 228)
2 tablespoons chopped coriander roots
4 bream fillets
2 tablespoons chopped coriander leaves

Preheat the oven to 180°C/Gas Mark 4.

Heat the oil in a pan and sauté the onions with all the spices, the tamarind water and the coriander roots until the onions soften. Remove from the heat.

Cut four 25cm squares of kitchen foil or baking parchment. Divide the onion mixture into eight equal batches. Place one batch in the centre of each piece of foil. Place a fillet of fish on top, then cover with the remaining onion mixture. Sprinkle with the chopped coriander. Seal the foil into parcels, then place on a baking tray.

Bake for 10–12 minutes or until the fish is cooked: check with the tip of a knife. Serve with a salad of your choice.

PAKISTANI BAKED FISH CURRY

BANG KRASSOP PRAWN AND VEGETABLE STEW

Bang Krassop is a place with a small population in the Cambodian province of Koh Kong on the border with Thailand. I learnt this recipe from one of my trainee chefs who comes from this region. His spice paste was slightly different from the one I have created, but the dish is the same in essence and still tastes delicious.

SERVES 4

200g jasmine rice
3 tablespoons vegetable oil
300g raw prawns, peeled, cleaned and deveined
1 tablespoon finely chopped fresh ginger
3 tablespoons Kroeung (Cambodian Spice Paste; see page 224)
500ml fish stock
2 carrots, diced
100g green beans, cut into small pieces
1 mooli, peeled and cut into small dice
4–5 small tomatoes, halved
4 tablespoons fish sauce
1 tablespoon palm or brown sugar
a few coriander sprigs, to garnish
1 lime, cut into wedges, to serve

Toast the rice in a dry pan or wok, then roughly crush in a mortar or pulse in a blender. Keep aside until required.

Heat the oil in the wok and sauté the prawns with the ginger for 3–4 minutes or until the prawns turn pink and opaque. Remove and set aside. Add the spice paste to the wok and sauté for 2–3 minutes until fragrant. Add the fish stock, vegetables, toasted crushed rice, fish sauce and sugar and stir to mix. Bring to the boil, then simmer gently for 8–10 minutes or until the vegetables are just cooked.

Add the prawns and simmer for a further 2–3 minutes to heat through. Correct the seasoning with fish sauce and serve garnished with coriander sprigs and lime wedges.

CHILLI CRAB

Anyone visiting Singapore has to eat chilli crab and pepper crab; they are practically the national dishes and are unsurpassed in other parts of the world. It is the quality of the ingredients that makes them so special. Apparently you need to ask the locals for the names of the best places to find them, although they are closely guarded secrets and you might have a hard time getting the Singaporeans to divulge their favourites!

SERVES 4

3 large fresh crabs, still in the shell, cut into 4–6 pieces (you could ask your fishmonger to do this), cleaned
oil for deep-frying
300ml fish stock
1 egg, beaten
1 tablespoon cornflour, mixed with 50ml water
salt and white pepper

For the sauce
3 tablespoons vegetable oil
1 large onion, chopped
2 tablespoons finely chopped garlic
a small knob of fresh ginger, scraped and thinly sliced

1 tablespoon black bean paste
4–6 large red chillies, deseeded and sliced
2 medium tomatoes, diced
4 tablespoons sweet chilli sauce
4 tablespoons tomato ketchup
1 teaspoon toasted sesame oil
1 tablespoon soy sauce
1 tablespoon brown sugar
1 teaspoon red chilli powder
1–2 teaspoons ground white pepper

To garnish
2–3 spring onions, thinly sliced
coriander cress or coriander sprigs

Crack the crab claws to allow the spices to penetrate the meat. Heat enough oil for deep-frying in a large, deep pan or wok. When it is hot (about 190°C), deep-fry the crab pieces for 2–3 minutes or until the shell turns deep red. Drain on kitchen paper and keep aside until required.

To make the sauce, heat the oil in a wok over a high heat and sauté the onion, garlic, ginger, black bean paste and chillies for 1–2 minutes or until lightly coloured and fragrant. Add the tomatoes, chilli sauce, ketchup, sesame oil, soy sauce and sugar. Cook, stirring, for a further 2 minutes. Add the chilli powder and season with the white pepper.

Add the fried crabs and coat with the sauce. Pour in the stock and stir well. Bring to a simmer over a high heat, cook for 1–2 minutes, then add the beaten egg and cornflour mixture and continue to simmer, stirring, until the sauce thickens. Season with salt and pepper, then serve garnished with spring onions and coriander cress.

CRAB CURRY

KAKULUWO CURRY

Sri Lankan crab curries are wonderful. I have tasted many versions, from Jaffna to Dondra and Colombo to Trincomalee, and they are so different from each other. It is the spice mix that creates the magic, so when making this recipe choose your curry powder carefully.

SERVES 4

3 tablespoons coconut or vegetable oil
1 teaspoon black mustard seeds
1 teaspoon fennel seeds
1/4 teaspoon fenugreek seeds
a 1cm piece of cinnamon stick
1 large red onion, thinly sliced
1 tablespoon finely chopped green chillies
1 tablespoon finely chopped fresh ginger
10–12 curry leaves
2 large fresh crabs, still in the shell, cut into 4–6 pieces (you could ask your fishmonger to do this), cleaned

1/2 teaspoon ground turmeric
2 tablespoons Jaffna Curry Powder (see page 223)
1 teaspoon red chilli powder or paprika
600ml coconut milk
4 tablespoons Tamarind Water (see page 228)
2 tablespoons lime juice
2 tablespoons finely chopped coriander leaves
salt

For the coconut paste
150g freshly grated coconut
1 teaspoon black peppercorns
1 teaspoon cumin seeds
4 garlic cloves, peeled
3–4 tablespoons coconut milk

For the paste, toast the grated coconut, peppercorns and cumin seeds in a dry pan, toasting one after the other, until each is lightly coloured. Leave to cool, then blend with the remaining coconut paste ingredients until smooth.

Heat the oil in a wok and sauté the seeds and cinnamon until the spices crackle. Add the onion, green chillies, ginger and curry leaves and sauté for a minute. Put the pieces of crab into the pan and sauté, turning so the shell colour changes to red all over. Add all the ground spices, stir well and cook for 2–3 minutes.

Add the coconut paste and stir well for 2–3 minutes, then pour in the coconut milk and tamarind water. Simmer very gently for a few more minutes until the crab is cooked. Check the seasoning. Finish with the lime juice and chopped coriander and serve with rice.

FISH BALLS CURRY

MACHER KOFTA

In a family household, such as mine, leftovers are a common occurrence. This is a great recipe for using up an excess of fish; any firm fish can be used.

SERVES 4

For the fish balls
600g skinless snapper, bream or sea bass fillet
1 small onion, finely chopped
1 tablespoon finely chopped fresh ginger
1 teaspoon finely chopped garlic
1/2 teaspoon toasted cumin seeds, crushed
1/2 teaspoon crushed black peppercorns
a pinch of grated nutmeg
2 small green chillies, chopped
breadcrumbs, if needed
salt

For the sauce
4 tablespoons vegetable oil
3 small onions, thinly sliced
1 bay leaf
1 teaspoon Ginger-Garlic Paste (see page 223)
1 teaspoon red chilli powder
1/2 teaspoon ground turmeric
1 teaspoon ground cumin
1 teaspoon ground coriander
200g tomatoes, skinned, deseeded and chopped
1 tablespoon kasoori methi (dried fenugreek leaves)
600ml fish stock
1 tablespoon finely chopped coriander leaves

Put the fish into a food processor and pulse until roughly minced. Mix with all the remaining ingredients for the fish balls with salt to taste. Shape into small golf-ball-sized balls. If the paste is a little too soft to shape, mix in some breadcrumbs. Keep in the refrigerator until required.

In a wok, heat the vegetable oil and sauté the onions with the bay leaf until light brown. Add the ginger-garlic paste and sauté for 1–2 minutes until the raw smell of garlic goes away. Add all the ground spices and sauté for a further 2 minutes. Add the chopped tomatoes and cook on a low heat for 8–10 minutes, stirring occasionally.

Add the kasoori methi and sauté for 2 minutes to release the flavour. Pour in the fish stock and bring to the boil, then reduce the heat to simmer gently. Place the fish balls in the sauce and cook on a low heat for 4–5 minutes or until the fish balls are cooked through (the fish will turn opaque and the balls will feel firmer to the touch). Sprinkle with the coriander and serve with rice.

(LEFT) BANGLADESHI CURRIED PRAWN BALLS
(RIGHT) EAST AFRICAN PRAWN CURRY

CURRIED PRAWN BALLS

CHOTO CHENGRI KOFTA KARI

In the last 20 or so years I have been cooking, I must have used prawns from all over the world and I have to say that I am a big fan of prawns from the Indian Ocean and also the freshwater prawns that are from West Bengal and Bangladesh. They naturally have a sweeter taste that give whatever dish I'm cooking a new life because its basic raw ingredient is so good. This Bengali curry shows off the region's wonderful ingredients to great effect.

SERVES 4

For the kofta
500g raw prawns, peeled, cleaned and deveined
1 tablespoon chopped fresh ginger
3 garlic cloves, peeled
2 green chillies
1/4 teaspoon ground turmeric
2 tablespoons besan (chickpea flour)
1/2 teaspoon freshly crushed black peppercorns
1 tablespoon chopped coriander leaves
salt

For the curry sauce
1 tablespoon ghee
a 2.5cm piece of cinnamon stick
2 green cardamom pods
2 cloves
1 bay leaf
1 onion, finely chopped
1/4 teaspoon ground turmeric
1 tablespoon Ginger-Garlic Paste (see page 223)
500ml coconut milk
1 teaspoon sugar
1 tablespoon lime juice

coriander sprigs, to garnish

Put all the ingredients for the kofta, with salt to taste, in a food processor and pulse until minced. Shape the mixture into small golf-ball-sized balls and set aside until required.

Heat the ghee in a pan and sauté the whole spices and bay leaf for a minute. Add the onion and sauté until translucent, then add the turmeric and ginger-garlic paste. Stir well, then add the coconut milk and sugar and bring to a simmer.

Gently place the prawn koftas in the sauce, then leave to simmer for 6–9 minutes or until the koftas are cooked through. Add the lime juice and garnish with a few sprigs of coriander, and a few finely sliced green chillies, if you wish. Some tomatoes on the vine make for a dramatic presentation (optional). Serve hot with rice.

EAST AFRICAN PRAWN CURRY

Africa has a wealth of exotic ingredients and this dish is usually served with some of its best: fried onion rings, chopped bananas, chopped cucumber, pineapple chutney and grated coconut. For a dinner party or more elaborate meal, try serving it with some of these, or just keep it simple and serve it with rice – its warm colours and spices will still bring home a taste of the sunshine.

SERVES 4

3 medium potatoes, peeled and cut into 1cm dice
45g butter or 3 tablespoons vegetable oil
2 onions, finely chopped
1 tablespoon finely chopped garlic
1 tablespoon East African Curry Powder (see page 222)
1 teaspoon ground turmeric
1/2 teaspoon red chilli powder
500ml coconut milk
800g raw prawns, peeled, cleaned and deveined
2 tablespoons lemon juice
1 tablespoon finely chopped coriander leaves
salt

Blanch the potatoes in a pan of boiling water for 7–10 minutes or until just cooked. Drain and set aside.

Melt the butter in a pan and fry the onions until translucent. Add the garlic, curry powder, turmeric and chilli powder and cook, stirring, for 2 minutes. Add the prawns, potatoes, coconut milk, 150ml water and salt to taste. Bring to the boil, then simmer for 10–12 minutes or until the potatoes and prawns are cooked through. Stir in the lemon juice, garnish with a slice of lemon or lime and some chopped coriander, and serve with rice or salad.

MIDDLE EASTERN FISH CURRY

FISH CURRY

SAMAK QUWARMAH

Here is a recipe for a Middle Eastern korma (see page 46 for more on Indian and UK kormas). The spicing of kormas (Quwarmah) in the Gulf countries is gentle and subtle, their Baharat spice powder adds warmth and sweetness rather than fiery heat.

SERVES 4

4 sea bream fillets or salmon
    steaks
4 tablespoons ghee or
    vegetable oil
2 onions, finely chopped
1 teaspoon finely chopped
    fresh ginger
1 tablespoon finely chopped
    garlic
1/2 teaspoon red chilli powder
1 teaspoon Baharat (Middle
    Eastern spice powder; see

page 220)
1 teaspoon ground turmeric
a 2.5cm piece of cinnamon
    stick
200g tomatoes, skinned and
    chopped
2 loomi (dried limes) or
    thinly pared rind of
    1 lemon
100ml fish stock or water
salt

Season the fish with salt and leave it, covered, in the fridge until required.

Heat 2 tablespoons of the ghee in a pan and sauté the onions until translucent. Add the ginger, garlic, red chilli powder, baharat, turmeric and cinnamon and sauté for 2–3 minutes. Add the tomatoes, loomi and stock. Bring to the boil, then simmer gently for 5 minutes or until the tomatoes melt in the sauce.

Slash the fish skin. Heat a frying pan over a medium–high heat until hot, then add the remaining ghee. Place the fillets in the pan, skin-side down, and sear for 2 minutes, or until the skin is crisp, then flip over and fry on the other side for about a minute, or until cooked through.

To serve, remove the loomi from the sauce and spoon the sauce into serving plates. Add a bed of rice or salad to the middle and place the fish on top. An optional garnish of rose petals finishes the dish attractively. Serve immediately.

FISH CURRY

KARE IKAN

For this Indonesian curry, use a firm fish like haddock, salmon or even swordfish – you need a strong flesh to stand up to the spices.

SERVES 4

4 tablespoons vegetable oil
800g skinless haddock fillet,
    cut into 5cm dice
2 onions, thinly sliced
1 tablespoon finely chopped
    garlic
1 teaspoon finely chopped
    fresh ginger
1 tablespoon finely chopped
    lemongrass (white part
    only)
1 teaspoon red chilli powder

2 teaspoons ground coriander
1 bay leaf
1/2 teaspoon ground turmeric
100ml Tamarind Water
    (see page 228)
250ml coconut milk
salt

To garnish
mint sprigs
sliced cucumber
red chilli, thinly sliced

Heat the oil in a wok and fry the pieces of fish until lightly coloured; remove with a slotted spoon and keep aside until required. Add the onions and garlic to the wok and sauté until translucent. Add the ginger, lemongrass, chilli powder, coriander, bay leaf and turmeric and stir to mix. Sauté for a minute to cook the spices, then add the tamarind water and 100ml water. Bring to the boil, then reduce to a simmer.

Return the fried fish pieces to the wok and simmer for 5–7 minutes or until the fish is almost cooked. Pour in the coconut milk, stir and simmer for a further 2 minutes. Serve with rice, garnished with mint sprigs, sliced cucumber and red chilli.

FISH CURRY WITH TOMATO

NGA SIPYAN

This is an everyday fish curry that works well with rice and a simple vegetable side dish. I like to use either sea bass or whiting for this recipe.

SERVES 4

4 sea bass fillets, about 150g each
1 teaspoon ground turmeric
2 tablespoons fish sauce
1 large onion, roughly chopped
6–7 garlic cloves, peeled
2–3 dried red chillies, soaked in lukewarm water to

soften and drained
4 tablespoons rapeseed or vegetable oil
1/2 teaspoon red chilli powder
12–14 small ripe tomatoes, quartered
100ml fish stock
2 tablespoons finely chopped coriander leaves

Place the fish fillets in a dish and sprinkle over the turmeric and fish sauce. Turn to coat, then leave to marinate in a cool place for 30 minutes.

In a mortar and pestle, roughly crush the onion, garlic and chillies together to make a coarse paste. Heat the oil in a saucepan and sauté the onion paste until caramelised. Add the chilli powder and mix in, then add the tomatoes and fish stock. Bring to the boil.

Drop the fish fillets into the sauce and simmer for 5–7 minutes or until the fish is just cooked. Correct the seasoning with fish sauce. Sprinkle with the coriander and serve.

FISH HEAD CURRY

I know, this recipe does sound spooky but in the Eastern world fish head curry is a delicacy. You can replace the fish head with fish fillet if you prefer but I'd urge you to give the fish heads a try – I think they're delicious.

SERVES 4

4 tablespoons vegetable or coconut oil
1/2 teaspoon mustard seeds
1/2 teaspoon fenugreek seeds
4 shallots, finely chopped
10 curry leaves
4 tablespoons fish curry powder or mild curry powder
600ml fish stock
600ml coconut milk
2 large fish heads (John Dory or sea bream), cut in half lengthways
2 tablespoons Tamarind Water (see page 228)
10–12 small okra, tip and tail removed

2 small aubergines, quartered lengthways
2 tomatoes, quartered
1 tablespoon sugar
salt

For the spice paste
2 lemongrass stalks, thinly sliced
a 5cm knob of fresh turmeric or 1 teaspoon ground turmeric
1 tablespoon Ginger Paste (see page 223)
4–5 red chillies, thinly sliced
20 shallots, sliced
8–10 garlic cloves, peeled

Blend or pound together the ingredients for the spice paste until fine.

Heat the oil in a wok and sauté the mustard and fenugreek seeds until fragrant, then add the shallots, spice paste and curry leaves. Sauté for 5 minutes to colour lightly, then add the curry powder and stir well. Sauté for a further 2 minutes or until fragrant.

Pour in half the stock and stir to mix. Bring to the boil, then simmer for 5 minutes. Add the rest of the stock, the coconut milk and fish heads and simmer for 2 minutes. Add the tamarind water, okra and aubergines and simmer for 8–10 minutes or until all the vegetables are cooked.

Add the tomatoes, sugar, salt to taste and cook for a further 5 minutes. Serve with rice.

FISH HEAD CURRY

MACHER MOORIGHUNTO

Fish head curries in Malaysia, Singapore and Bangladesh are hugely popular. Though perhaps not the first choice for many in the west, it's well worth making the effort to source the carp fish heads for this Bengali favourite.

SERVES 4–6

150g mung daal (split mung beans)	1 tablespoon Ginger-Garlic Paste (see page 223)
1 tablespoon vegetable oil	2 teaspoons red chilli powder
2 carp heads (or 4 fillets)	$1/2$ teaspoon ground turmeric
15g butter or 1 tablespoon ghee	2 teaspoon ground coriander
	$1/2$ teaspoon ground cumin
2 bay leaves	2 carrots, cut into roundels
1 teaspoon cumin seeds	2 aubergines, cut into roundels
4 green cardamom pods, lightly bruised	
a 5cm piece of cinnamon stick	4 green chillies, slit
	salt
6–8 cloves	3 tablespoons chopped coriander leaves, to garnish
3 small red onions, sliced	lemon wedges, to serve

Dry-roast the mung daal in a pan until lightly browned and aromatic. Rinse and return to the pan, then add 500ml boiling water and cook for 10–12 minutes, until al dente. Remove from the heat and set aside.

Heat the oil in a wok and sauté the fish heads, turning them, until lightly coloured on all sides. Remove and keep aside until needed.

Heat the butter or ghee in the pan and sauté the bay leaves with the whole spices until fragrant. Add the onions and sauté until translucent. Add the ginger-garlic paste and ground spices, then stir in 50ml water. Cook on a medium heat for 2–3 minutes to cook the onion and spices.

Return the fish heads to the pan and add the carrots and aubergines. Mix well, then add 200ml water and bring to a simmer, then cook for 10–12 minutes. Add the cooked daal and its stock. Bring to the boil and simmer until the fish heads and vegetables are cooked – the meat should come away from the bone easily. Add the green chillies. Serve garnished with the coriander, accompanied by lemon wedges and rice.

SUMATRAN (PADANG) FISH CURRY

GULAI IKAN MASIN

Unlike most other recipes, this tilapia curry is delicious if served slightly warm rather than piping hot. Strong spices such as cardamom, cinnamon and cloves need to be experienced at higher temperatures for the full weight and depth of the spice to come through, but here the more gentle flavours work their magic at more moderate temperatures. Bream or sea bass would also work well in this dish.

SERVES 4

2 tablespoons groundnut oil	salt
2 thick lemongrass stalks, tied together	
	For the spice paste
4 kaffir lime leaves, preferably fresh	6 shallots, chopped
	2 garlic cloves, chopped
6 green or red Thai chillies, stem removed	$1/2$ teaspoon ground turmeric
	1 tablespoon chopped fresh ginger
300ml coconut milk	
1 teaspoon sugar	3–4 macadamia nuts or candlenuts
4 tilapia fillets	

Blend or pound together the ingredients for the spice paste to make a fine paste. Heat the oil in a pan and sauté the spice paste with the lemongrass, kaffir lime leaves and chillies for 3–5 minutes or until fragrant. Add the coconut milk, sugar, salt to taste and 200ml water. Bring to the boil, then simmer for 5–7 minutes.

Gently place the fish in the sauce and cook over a low heat for 5–7 minutes or until the fish is perfectly cooked. Remove from the heat and leave to cool for 10 minutes, then serve with rice.

GOAN FISH CURRY

This recipe is inspired by one of my culinary heroes – Arvind Saraswat, a renowned Indian chef who is a veteran of the culinary world and has cooked at banquets for world leaders. I have followed his work for years but have not yet had the pleasure of meeting him – maybe one day!

SERVES 4

4 tablespoons vegetable oil
1 onion, chopped
2 tomatoes, chopped
1 tablespoon tomato paste
300ml coconut milk
4 salmon or swordfish steaks
2 green chillies, sliced
salt

For the paste
6–7 red chillies or 2

teaspoons red chilli powder
100g freshly grated coconut
1 tablespoon coriander seeds
1 teaspoon cumin seeds
2 tablespoons Tamarind
 Water (see page 228)
2 tablespoons chopped garlic
2 tablespoons chopped fresh
 ginger
1 teaspoon ground turmeric

Place all the paste ingredients in a blender and blend to a fine paste.

Heat the oil in a wok or pan and sauté the onion until light brown in colour. Add the tomatoes, tomato paste and the spice paste and sauté for 3–4 minutes to cook the mixture. Add the coconut milk, bring to a simmer, then add the fish and chillies and simmer for 7–10 minutes, until the fish is just cooked. Adjust the seasoning and serve with rice.

FISH LEMON STEW

THORA MALU ISTUWA

If I were cooking this stew in Sri Lanka, where it originates, I'd use king mackerel, also called kingfish, which is one of the best catches from the Indian Ocean. In the UK other meaty fishes such as turbot, salmon or swordfish are good substitutes.

SERVES 4

600g kingfish, swordfish or
 salmon steaks
1 teaspoon ground white
 pepper
4 tablespoons vegetable oil
3 red onions, 1 chopped and
 2 sliced into rings
2 pandan leaves, cut into 5cm
 pieces
2 sprigs of curry leaves
4 garlic cloves, chopped
2 green chillies, thinly sliced

4 green cardamom pods,
 crushed
1/2 teaspoon fenugreek seeds
a 2.5cm piece of lemongrass
 stalk, finely sliced
2 teaspoons ground coriander
1 teaspoon ground cumin
1/2 teaspoon ground turmeric
250ml coconut milk
juice of 1 lemon
salt

Season the fish steaks with the pepper and some salt. Heat the oil in a large frying pan until very hot and sear the steaks on both sides. Remove with a fish slice and keep aside until required.

Heat the oil again and sauté the chopped onions with the pandan and curry leaves, garlic, green chillies, cardamom pods, fenugreek seeds and lemongrass over a medium heat until fragrant and the onions are translucent. Add the ground spices and sauté for a minute, then add the coconut milk. Bring to a simmer. Lower the heat and add the fish steaks and onion rings. Simmer gently for 10–15 minutes or until the fish is cooked through. Remove from the heat and stir in the lemon juice. Place the fish steak onto a plate, pour the sauce over it and serve with a salad of your choice.

SRI LANKAN FISH LEMON STEW

HOT AND SWEET SQUID CURRY

MAKALI PATIA

This is a renowned Parsee curry. The Parsee community has lived in India for over 1,300 years after they moved from Iran, fleeing persecution. They are a creative lot – on moving to India, they adopted and adapted the style, life and cuisine of India yet also enriched India with their heritage and culinary traditions. I grew up among the Parsee community in Jamshedpur and know them well (hello Cyrus!).

SERVES 4

1 tablespoon chopped garlic
2 green chillies, chopped
1 teaspoon cumin seeds
4 tablespoons vegetable oil
2 large onions, finely chopped
1/2 teaspoon ground cumin
1 teaspoon ground coriander
1/2 teaspoon red chilli powder
1 teaspoon Garam Masala
  (see page 223)
1/2 teaspoon ground turmeric

2 tomatoes, chopped
4 tablespoons Tamarind
  Water (see page 228)
1 teaspoon palm sugar
12–15 curry leaves
50g coriander leaves, chopped
600g squid rings
2 bunches of spring onions,
  chopped
salt

Place the garlic, green chillies and cumin seeds in a blender and process to a smooth paste.

Heat 3 tablespoons of the oil in a pan and sauté the onions until light brown in colour. Add the spice paste and sauté for 2–3 minutes over a medium heat, then add the cumin, coriander, red chilli, garam masala and turmeric. Stir well for a minute, then add the chopped tomatoes, tamarind water, palm sugar, curry leaves, coriander leaves and salt to taste. Adjust the sweet and sour flavours and keep the sauce warm.

In another pan, heat the remaining tablespoon of oil and sauté the squid rings for 5–8 minutes to lightly colour and cook. Add the spring onions to the squid, sauté for another minute, then tip into the sauce. Stir well, then serve with rice.

MALABAR LOBSTER CURRY

KONCH KARI

I love this recipe and first ate it in Kerala with crayfish. I have converted it into a lobster dish and it works so well, although for something a little less extravagant it's also great made with prawns, crayfish or squid.

SERVES 4

3 tablespoons vegetable oil
1/2 teaspoon black mustard
  seeds
12 curry leaves
1 onion, thinly sliced
1 teaspoon finely chopped
  fresh ginger
1 teaspoon finely chopped
  garlic
2 small green chillies, slit
  open
1 dried red chilli
1/2 teaspoon ground paprika
1/2 teaspoon ground turmeric
1 teaspoon ground coriander
1/2 teaspoon ground cumin

a pinch of ground cinnamon
2 tomatoes, chopped
1 tablespoon Tamarind Water
  (see page 228)
500ml coconut milk
400g raw lobster or crayfish
  tails, cut into 2.5cm pieces
salt

For the tempering
2 tablespoons coconut oil
  or ghee
2 shallots, thinly sliced
2 green chillies, slit
5–6 curry leaves

Heat the oil in a wok or a frying pan and sauté the mustard seeds and curry leaves until fragrant, then add the onion. Sauté, stirring, for 4–5 minutes until lightly coloured. Add the chopped ginger, garlic and green chillies and sauté for a minute, then add the ground spices with 50ml water and cook over a medium heat for a minute, making sure the spices don't burn. Add the chopped tomatoes, tamarind water and 100ml water and simmer until the tomatoes soften. Add the coconut milk and lobster and simmer for 5–8 minutes, until the lobster pieces are cooked through. Season with salt.

In a small pan, heat the coconut oil or ghee and sauté the shallots, chillies and curry leaves. Pour over the lobster curry just before serving. Serve with rice.

MALAYSIAN BUTTER PRAWNS

This is an unusual recipe that uses curry leaves with soy sauce: India meets China in Malaysia...

SERVES 4

500g large raw prawns, peeled, cleaned and deveined	1 teaspoon palm sugar
	1½ teaspoons soy sauce
oil for deep-frying	1 tablespoon rice wine
45g butter	6 tablespoons grated fresh
3 bird's eye chillies, chopped	coconut, lightly toasted,
10–12 curry leaves	or kerisik (toasted ground
3 garlic cloves, chopped	coconut; see page 224)
	salt

Heat enough oil for deep-frying in a wok or large, deep pan. When it is hot (180–190°C), deep-fry the prawns until they turn pink and opaque. Drain on kitchen paper and set aside.

Melt the butter in a pan and add the chillies, curry leaves and garlic. Fry for 2 minutes or until fragrant. Add the prawns, sugar, soy sauce, wine and grated coconut. Cook over a high heat for 1–2 minutes, stirring frequently, then serve immediately.

SPICY SNOW CRAB STIR FRY

Canadian snow crab is harvested throughout the Atlantic provinces (Newfoundland, New Brunswick, Nova Scotia, Prince Edward Island) and Quebec. I have family in Canada whom I visit often and this is one of my favourite snow crab recipes – the flavour of the meat is so beautifully sweet and delicate. Back in the UK we have a wealth of crabs available on our shores, so here I substitute brown crabs for the snow crabs. The flavours in this dish are very delicate so be careful not to over-spice it.

SERVES 4

2 tablespoons coconut oil	until al dente
1 teaspoon black mustard seeds	pinch of sugar
	¼ teaspoon red chilli powder
1 teaspoon finely chopped fresh ginger	¼ teaspoon ground turmeric
	400g fresh white or brown
1 teaspoon finely chopped green chilli	crab meat
	1 tablespoon lime juice
1 onion, finely chopped	1 tablespoon finely chopped
12–15 curry leaves, chopped	coriander leaves
100g frozen peas	salt
1 carrot, diced and blanched	

Heat the oil in a wok and sauté the mustard seeds until they pop. Add the ginger and green chilli, sauté for a minute to infuse their flavour, then add the onion and curry leaves. Sauté until the onions are translucent, then add the peas, carrot, sugar, spices and salt to taste. Sauté for couple of minutes, then add the crab meat and lime juice and mix well. Stir in the chopped coriander and serve warm with mixed salad leaves.

PINEAPPLE, PRAWN AND SCALLOP CURRY

GANG PIT MOCK NUT

Seafood such as prawns and scallops have an innate sweetness, which marries beautifully with a sweet fruit, such as pineapple. In a curry, this sweetness will be balanced with other flavourings – a sour and a salty element, for example – as is exemplified in this Laotian curry. For a more modern presentation, you can cook the sauce without the seafood, frying the prawns and scallops separately in a little oil and butter (leaving the prawns unpeeled adds to the presentation). Finish by serving with the sauce drizzled over, as in the picture opposite.

SERVES 4

2 tablespoons groundnut or vegetable oil
3 tablespoons Laotian Curry Paste (see page 224)
300g raw prawns, peeled, cleaned and deveined
200g scallops, coral removed
2 tablespoons fish sauce
1 tablespoon sugar
4 kaffir lime leaves
500ml coconut milk
1 small pineapple, peeled and diced
4 spring onions, cut into 2.5cm pieces
handful of holy basil or ordinary basil leaves, plus extra to garnish

Heat the oil in a wok and sauté the curry paste for a minute until fragrant. Add the prawns and scallops. Cook for 2–3 minutes, stirring, then add the fish sauce, sugar and kaffir lime leaves. Stir for a minute. Use a slotted spoon to remove the seafood from the wok and keep warm.

Add the coconut milk to the wok and bring to the boil, then simmer for 2–3 minutes. Add the pineapple and simmer for 5 minutes. Return the seafood to the wok and add the spring onions and basil leaves. Cook, stirring, for a couple of minutes, then transfer to serving bowls. Garnish each with a sprig of basil and serve with rice, shredded lettuce and sliced cucumber.

PADANG FISH CURRY WITH ASPARAGUS

PANGEK IKAN

Starfruit is native to Indonesia, India and Sri Lanka. The flesh has a citrusy tang and can taste slightly sweet but the degree to which it is sweet or sour depends on how ripe the fruit is when it is picked. The yellower starfruit, often with brown edges, are riper and sweeter than the fruits that are green and only tinged with yellow edges. Use whichever type you prefer in this aromatic Indonesian curry.

SERVES 4

500ml coconut milk
1 lemongrass stalk, lightly bruised at the bulb
4 trout fillets, with skin
16 small green asparagus spears, trimmed
1 starfruit, thickly sliced
10 mint leaves
10 basil leaves

For the spice paste
5 shallots, chopped
2 garlic cloves, peeled
1 teaspoon chopped fresh ginger
1/2 teaspoon chopped galangal
4–6 macadamia nuts or candlenuts
1 teaspoon ground coriander
1 teaspoon ground turmeric
3–4 tablespoons coconut milk
2 tablespoons coconut or vegetable oil
salt

Preheat the oven to 150°C/Gas Mark 2.

Blend or pound together all the ingredients for the spice paste, with salt to taste, to make a fine paste. Place the paste in a heavy-bottomed pan and simmer, stirring well, for 5 minutes.

Add the 500ml of coconut milk and simmer for 10 minutes, stirring occasionally. Remove from the heat and keep aside until required.

Put the lemongrass in a shallow baking dish and place the fish on top, together with the asparagus, starfruit and mint and basil leaves. Pour the sauce over. Bake for 30–40 minutes or until the fish is cooked. (Alternatively, you can simmer the fish very gently on the hob.)

LEFT: LAOTIAN PINEAPPLE, PRAWN AND SCALLOP CURRY

FRIED FISH

LAHORI TALI MACHCHI

Lahore is a landlocked city so the local fish supply traditionally comes either from the local rivers or ponds; sea fish is only available in the markets. This is a popular street food dish – simple and easily prepared and cooked, yet utterly delicious.

SERVES 4

4 firm fish steaks, such as salmon or swordfish, 120–150g each
oil for deep-frying
2 onions, cut into rings
4 green chillies
2 lemons, cut into wedges

For the marinade
1 tablespoon coriander seeds
1 teaspoon cumin seeds

6 tablespoons besan (chickpea flour)
1 tablespoon Ginger-Garlic Paste (see page 223)
2 tablespoons Tamarind Water (see page 228)
1 teaspoon red chilli flakes
1 teaspoon red chilli powder
1 teaspoon ground turmeric
salt

Toast the coriander and cumin seeds in a small dry pan, then grind to a coarse powder. Mix with the remaining ingredients for the marinade, seasoning with salt to taste, and add 3–4 tablespoons of water to make a thick paste.

Smear this paste onto both sides of the fish steaks, then leave to marinate in a cool place for 10–15 minutes.

Heat enough oil for deep-frying in a wok or deep pan. When it is hot (180–190°C), deep-fry the fish steaks, one or two at a time, until deep golden – it shouldn't take more than 3–4 minutes for each steak, depending on their size. Drain on kitchen paper and serve immediately with the onion rings, green chillies and lemon wedges.

PRAWN AND PINEAPPLE CURRY

UDANG MASAK

I have to thank my friend Maria Mustafa – an accomplished cook, TV personality, and dedicated family woman – for teaching me so much about Malaysian food in such a short time. Her recipes are sensational and extremely inspirational – here's one I have tried to recreate.

SERVES 4–6

3 tablespoons vegetable or groundnut oil
flesh from 1/2 small pineapple, peeled and diced
2 tablespoons palm sugar
500g raw prawns, peeled but with tails left on, cleaned and deveined
3 small tomatoes, cut in quarters
300ml coconut milk
salt

For the paste
2 thick lemongrass stalks, thinly sliced
3 shallots, chopped
1 garlic clove, finely chopped
3 red chillies, chopped
1 green chilli, chopped
1 teaspoon ground turmeric
4–6 candlenuts or macadamia nuts

a few spring onions, chopped into 2.5cm lengths to garnish

Pound or blend together all the paste ingredients with 2–3 tablespoons of water to make a fine paste.

Heat the oil in a wok and fry the paste over a medium heat for 5–8 minutes or until well cooked (there should be no smell of raw garlic and the oil should have started to separate out).

Add the pineapple and sauté for 2–3 minutes, then add the sugar, some salt and 400ml water. Bring to the boil, then simmer for 3–5 minutes or until the pineapple softens.

Add the prawns and continue to simmer for 4–5 minutes or until the prawns turn pink and opaque. Add the tomatoes and cook for a further 2–3 minutes, then pour in the coconut milk. Bring back to the boil, stirring well. Simmer gently for a further 3–5 minutes, then serve, garnished with a few batons of spring onion.

MALAYSIAN PRAWN AND PINEAPPLE CURRY

SWEET AND SOUR PRAWNS AND MANGOES

The mangoes I've used in this recipe are small and green, which means that they were under-ripe when picked and have a sour flavour. The choice is deliberate and is what gives this dish its sour note. It's a really interesting and perhaps slightly unexpected way of using fruit and works beautifully when contrasted with the sweetness in the dish, which comes from the sugar and the prawns.

SERVES 4

2 tablespoons vegetable oil
60g medium raw prawns, peeled, cleaned and deveined
6 garlic cloves, chopped
1 green chilli, sliced
5 tablespoons palm sugar
4 tablespoons fish sauce
2 tomatoes, quartered

2 small green mangoes, peeled and diced
1/4 teaspoon ground turmeric
1/4 teaspoon ground coriander
10–12 Thai basil leaves, to garnish
10–12 sprigs of coriander, to garnish

Heat the oil in a wok over a high heat and sauté the prawns until opaque and light golden; remove with a slotted spoon and keep aside until required. Add the garlic to the wok, sauté to brown lightly, then add the green chilli, sugar and fish sauce. Cook, stirring, to caramelise the mixture.

Add the tomatoes and mangoes and stir-fry for 2–3 minutes. Return the prawns to the wok and add the ground spices. Mix well, then remove from the heat and garnish with Thai basil and coriander leaves.

RED SNAPPER CURRY

The varieties of basil used in Asia are very different to those that are commonly employed in European cuisine. As you might expect, Asian cultivars have spicier notes – many of them, including Thai basil and holy basil, have an aniseed or lemon flavour. Asian varieties have also been cultivated to stand up well to the high temperatures of stir–fries or to extended cooking times.

SERVES 4–6

6 red snapper or sea bass fillets, with skin
2 tablespoons fish sauce
1 teaspoon ground turmeric
1/2 teaspoon finely chopped red chilli

For the sauce
2 tablespoons vegetable oil
2 onions, finely chopped
3 spring onions, thinly sliced
2 large red chillies, chopped
2 bird's eye chillies, chopped (optional)
1 tablespoon Garlic Paste (see page 223)
1 tablespoon finely chopped fresh ginger
2 lemongrass stalks, chopped

1/2 teaspoon ground cinnamon
1 teaspoon ground coriander
1/2 teaspoon ground fennel
1 teaspoon ground turmeric
2 tablespoons fish sauce
250ml fish stock
4 kaffir lime leaves, shredded
2 star anise
400ml coconut milk
300g snake beans or green beans, cut into 5cm pieces
1 teaspoon palm sugar
1 tablespoon lime juice
4 leaves of Thai basil, shredded
a few coriander sprigs, to garnish
lime wedges, to serve

Make a few deep slashes in the fish, then place in a dish and add the fish sauce, turmeric and red chilli. Turn to coat, then keep aside until required.

For the sauce, heat the oil in a wok and sauté the onions, spring onions, chillies, garlic paste, ginger, lemongrass and ground spices for 2–3 minutes, stirring well. Add the fish sauce, fish stock, kaffir lime leaves and star anise. Bring to the boil, then simmer for a couple of minutes to cook the spices. Add the coconut milk and beans simmer for 5 minutes, until the beans are tender.

Meanwhile, heat a frying pan over a medium–high heat until hot, then add the olive oil. Place the fillets (skin-side down) in the pan and sear for 2 minutes, or until the skin is crisp, then flip over and fry on the other side for about a minute, or until cooked through.

To serve, add the palm sugar, lime juice and basil to the sauce and bring back to a simmer. Serve the sauce in serving bowls, topped with the fish and garnished with coriander sprigs. Serve with lime wedges accompanied by rice.

RIGHT: VIETNAMESE RED SNAPPER CURRY

CARIBBEAN PRAWN SKEWER CURRY

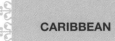

PRAWN SKEWER CURRY

Caribbean food is a mélange of cuisines and cultures and this recipe is the perfect example of the richness of the islands' diverse culinary heritage. Blending spices such as peppercorns and coriander from the East with paprika and herbs, such as parsley and thyme, from the West creates a unique and fascinating cuisine that is bold, flavoursome and bursting with colour and freshness. Here's an easy dish – juicy prawns marinated and grilled, then served with rice and curry.

SERVES 4

24 medium raw prawns, peeled but with tails left on, cleaned and deveined
1 large green pepper, deseeded and cut into large square pieces
2 red onions, cut into large square pieces
vegetable oil, for basting
limes, to serve

For the marinade
3 tablespoons finely chopped garlic
2 green chillies, finely chopped
2 tablespoons lime juice
4 sprigs of thyme, chopped
2 tablespoons chopped parsley
1 tablespoon smoked paprika
2 tablespoons vegetable oil
1/2 teaspoon freshly cracked black peppercorns
1 tablespoon ground coriander
3 tablespoons finely chopped coriander leaves

For the sauce
2 tablespoons vegetable oil
1/2 teaspoon fenugreek seeds
1 onion, finely chopped
2 tablespoons finely chopped fresh ginger
3 tablespoons Caribbean Curry Powder (see page 220), mixed with 100ml water
300ml coconut milk
1/2 Scotch bonnet chilli, deseeded and finely chopped
10–12 cherry tomatoes, or 1 large tomato, diced
2 tablespoons finely chopped coriander leaves
salt

The night before, put 8 bamboo or wooden skewers in a bowl of water and leave to soak overnight.

Mix together all the ingredients for the marinade in a bowl and add the prawns, pepper and onions. Leave in a cool place to marinate for 30 minutes.

To make the sauce, heat the oil in a pan and sauté the fenugreek seeds just until they change colour. Add the onion and ginger and sauté until translucent. Stir in the curry powder slurry and cook for 2–3 minutes. Add the coconut milk and Scotch bonnet chilli, bring to a simmer and simmer for 3–5 minutes or until the sauce thickens. Add the tomatoes and chopped coriander, season with salt and stir to mix. Keep warm while you cook the prawns.

Prepare a charcoal fire in a barbecue or preheat the grill to medium. Thread three prawns on to each skewer, alternating with pepper and onion. Grill the prawns, basting with oil and turning, until they are lightly charred and cooked. Squeeze lime juice over the prawn skewers and serve with the hot sauce and rice. Garnish with a few sprigs of coriander.

PRAWN CURRY

PRAWN AND TAMARIND CURRY

MEEN VEVICHATHU

Thai food is incredibly vibrant; it has colour, punchy aromatic flavours and many textures. Sweet with sour, hot with nutty and many other pairings make this cuisine stand out among other spicy cuisines.

SERVES 4

3–4 tablespoons vegetable oil
½ teaspoon sugar
2 tablespoons fish sauce
100ml Tamarind Water (see page 228)
16–20 medium raw prawns, peeled, cleaned and deveined
4–5 betel leaves (optional)
2 heads of pak choi, shredded
a few sprigs of coriander leaves, to garnish

For the spice paste
8 dried long red chillies,

soaked in lukewarm water to soften, deseeded and drained
1 lemongrass stalk, chopped
3 tablespoons chopped fresh turmeric, or 1 teaspoon ground turmeric
4 red shallots, chopped
3 tablespoons chopped garlic
1 teaspoon white peppercorns
1 teaspoon kapi (dried shrimp paste; see page 222; optional)
salt, to taste

Place all the spice paste ingredients in a blender and blend to make a fine paste.

Heat the oil in a wok, add the paste and sauté over a medium heat for 3–4 minutes until fragrant and lightly coloured. Add the sugar, fish sauce and tamarind water and mix well. Add the prawns and sauté for 3–5 minutes, until the prawns are almost cooked. Add the betel and pak choi leaves and toss gently to wilt the leaves. Serve hot, garnished with coriander and accompanied by rice.

This is a great recipe from Kerala, traditionally made with fish tamarind (or Malabar tamarind, kudampuli or gambooge as it is also known), which is very particular to Keralan cooking. The ripe, yellow, pumpkin-shaped fruit is picked from the tree then left to dry, either in the sun or above the stove, then smoked, which gives it a very distinctive flavour. It's unlike anything I've tasted – some people love it and others really dislike it, so while I would urge you to give it a try, I'd also say proceed with caution. Perhaps try it in a smaller quantity the first time you cook with it. In the absence of fish tamarind, or if you'd prefer not to risk it, just use plain tamarind.

SERVES 4

a walnut-sized piece of seedless dried tamarind or half the quantity of fish tamarind
1 tablespoon rapeseed oil
1 teaspoon black mustard seeds
1 teaspoon fenugreek seeds
2 shallots, chopped
2 green chillies, slit
1 tablespoon chopped fresh ginger
15–20 curry leaves
20–24 medium raw prawns, peeled, but with tails left

on, cleaned and deveined
salt

For the spice paste
5 shallots
2 garlic cloves
a 5cm piece of cinnamon stick
2 cloves
½ teaspoon fennel seeds
1 teaspoon red chilli powder
2 teaspoons ground coriander
1 teaspoon ground turmeric
½ teaspoon ground black pepper

Soak the dried tamarind in 200ml lukewarm water for 15–20 minutes.

Place all the spice paste ingredients in a blender with 4–5 tablespoons of water and blend to a fine paste.

Heat the oil in a pan, add the mustard seeds and sauté until they pop, then add the fenugreek and shallots, Sauté until the shallots are light brown in colour. Add the green chillies, ginger, curry leaves and salt. Cook over a medium heat for 3–5 minutes. Mix in the spice paste, sauté for 2–3 minutes, until fragrant, then add the prawns. Add the tamarind with its soaking liquid and cook for 10–12 minutes until the prawns are cooked. You can garnish with a few crisp-fried curry leaves. Serve with rice.

RIGHT: SOUTH INDIAN PRAWN AND TAMARIND CURRY

PRAWNS IN TOMATO SAUCE

GOLDA CHINGRI

Golda chengri is the name given to the very large freshwater prawns or crayfish found in Bangladesh. For this curry, the prawns are cooked whole with the head on to give extra flavour and richness to the sauce.

SERVES 4

4 tablespoons mustard oil or vegetable oil
1 teaspoon cumin seeds
1 bay leaf
1 large onion, thinly sliced
1 tablespoon Ginger Paste (see page 223)
1/2 teaspoon ground turmeric
1 teaspoon red chilli powder
1 tablespoon ground coriander

4–6 large raw prawns
2 large tomatoes, skinned, deseeded and puréed
100ml coconut milk
2 red chillies, sliced
2 green chillies, sliced
1/4 teaspoon Garam Masala (see page 223)
salt
2 tablespoons finely chopped coriander leaves, to garnish

Heat the oil in a pan and sauté the cumin seeds and bay leaf for a minute. Add the onion and sauté until translucent. Add the ginger paste and sauté for 2 minutes, then stir in all the ground spices except the garam masala. Sauté for a minute.

Add the prawns and sauté briefly to sear on both sides. Add the puréed tomato and 100ml water and season with salt. Bring to the boil and simmer until the prawns turn pink and opaque. Add the coconut milk and simmer for a further 5 minutes.

Sprinkle over the red and green chillies and the garam masala, then garnish with the coriander and serve with rice.

SEYCHELLES FISH CURRY

Seychelles cuisine echoes the influences of the different people that inhabit the islands – Chinese, Indian and French to name but a few. Needless to say seafood forms a huge part of the diet – it is said that over 1,000 species of fish can be found around the Seychelles – so there is much to choose from.

SERVES 4

4 tablespoons vegetable oil
2 onions, chopped
2 tablespoon Seychelles Curry Paste (see page 227)
1/2 teaspoon ground turmeric
1 tablespoon finely chopped garlic
1 tablespoon finely chopped fresh ginger

3 tablespoons Tamarind Water (see page 228)
2 sprigs of thyme
1 star anise
500ml fish stock
4 red snapper or sea bass fillets, with skin on
salt and pepper

Heat 2 tablespoons of the oil in a pan and sauté the onions until lightly browned. Add the curry paste, turmeric, garlic and ginger and sauté, stirring, until fragrant. Add the tamarind water, thyme, star anise, stock and salt and pepper to taste. Bring to the boil, then simmer for 10–12 minutes.

Meanwhile, slash the skin of the fish and season with salt and pepper. In a separate pan, heat the remaining oil, then place the fillets in the pan, skin-side down, and sear for 2 minutes or until the skin is crisp. Add to the sauce and simmer for a final 2–3 minutes or until the fish is cooked through. Serve immediately with rice.

SEYCHELLES FISH CURRY

MY UNCLE AND AUNT'S LOBSTER CURRY

My uncle moved to Canada years ago and is now a true Canadian; he struggles to talk in Hindi. My aunt is from New Brunswick so lobster has been a staple ingredient in their household. They are both amazing cooks and this recipe was inspired by them.

SERVES 4

4 live lobsters
3 tablespoons coconut or vegetable oil
a 2.5cm piece of cinnamon stick
2 green cardamom pods
4 cloves
1 tablespoon finely chopped fresh ginger
2 garlic cloves, sliced
1 large onion, sliced
10 curry leaves
1 teaspoon ground turmeric
1/2 teaspoon red chilli powder
1 teaspoon ground coriander
1/4 teaspoon crushed black peppercorns
2 tomatoes, chopped
5–6 cashew nuts, soaked in lukewarm water for 1 hour then blended to a fine paste
400ml coconut milk
salt
coriander sprigs, to garnish

Put the lobsters in the freezer for 2 hours, until almost frozen – this will render them unconscious. Then add them to a very large pan of boiling salted water and simmer for 2 minutes. Remove from the pan, immerse them in chilled water, then drain. Remove all the meat from the shells, keeping it whole – discard the black intestinal vein that runs down the tail flesh and the stomach sac and gills from the head. The meat will just be blanched, not completely cooked, at this stage.

Heat 2 tablespoons of the oil in a pan over a medium heat and briefly sauté the cinnamon, cardamom and cloves. Add the ginger and garlic and sauté for a minute, then add the onion and curry leaves. Sauté until the onion is translucent, then add the turmeric, chilli, coriander and peppercorns. Add the chopped tomatoes and cook for 2–3 minutes. Add the cashew nut paste and half the coconut milk and simmer for 10–12 minutes until the sauce thickens. Add the remaining coconut milk and simmer for a further 2–3 minutes to heat through.

In a separate pan, heat the remaining oil and sauté the lobster meat to brown lightly. Add it to the sauce, bring to a simmer, then remove from the heat. Garnish with coriander and serve with rice.

PRAWNS IN COCONUT MILK

NARKOL CHENGRI MOLAIKARI

This curry from Bangladesh demonstrates the Bengali love of sweet flavours. Coconut milk, almonds, yoghurt and cream, gently spiced with cardamom, make this a sweetly perfumed, rich dish but as part of an elaborate meal it really stands out. It's the sort of dish that would be served at a festive occasion, such as Diwali.

SERVES 4

2 tablespoons vegetable oil
2 green cardamom pods
1 bay leaf
2–3 cloves
1 onion, finely chopped
1 teaspoon red chilli powder
1/4 teaspoon crushed black peppercorns
1/2 teaspoon Ginger Paste (see page 223)
1/4 teaspoon ground turmeric
1 medium tomato, puréed whole
500g raw tiger prawns, peeled, cleaned and
deveined
50g plain yoghurt, whisked
1 tablespoon single cream
50g almonds, soaked in lukewarm water for 1 hour then blended to a fine paste
1 teaspoon ghee
100ml coconut milk
salt

To garnish
1 tablespoon flaked almonds, toasted
1 tablespoon finely chopped coriander leaves

Heat the oil in a wok and sauté the cardamom pods, bay leaf and cloves for a minute. Add the onions and sauté until translucent. Add the chilli powder and black pepper and stir to mix, then sauté for a minute until fragrant. Add the ginger paste, turmeric and puréed tomato and cook for 3–4 minutes, stirring well.

Add the prawns and sauté briefly to sear on both sides, then add 100ml water. Bring to a boil and simmer until the prawns turn pink and opaque. Whisk in the yoghurt, cream, almond paste, ghee, coconut milk and salt to taste. Continue simmering until the sauce thickens.

Garnish with the toasted almonds and chopped coriander leaves and serve.

SALMON AND PRAWN PARCELS

IKAN UDANG PAKET

In Indonesia, these parcels are always made with banana leaf but I like to use wonton wrappers as they're easier to find in the UK and they're also edible, which means less fuss and less mess. You could also use foil or greaseproof paper to wrap the parcels.

SERVES 4

4 pieces of salmon fillet with skin, about 100g each
1 teaspoon lime juice
200g raw prawns, peeled, cleaned and deveined
3 spring onions, shredded
4 large wonton wrappers
salt

For the spice paste
1 teaspoon Sambal Olek (chilli paste; see page 227)
4 macadamia nuts
3 shallots, chopped
2 garlic cloves, peeled
1 teaspoon chopped fresh ginger
1 teaspoon terasi (dried shrimp paste; see page 222; optional)
1 tablespoon Tamarind Water (see page 228)
2 red Thai chillies, sliced
1 tablespoon finely chopped lemongrass (white part only)
3 kaffir lime leaves, finely chopped
150ml coconut milk

Sprinkle the fish with the lime juice and some salt and set aside in a cool place to marinate. Preheat the oven to 200°C/Gas Mark 6.

Place all the ingredients for the spice paste, with salt to taste, in a blender and blend to a fine paste. Heat the paste in a wok and cook, stirring, until it becomes thick. Add the prawns and cook for 3–5 minutes, until they turn pink and opaque, then remove from the heat.

Divide the spring onions between the wonton wrappers, place a fish fillet on, then place a generous amount of the prawn mixture on top. Wrap up neatly and place on a baking tray. Bake for 10–12 minutes or until the fish is cooked and the wrappers are golden brown. Insert a thin skewer into a parcel to check if the fish is cooked – it should go through the fish with ease. Serve immediately with a lentil salad.

SHRIMP COCONUT CURRY

As you would expect, seafood is a major part of Sri Lankan cuisine, and spices, coconut and seafood is a combination you come across time and again. To a Western palate that might sound repetitive but each dish and recipe has its own character due to the variety of flavours available and the different combinations and quantities of spices used.

SERVES 4

2 tablespoons rapeseed oil
2 onions, thinly sliced
6 garlic cloves, finely chopped
1 tablespoon finely chopped fresh ginger
a sprig of curry leaves
a 5cm piece of cinnamon stick
2 green chillies, slit
4 teaspoons Ceylon Curry
Powder (see page 221)
1 teaspoon red chilli powder
1 teaspoon ground turmeric
1 large tomato, chopped
600g medium raw prawns, peeled (tails left on), cleaned and deveined
400ml coconut milk
salt

Heat the oil in a pan and sauté the onion with the garlic, ginger, curry leaves, cinnamon and green chillies until lightly browned. Add the curry powder, chilli powder, turmeric and chopped tomato with salt to taste. Cook over a medium heat, stirring frequently, for 10 minutes or until the tomatoes have broken down.

Add the prawns and cook for 3–5 minutes, stirring well, then add the coconut milk and simmer until the prawns are cooked through. Serve hot.

SEAFOOD KORMA

In India, the korma is a dish that can be traced back to the 16th century, when it was introduced to northern India by the Mughlai. It is now found all over India and other parts of Asia (see also the recipes on pages 78 and 147) and it either mildly or heavily spiced, depending on the region or country. The word 'korma' actually refers to the cooking technique, which in Hindi and Urdu means 'to braise'. In northern India a korma is traditionally made from a 'shahi' – a gravy made out of boiled onion paste is then thickened with almond paste and cream or yoghurt, cooked slowly over a long period. In the UK, the korma common to British curry houses simply refers to a curry that is only mildly spiced, which has a thick cream – or coconut-based sauce. Some kind of nut, most commonly almonds, generally features, but there are no onions used. It is in fact not dissimilar to the southern Indian kormas, which are also made out of coconut milk and do not use any onion either, but the cooking method will differ and there won't be any cream used. To me, all versions are delicious, although in different ways. This recipe is very definitely a UK korma, prepared and cooked very quickly and easily.

SERVES 4

4 tablespoons vegetable oil
2 cloves
2 green cardamom pods
3 tablespoons ground almonds
3 tablespoons Onion Masala Gravy (see page 226)
$^1/_2$ teaspoon ground cumin
$^1/_2$ teaspoon ground coriander
$^1/_4$ teaspoon red chilli powder
150ml coconut milk
150ml single cream
2 tablespoons butter
8 king-sized scallops, coral removed
80g squid rings
8 large raw prawns, peeled (tails left on), cleaned and deveined
8 green lip mussels
salt and black pepper

To garnish
finely chopped coriander and mint leaves
1 green chilli, finely chopped
1 teaspoon finely chopped fresh ginger

Heat half the oil in a pan and sauté the cloves and cardamoms for a minute until the spices sizzle. Add the ground almonds and sauté for 30 seconds, then add the onion masala gravy, cumin, coriander and red chilli powder and sauté for 2 minutes. Add the coconut milk and simmer for 3–4 minutes, then add the single cream and correct the seasoning with salt and pepper.

In a frying pan, heat the remaining oil and the butter and sauté the seafood pieces one type after the other, for 1–2 minutes, to seal and sear. Remove each batch with a slotted spoon before adding the next. Set aside until required.

Bring the sauce to a simmer and add all the seafood and juices and simmer for 3–5 minutes or until completely cooked. Serve garnished with the chopped coriander, mint, chilli and ginger. I like to add a finishing flourish by presenting at the table with a few edible flowers.

BURMESE SIMPLE PRAWN CURRY

SIMPLE PRAWN CURRY

PAZUN HIN

Curry and rice is the staple diet in Burma and this curry is a good example of a typical meal. Burmese cuisine generally uses fewer spices than Indian, and garlic and ginger feature more prominently. The cooking method might be more elaborate in some versions of this recipe but I've chosen to keep it simple – this can be prepared and cooked quickly and easily making it ideal for a midweek curry.

SERVES 4

4 tablespoons groundnut or rapeseed oil
2 onions, chopped
1 tablespoon finely chopped garlic
1 tablespoon finely chopped fresh ginger
$1/2$ teaspoon ground turmeric
1 teaspoon curry powder
1 teaspoon sweet paprika
20 medium raw prawns, peeled, cleaned and deveined
2 courgettes, cut into large dice
3 green chillies, slit
1 tablespoon fish sauce
100ml fish stock or water
3 tomatoes, chopped
1 tablespoon chopped coriander leaves

Heat the oil in a pan and sauté the onions for 12–15 minutes or until lightly caramelised. Add the garlic and ginger and sauté for a further 2–3 minutes. Add the turmeric, curry powder and paprika and sauté for 2 minutes, stirring well.

Add the prawns, courgettes, green chillies, fish sauce and stock. Bring to the boil, then simmer gently for 4–5 minutes, until the prawns turn pink and opaque. Correct the seasoning with fish sauce. Add the chopped tomatoes and coriander, and serve. Garnish with onion rings and red chilli (optional).

SQUID CURRY

KANAWAI KARI

Squid is one fish that is better frozen than fresh. After thawing, the protein in the squid relaxes, making it far more tender to eat than the fresh fish, which can be rubbery. To keep it tender, you must either cook it very quickly, over a high heat, for just a minute or two, or cook it for a long period.

SERVES 4

1kg frozen squid, cleaned and cut into rings
$1/4$ teaspoon ground turmeric
$1/2$ teaspoon red chilli powder
2 tablespoons Jaffna Curry Powder (see page 223)
2 tablespoons finely chopped fresh ginger
1 tablespoon finely chopped garlic
10–12 curry leaves
$1/4$ teaspoon fenugreek seeds
1 star anise
a 2.5cm piece of cinnamon stick
1 lemongrass stalk, bruised
1 large red onion, finely chopped
5–6 tablespoons Tamarind Water (see page 228)
1 tablespoon coconut oil
600ml coconut milk
salt

Heat a frying pan over a high heat until very hot. Add a splash of oil to the pan and toss in the squid. Sear very quickly for 1–2 minutes, until just cooked. Remove from the pan and set aside.

Mix all the remaining ingredients (except the coconut milk) in a heavy-based pan on a low heat for 2–3 minutes to heat up the mixture. Add the coconut milk, 50ml water and salt to taste and stir to mix. Bring to a simmer and cook for 10–15 minutes. Add the squid and simmer for 1 minute to reheat, then serve immediately.

FISH CURRY

CURRY TRE RUAA

France's role in Cambodian history has left its mark on the cuisine in the form of the French baguette, which is a hugely popular food in Cambodia and is often to be found served alongside curries. It's a great vehicle for mopping up sauce! Its prevalence is perhaps somewhat ironic in a country that relies so heavily on rice but that's the sort of diversity that Cambodia offers in its cuisine.

SERVES 4

3 tablespoons vegetable oil
500ml coconut milk
100ml Tamarind Water (see page 228)
2 tablespoons sugar
2 tablespoons fish sauce
600g skinless snapper, bream or sea bass fillet, cut into 4 pieces
200g aubergine, sliced on the diagonal 2.5cm thick
100g runner or green beans, cut into 5cm pieces
salt
thinly sliced bird's eye chillies, to garnish

For the spice paste
1 tablespoon vegetable oil

3 dried red chillies
a 2.5cm piece of cinnamon stick
$1/2$ nutmeg, grated
2 star anise
5 green cardamom pods
$1/2$ lemongrass stalk
3 tablespoons chopped coriander leaves
4 garlic cloves, peeled
2 shallots, chopped
1 tablespoon chopped galangal
1 tablespoon chopped fresh ginger
$1/2$ teaspoon ground turmeric
2 teaspoons prahoc or kaapi (dried shrimp paste)

First make the spice paste. Heat the oil in a wok and sauté all the ingredients for the paste (except the shrimp paste) until lightly browned. Tip into a blender and add the shrimp paste and 200ml water, then blitz to make a fine paste. Set aside until required.

To make the curry, heat the oil in another wok, add the coconut milk and simmer for 3–4 minutes. Add the spice paste, tamarind water, sugar, fish sauce and salt to taste and simmer gently for 3–5 minutes to blend the flavours, stirring well. Gently add the fish, aubergine and beans and cook for 5–7 minutes or until the fish is tender and the vegetables are cooked. Serve garnished with sliced red chillies and accompanied by rice.

MANGO AND FISH CURRY

MEEN MANGA KARI

South Indian cuisine is robust, rustic and hearty; it reflects the geography of the region and that's what makes it intriguing. Fish, mangoes, curry leaves, green chillies, ginger, garlic all feature heavily, as this recipe demonstrates.

SERVES 4

4 medium swordfish steaks or mackerel or sea bass fillets
1 large unripe mango, peeled and sliced
1 onion, sliced
4 green chillies, slit
1 tablespoon finely chopped fresh ginger
15 curry leaves
1 tablespoon rapeseed oil
salt

For the spice paste
8 garlic cloves
1 large green chilli
$1/4$ teaspoon ground turmeric

2 teaspoons ground coriander
$1/2$ teaspoon red chilli powder

For the coconut paste
$1/2$ medium coconut, grated

For the seasoning
1 tablespoon vegetable oil
1 teaspoon black mustard seeds
1 dried red chilli, torn into pieces
4–5 shallots, chopped
6 curry leaves
$1/2$ teaspoon ground fenugreek

To make the spice paste, place all the ingredients in a blender with 4 tablespoons of water and blend to a fine paste. Tip into a bowl and set aside until required. Wash the blender and make the coconut paste by blending the grated coconut into a fine paste with 100ml water.

Place the fish, mango, onion, green chillies, ginger, curry leaves, oil, salt and spice paste in a pan and mix with 250ml water. Bring to a simmer and cook for 6–8 minutes, until the fish is just cooked. Add the coconut paste and simmer for 3–4 minutes – the sauce should begin to thicken.

For the seasoning, heat the oil in another pan, add the mustard seeds and when they pop add the chilli, shallot and curry leaves. Fry until fragrant, then remove from the heat and add the ground fenugreek. Pour the seasoning over the fish curry and serve with rice.

SOUTH INDIAN MANGO AND FISH CURRY

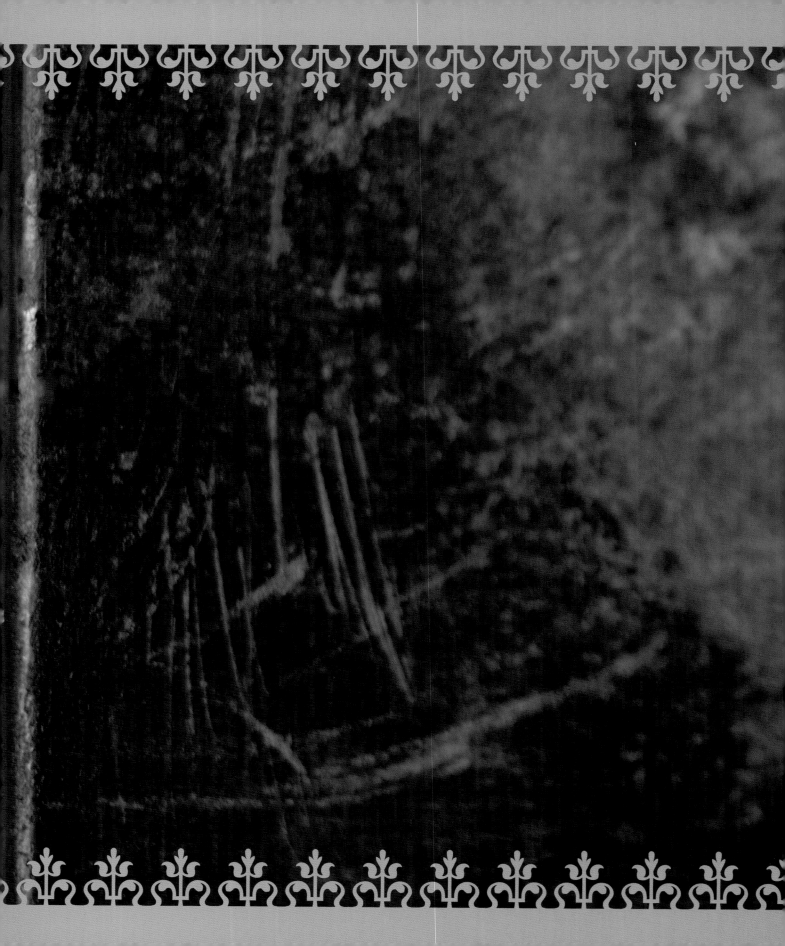

CHICKEN

AROMATIC GRILLED CHICKEN

AYAM PERCIK

On my trip round Malaysia filming a television series, the crew and I were very fortunate to be invited to do some filming in gardens belonging to Malay royalty. I was given the opportunity to cook with one of the royal chefs, although my tutor for the recipe was in fact a Malay princess, who watched closely as the chef distilled his secrets for making the dish. This is one of the recipes that really stood out on my trip – I loved the combination of the spices with the sweet and sour flavours of the coconut and tamarind.

SERVES 2

¹/₂ teaspoon coriander seeds
¹/₂ teaspoon fennel seeds
6–8 peppercorns
a 5cm cinnamon stick
6 shallots, peeled
4 garlic cloves, peeled
a 1cm piece of fresh ginger, peeled
2 tablespoons groundnut or vegetable oil
2 lemongrass stalks, finely chopped
3 small red chillies, sliced
1 teaspoon ground turmeric
300ml coconut milk
palm sugar or muscovado sugar, to taste
2 tablespoons Tamarind Water (see page 228)
2 medium boneless chicken breasts, with skin
salt

Toast the whole spices lightly in a dry non-stick frying pan until aromatic. Remove from the pan and set aside to cool.

Pound the shallots, garlic and ginger in a mortar to make a paste. Heat the oil in the frying pan, add the paste and sauté until opaque. Add the lemongrass and continue frying over gentle heat, stirring occasionally.

Meanwhile, pound the chillies to a paste in the mortar. Add to the pan together with the turmeric and stir well. Continue cooking gently.

Grind the toasted spices to a fine powder and add to the pan. Stir in the coconut milk, then add sugar to taste. Season with salt and add the tamarind. Stir well. Add 1–2 tablespoons water if the sauce is too thick. Add the chicken to the pan and braise gently in the sauce for 15–20 minutes or until cooked through.

Prepare a charcoal fire in the barbecue or preheat the oven grill to high. Grill over the hot coals or on a baking tray under the grill, basting with the sauce from time to time, for 5–10 minutes or until the chicken is lightly charred all over but still moist. Serve with a salad and the remaining sauce.

CAMBODIAN CHICKEN CURRY

KARRY SACH MOAN KHMER

Kroeung, the Cambodian curry paste, has an amazing blend of spicy flavours that are unique to this country, including turmeric, lemongrass and galangal. Spicy and rich, with a sour flavour cutting through – that's the balance required for curries from this part of the world.

SERVES 4

3 tablespoons vegetable or groundnut oil
500g potatoes, peeled and cut into wedges
4–6 tablespoons Kroeung (Cambodian Spice Paste; see page 224)
500ml coconut milk
8–10 chicken drumsticks, with skin
1 onion, thinly sliced
2 tablespoons fish sauce
4 teaspoons sugar
4 star anise
a 5cm cinnamon stick
salt
a handful of baby spinach leaves
pink pickled onions, to garnish

Heat 2 tablespoons of the oil in a frying pan and fry the potatoes over a medium heat until lightly coloured. Remove with a slotted spoon and set aside until required. Add the chicken to the pan and, using the same oil, fry over a medium heat until lightly coloured all over.

Heat the remaining tablespoon of the oil in a wok and sauté the kroeung paste on a medium heat for 5–7 minutes or until aromatic. Add half the coconut milk and simmer slowly to reduce until the paste becomes shiny and the oil starts separating out.

Add the onion, fish sauce, sugar, star anise, cinnamon and salt to taste. Sauté for 2–3 minutes, then add the chicken and the remaining coconut milk and simmer for about 15 minutes. Add the potatoes and mix them in, then continue simmering until they are completely tender and the chicken is cooked through. Add the spinach leaves, stir and remove them as they wilt. Serve with rice and garnish with the pickled onions.

CAMBODIAN CHICKEN CURRY

SOUTH INDIAN CHICKEN CHETTINAD

CHICKEN CHETTINAD

CHETINAAD KOZHI KOZHAMBU

In culinary terms Chettinad is a very influential region in the southern Indian state of Tamil Nadu. The food is generally dry and spicy. Cooks use spices that are unique to the region and often have a heady smell and flavour: spices such as Marathi mukku (looks like a large clove) and kalpasi (a stone fungus that grows near sea shores) are typical examples. If you can't find these spices you will have to attempt the recipe without them, but you will need to increase the quantities of each of the other spices by a teaspoon.

SERVES 4

5 tablespoons oil
600g skinless, boneless
   chicken thighs

For the spice powder
1 star anise
2 Marathi mukku (optional)
3–4 pieces of kalpasi (black
   stone fungus)
2 teaspoons black
   peppercorns
2 whole dried red chillies
2 teaspoons fennel seeds
1 teaspoon cumin seeds
2 teaspoons coriander seeds
3 tablespoons desiccated
   coconut
a 5cm piece of cinnamon

stick
2 cloves
2 green cardamom pods
2 tablespoons roasted channa
   daal
2 teaspoons poppy seeds

For the sauce
1 bay leaf
3 onions, thinly sliced
1 teaspoon red chilli powder
1 tablespoon Ginger-Garlic
   Paste (see page 223)
10 curry leaves
2 tomatoes, chopped
300ml coconut milk
salt

Heat a pan and toast all the spices for the spice powder, toasting one after the other, until each is lightly coloured and fragrant. Allow to cool a little, then tip all the spices into a blender and blend to a fine powder.

Heat the oil in a wok and sauté the chicken pieces until sealed and lightly coloured. Remove with a slotted spoon and set aside.

Reheat the oil and sauté the bay leaf and onions for 10–12 minutes over a medium heat until lightly coloured. Add the powdered spices, red chilli powder, ginger-garlic paste and curry leaves and sauté for 1–2 minutes, then add the chopped tomatoes, chicken and 100ml water and cook over a low heat until the chicken is cooked through – check this by pricking the thickest part of the meat with the end of a sharp knife to see if the juices run clear. Add the coconut milk and bring to the boil, then simmer for 2 minutes. Check the seasoning. You can garnish with a few crisp-fried curry leaves. Serve with steamed rice.

BENGALI CHICKEN STEW

MURGI JHOL

Chicken is one of the most favoured meats in Bangladesh. I love the simplicity of this recipe; it is an everyday curry in the average Bengali household but each housewife will add something 'special' to make the recipe her own, generally in the form of her own garam masala.

SERVES 4

2 tablespoons mustard oil or
   vegetable oil
800g skinless, boneless
   chicken thighs, cut into
   smaller pieces
1 teaspoon Panch Phoran
   (Bengal spice mix; see page
   226) or Chinese five-spice
   powder
1 bay leaf
2 cloves
1 teaspoon Ginger-Garlic
   Paste (see page 223)
2 medium potatoes, cut into

wedges
2 small cauliflower, broken
   into florets
$1^1/_2$ teaspoons ground
   turmeric
400ml chicken stock
2 medium tomatoes, cut into
   wedges
$1/_4$ teaspoon Garam Masala
   (see page 223)
1 tablespoon chopped
   coriander leaves
salt

Heat the oil in a pan, add the chicken pieces and sauté for 2–3 minutes, until sealed but with very little colour. Remove the pieces and set aside until required.

Reheat the oil, then add the panch phoran, bay leaf and cloves and sauté until the spices begin to pop. Add the ginger-garlic paste and sauté for 2 minutes, then add the potato wedges and cauliflower florets together with the turmeric. Sauté, stirring well, for 5–8 minutes or until the vegetables are almost cooked.

Return the chicken to the pan and add the stock and some salt. Bring to the boil, then simmer on a low heat until the chicken and potatoes are cooked. Add the tomatoes and simmer for a further 2–3 minutes, until the tomatoes soften. Sprinkle with the garam masala and chopped coriander before serving.

BURMESE CHICKEN CURRY

KYET THAR SIPYAN

Sipyan means 'curry' in Burmese, and roughly translates as 'floating oil' – oil floating on a curry is a sure sign that it is perfectly cooked. This recipe is really simple. The flavour of the curry relies on the chicken and onions only rather than any dominant spice.

SERVES 4

8–10 chicken drumsticks, with skin
3 tablespoons fish sauce
1 teaspoon groundnut or rapeseed oil
1 teaspoon ground turmeric
salt

For the onions
6 tablespoons groundnut or rapeseed oil
2 onions, thinly sliced

For the curry
1 tablespoon groundnut or rapeseed oil
1 tablespoon finely chopped garlic
1 teaspoon red chilli flakes
3 medium tomatoes, chopped
400ml chicken stock or water
1 tablespoon finely chopped coriander leaves

Place the chicken drumsticks in a dish, add the fish sauce, oil, turmeric and some salt and turn to coat. Leave to marinate in a cool place for 30–40 minutes.

Next prepare the onions. Heat the oil in a wok and fry the onions in small batches until light golden in colour. As they are cooked, remove to kitchen paper to drain, leaving as much oil as possible in the wok. Reheat the same oil and fry the chicken drumsticks until lightly browned all over. Remove and set aside.

Pour off the frying oil from the wok, then heat the 1 tablespoon oil and sauté the garlic with the chilli flakes until lightly coloured and fragrant. Add the onions and chicken to the wok and stir-fry for 2–3 minutes. Add the tomatoes and stock. Bring to the boil, then simmer for 25–30 minutes or until the chicken is perfectly cooked. Check the seasoning, add the coriander and serve with steamed rice.

CHICKEN COCONUT CURRY

KUKU PAKA

This is a traditional East African coastal dish of chicken, coconut and spices. 'Kuku' is the Swahili word for 'chicken' but the actual origins of the dish are difficult to trace and it is now widespread through the region. The Indian influence on the dish and region is evident in the spices used.

SERVES 4–6

4 medium potatoes, peeled and quartered
6 tablespoons vegetable oil
1 chicken, about 1.5kg, skin removed, cut into 8 or 12 pieces
2 onions, finely chopped
4 cloves
1 teaspoon finely chopped fresh ginger
1 teaspoon finely chopped garlic
1 tablespoon Malawi Curry Powder (see page 225)
2 green peppers, deseeded and cut into small dice
3 tomatoes, cut in quarters
600ml coconut milk
1 tablespoon lemon juice
1 tablespoon finely chopped coriander leaves
salt

Bring a saucepan of water to the boil and blanch the potatoes for 8–10 minutes or until just cooked. Drain.

Heat the oil in a frying pan and fry the chicken pieces until lightly brown; remove and set aside. Add the potatoes to the pan and brown lightly; remove and set aside until required.

Reheat the oil and sauté the onions with the cloves, ginger and garlic until lightly coloured. Stir in the curry powder, then return the chicken and potatoes to the pan. Add the green peppers and salt to taste. Sauté for a minute, then add the tomatoes and coconut milk. Simmer until the chicken is cooked, adding a little water, if needed. Stir in the lemon juice and coriander leaves. Serve hot with rice or bread. Garnish with a julienne of green peppers.

MALAWI CHICKEN COCONUT CURRY

CHICKEN CURRY NOODLE SOUP KUALA LUMPUR-STYLE

KARE LAKSA A LA KL

The Malaysian cuisine is always growing, absorbing influences from other cultures. This soup – which could be called the unofficial national dish of Malaysia – is a good example. There are numerous versions, but the spicy one from Kuala Lumpur is my favourite.

SERVES 4

4 tablespoons groundnut or vegetable oil
a 2.5cm piece of cinnamon stick
2 thick lemongrass stalks, bruised and tied together
4 medium boneless chicken thighs, with skin, cut into small pieces
400ml coconut milk
150ml chicken stock or water
2 teaspoons palm sugar
200g fresh tofu, cut into dice
200g bean sprouts
2 tablespoons chopped coriander leaves and stalks
400g pre-cooked Chinese egg noodles, soaked in hot water to soften
salt

For the spice paste
3 tablespoons coriander seeds
1 teaspoon cumin seeds
1 teaspoon fennel seeds
1 clove
8–10 black peppercorns
$1/4$ teaspoon ground turmeric
2 small dried red chillies
1 teaspoon belacan (dried shrimp paste)
5 shallots, chopped

To garnish
1 large red chilli, thinly sliced
coriander and mint sprigs
1 lime, cut into quarters

First make the spice paste. Pound or grind the coriander, cumin and fennel seeds, the clove, peppercorns, turmeric and dried chillies to a fine powder. Add the dried shrimp paste, shallots and 100ml water and continue pounding or grinding to make a fine paste.

Heat 3 tablespoons of the oil in a wok and add the cinnamon stick followed by the spice paste. Reduce the heat and cook for 8–10 minutes or until the raw smell of shallots is gone. Add the lemongrass and chicken and cook until the chicken is golden all over.

Add the coconut milk, stock, palm sugar and salt to taste and bring to a gentle simmer. Simmer for about 12–15 minutes, until the chicken is cooked. Keep warm.

Meanwhile, heat enough oil for deep-frying in a wok. When it is hot (170–180°C), deep-fry the tofu for 2–3 minutes or until light golden. Drain on kitchen paper and set aside.

Lightly blanch the bean sprouts in boiling water; drain. Add the chopped coriander to the soup. Divide the bean sprouts among four large bowls, followed by the noodles, the chicken and tofu. Ladle the liquid into the bowls. Garnish with red chilli, coriander and mint sprigs and lime, and serve immediately.

CHICKEN AND VEGETABLE STEW

SAMLAA KAKO

This is one of the most common curries prepared in Cambodian homes. Every region boasts that theirs is better, but much of the end flavour depends on the freshness of the vegetables used.

SERVES 4

2 tablespoon groundnut or vegetable oil
2 garlic cloves, very finely chopped
1 tablespoon finely chopped galangal
2 red chillies, thinly sliced
2 tablespoons Kroeung (Cambodian Spice Paste; see page 224)
1 tablespoon palm sugar or brown sugar
12 skinless, boneless chicken thighs, cut into smaller pieces
4 tablespoons fish sauce

6–8 kaffir lime leaves
600ml coconut milk
300g yellow pumpkin flesh, cut into 2.5cm dice
200g aubergine, diced
100g green beans, cut into 5cm lengths
3 medium tomatoes, skinned, quartered and deseeded
100g baby spinach leaves
salt and pepper

To garnish
a small bunch of basil leaves
mint and coriander leaves or sprigs

Heat the oil in a wok and sauté the garlic, galangal and red chillies until lightly coloured. Add the spice paste and sugar and sauté, stirring, for a couple of minutes, then add the chicken, fish sauce, kaffir lime leaves and coconut milk. Stir to mix. Bring to the boil, then simmer on a low heat until the chicken is half cooked.

Add the pumpkin, aubergine and beans and simmer for 10 minutes or until the vegetables are just tender. Add the tomatoes and spinach leaves and cook for a further 5 minutes or until the chicken is perfectly cooked. Season to taste with salt and pepper, and stir in the basil, mint and coriander leaves. Serve with rice.

CHICKEN CURRY

CARI GA

This traditional Vietnamese curry can be made using different starches, such as taro, cassava, or potatoes as I've used here.

SERVES 4–6

800g skinless chicken thighs or drumsticks
400g potatoes, peeled and cut into 2.5cm dice
3 tablespoons vegetable oil
2 onions, finely chopped
2 bay leaves
3 lemongrass stalks, lightly bruised
2 red chillies
1 teaspoon sugar
600ml coconut milk
4 spring onions, thinly sliced
salt

For the paste
1 small knob of fresh ginger, peeled
3 lemongrass stalks
3 garlic cloves, peeled
2 teaspoons salt
1/2 teaspoon black peppercorns
2 red chillies
2 teaspoons curry powder – Malaysian or Vietnamese (see pages 225 and 228) or a shop-bought medium powder

Make a fine paste from the paste ingredients. Rub all over the chicken pieces, then leave to marinate in a cool place for 30 minutes.

Meanwhile, blanch the potatoes in boiling water for 8–10 minutes, until just cooked. Drain well. Heat the oil in a pan and fry the potatoes until lightly browned. Remove and set aside until required.

Reheat the oil in the pan and fry the chicken and onions until lightly coloured. Add the bay leaves, lemongrass, red chilli, sugar, coconut milk and salt to taste. Stir well, then simmer gently for 25–30 minutes or until the chicken is perfectly cooked. Add the potatoes and simmer for a couple of minutes to reheat. Garnish with the spring onions and serve.

CHICKEN CURRY WITH COURGETTES

This light curry works well with mild-flavoured vegetables, such as courgettes or pumpkins. Note the way turmeric is used in Burmese recipes – it is always rubbed or smeared on meat and poultry before marinating, which is an old way of making food safe for consumption.

SERVES 4

8 medium chicken thighs, with skin
1 teaspoon ground turmeric
3 tablespoons rapeseed or groundnut oil
2 onions, chopped
4 garlic cloves, chopped
1 teaspoon sweet paprika
1 teaspoon dried shrimps

2 lemongrass stalks, bruised
1 tablespoon fish sauce
400ml chicken stock or water
200g courgettes, cut into large dice
salt
3–4 green chillies, slit, to garnish

Rub the chicken thighs with a mixture of salt and turmeric, then set aside until required.

Heat the oil in a wok and sauté the onions and garlic for 10–15 minutes or until the onions are translucent. Add the paprika and dried shrimps and sauté for 2–3 minutes, stirring well. Add the chicken, lemongrass, fish sauce and stock. Bring to the boil, then simmer gently for 20–25 minutes or until the chicken is almost cooked.

Add the courgettes and cook for a further 5–7 minutes or until the chicken and courgettes are both perfectly cooked. Serve hot, garnished with the green chillies.

LEFT: VIETNAMESE CHICKEN CURRY

CHICKEN IN RED SAUCE

MASAK HABANG

Spicy, sweet and sour are the flavours that characterise Indonesian food and this dish is a good example of that vibrant cuisine. The nuts in the spice paste play really well against the hot spicy chillies.

SERVES 4–6

8 skinless, boneless chicken thighs, each cut into 4 pieces
1 tablespoon lime juice
6 medium tomatoes, skinned, deseeded and chopped
salt

For the spice paste
1 large onion, chopped
4 garlic cloves, peeled
3 large red chillies, deseeded and chopped

1 red pepper, deseeded and chopped
6–10 macadamia nuts, toasted
1 teaspoon terasi (dried shrimp paste)
1 teaspoon palm or brown sugar
3 tablespoons Tamarind Water (see page 228) or lime juice
3 tablespoons groundnut or vegetable oil

In a bowl, toss the chicken with the lime juice and some salt. Leave to marinate in a cool place for 30 minutes.

Meanwhile, blend or pound together all the ingredients for the spice paste to make a fine paste.

Transfer the paste to a saucepan and sauté for 5 minutes. Add the chicken pieces and cook, stirring, for 3–4 minutes. Pour in 500ml water. Bring to the boil, then simmer for 10–12 minutes or until the chicken is almost cooked and the sauce has reduced by half.

Add the chopped tomatoes and stir to mix, then cook for a further 3–4 minutes. Check the seasoning and serve with rice.

CHICKEN CURRY

QUWARMAH ALA DIJAJ

The Gulf states have always traded with India and they were major players during the spice route days. As a result there is a strong Indian influence on the cuisine in the region, which you can see in this recipe.

SERVES 4

2 teaspoons Baharat (Middle Eastern spice powder; see page 220)
1 teaspoon ground turmeric
1 tablespoon lemon juice
1 teaspoon oil vegetable oil
4–5 chicken legs (thigh and drumstick), with skin

For the curry
4 tablespoons ghee or vegetable oil
3 onions, thinly sliced
1 tablespoon finely chopped garlic

1 tablespoon finely chopped fresh ginger
1/4 teaspoon red chilli powder
a 2.5cm piece of cinnamon stick
200g tomatoes, skinned and chopped
2 loomi (dried limes), pierced all over, or pared rind of 1 lemon
200ml chicken stock or water
salt
1 tablespoon finely chopped parsley or coriander leaves, to garnish

Mix together the baharat, turmeric, lemon juice, oil and salt to taste. Rub this all over the chicken legs, then leave in a cool place for 30 minutes. Reserve the remaining spice rub.

Heat the ghee in a pan and seal the chicken pieces a few at a time; remove from the pan and set aside. Add the onions to the pan and fry until translucent. Add the garlic, ginger, the leftover spice rub, red chilli powder and cinnamon. Fry for 2–3 minutes, then add the chopped tomatoes, limes and stock plus salt to taste. Bring to the boil.

Return the chicken pieces to the pan. Reduce the heat and simmer for 45–50 minutes or until the chicken pieces are cooked and the sauce is thick. Garnish with chopped parsley or coriander and serve with rice.

MIDDLE EASTERN CHICKEN CURRY

CHICKEN CURRY KALIMANTAN STYLE

AYAM CINCANE

The Kalimantan is a region of Indonesia, comprising the southern part of the island of Borneo (the northern tip is made up of a part of Malaysia and Brunei). Kalimantan cuisine typically has a lot of meat and sweetness. This recipe demonstrates the Western influence on the region, as roasting meat is not a traditional cooking method. The roasted or grilled chicken is served with a sauce and relishes. I've suggested serving it with deep-fried crispy onions as well, which adds a lovely crunchy texture, and some turmeric rice, for a wonderful colour.

SERVES 4

4 chicken supremes, 100–120g each, with skin
1 teaspoon red chilli powder
1 tablespoon Garlic Paste (see page 223)
1 tablespoon lemon juice
1/4 teaspoon crushed black pepper
1 tablespoon vegetable oil
salt
a few chives, chopped, to garnish
Crispy Onions (see page 222), to serve
Turmeric Rice (see page 228), to serve

For the sauce
2 tablespoons vegetable oil
6 shallots, thinly sliced
1 tablespoon chopped garlic
2 large red chillies (Dutch), finely chopped
1 tablespoon finely chopped fresh ginger
1 teaspoon finely chopped galangal
1 teaspoon terasi (dried shrimp paste), lightly toasted and crumbled
1 bay leaf
1 tablespoon palm sugar
300ml coconut milk
100ml chicken stock

In a dish, mix the chicken with the chilli powder, garlic paste, lemon juice, black pepper and some salt. Leave to marinate in a cool place for 1 hour.

Preheat the oven to 180°C/Gas Mark 4. You can either sear the chicken pieces on a hot ridged grill pan or under a hot grill. Then place in the oven for 12–14 minutes, to finish the cooking.

To make the sauce, heat the oil in a pan and sauté the shallots until lightly coloured. Add the garlic, chillies, ginger, galangal, shrimp paste, bay leaf and sugar, and sauté for 3–5 minutes, until fragrant and lightly coloured. Pour in the coconut milk and stock. Bring to the boil, stirring well, then simmer until the sauce thickens.

Pour the sauce over the chicken and garnish with the chopped chives. Serve with crispy onions and turmeric rice.

CHICKEN RENDANG

RENDANG AYAM

Rendang is a dish of celebration in Malaysia and Indonesia, traditionally made with beef and often served at festive occasions, particularly weddings. The original recipe was time-consuming as beef was simmered in coconut milk and spices over several hours. This version, made with chicken, has a much shorter cooking time. It's a special treat whenever you make it!

SERVES 4

3 tablespoons groundnut or vegetable oil
a 5cm cinnamon stick
3 star anise
5–7 green cardamom pods, bruised to open
600ml coconut milk
a piece of dried asam gelugur (Malaysian equivalent of tamarind)
1 teaspoon palm sugar
4 kaffir lime leaves
500g skinless, boneless chicken thighs, cut into
2.5cm dice
salt

For the paste
3 lemongrass stalks, thinly sliced
5–6 shallots, chopped
2–3 garlic cloves, chopped
1 teaspoon ground turmeric, or a small knob of fresh turmeric
1 tablespoon chopped galangal
2–4 small dried red chillies

Pound or blend all the paste ingredients with 3–4 tablespoons water until fine.

Heat the oil in a wok and sauté the cinnamon stick, star anise and cardamom pods for 1–2 minutes or until the spices sizzle and change colour. Add the paste and sauté for 6–8 minutes, stirring constantly, until the raw garlic smell goes away and the oil separates out from the paste.

Add the coconut milk, asam gelugur, palm sugar, lime leaves and salt to taste. Bring to the boil, then simmer for 15–20 minutes, stirring often, until the liquid is reduced by a quarter.

Add the chicken pieces and stir to mix into the sauce. Lower the heat and simmer gently for 30–40 minutes or until the chicken is cooked and the sauce has reduced to a thick soup consistency. During cooking, stir well to prevent the curry from catching on the bottom of the pan.

Spoon off the excess fat, then continue to cook until the chicken pieces caramelise a bit and the sauce has a golden brown colour. Remove and discard the whole spices, asam gelugur and lime leaves. Transfer the chicken to a serving dish and serve with rice.

LEFT: INDONESIAN CHICKEN CURRY KALIMANTAN STYLE

PAKISTANI CHICKEN CURRY WITH FENUGREEK

CHICKEN CURRY WITH FENUGREEK

QASURI METHI MURG

Methi Murg, with its distinctive flavour of fresh fenugreek (methi), is an all-time favourite recipe of the people of Punjab. The best fenugreek in the world comes from Qasur, or Kasur, a small town south of Lahore.

SERVES 4

200g plain yoghurt
1 tablespoon crushed black pepper
salt
800g skinless, boneless chicken thighs, each cut into 2 or 3 pieces
plain yoghurt, to serve

For the sauce
5 tablespoons ghee or vegetable oil
5 green cardamom pods
1 black cardamom pod
4 cloves
a 2.5cm piece of cinnamon

stick
1 blade of mace
2 bay leaves
3 onions, thinly sliced
1 tablespoon Ginger-Garlic Paste (see page 223)
4 green chillies, sliced
1 teaspoon ground turmeric
2 tablespoons ground coriander
1 teaspoon red chilli powder
2 tomatoes, blended to a purée
2 tablespoons kasoori methi (dried fenugreek leaves)

Season the yoghurt with the pepper and salt to taste. Add the chicken pieces and turn to coat, then leave to marinate in a cool place for 1 hour.

Heat the ghee in a pan and sauté the whole spices with the bay leaves until they crackle. Add the sliced onions and sauté until golden brown. Add the ginger-garlic paste, green chillies and ground spices with 1 tablespoon water and cook for a minute, stirring well. Add tomatoes and cook for 15 minutes or until the fat starts to separate out.

Add the chicken with its marinade and 100ml water. Bring to a simmer and simmer over a low heat for 12–15 minutes, until the chicken is almost cooked. Adjust the seasoning, add the kasoori methi and mix well, then simmer for a further 3–5 minutes. Serve hot with dollops of thick yoghurt and breads or rice. Garnish with julienned ginger.

CHICKEN LIVER CURRY

This curry can be served as a main course with rice or as a snack with drinks, either placed neatly on small pieces of crisp naan bread or simply with a few toothpicks.

SERVES 4

1 tablespoon ground coriander
2 teaspoons ground cumin
2 tablespoons vegetable oil
1 tablespoon finely chopped garlic
1 tablespoon finely chopped fresh ginger
2 onions, finely chopped

$1/_2$ teaspoon ground turmeric
1 teaspoon red chilli powder
600g chicken livers, cleaned and diced
1 mango, peeled and diced
2 tomatoes, diced
2 tablespoons finely chopped coriander leaves
salt

Lightly toast the ground coriander and cumin in a small pan. Set aside until needed.

Heat the oil in a pan and sauté the garlic, ginger and onions together until lightly coloured. Add all the ground spices and sauté for a minute, then add the chicken livers and stir to coat them well with the spices. Cook, stirring, for 3–4 minutes or until the livers have lost their raw look. Add the mango, tomatoes and salt to taste and cook gently for 2–3 minutes or until the livers are cooked through. Serve hot, sprinkled with chopped coriander.

MALAY CHICKEN KURMA

I love this curry with its wonderfully fragrant aromas and subtle spicing. Very popular throughout much of South-East Asia, India and Pakistan – once tried you will return to it time and time again!

SERVES 4

120ml groundnut or
vegetable oil
6 shallots, thinly sliced
4 garlic cloves, finely chopped
seeds from 4 cardamom pods
2 star anise
a 3cm piece of cinnamon
stick
3 cloves
a 3cm piece of fresh ginger,
peeled and chopped
2 red chillies, sliced
4 tablespoons Malaysian

Kurma Powder
(see page 225)
600g skinless, boneless
chicken breasts, cut into
2.5cm pieces
700ml coconut milk
salt

To finish
1 large onion, finely sliced
2 red chillies, split and
deseeded

Heat the oil in a wok and sauté the shallots and garlic for 7–10 minutes, until translucent. Add the cardamom seeds, star anise, cinnamon, cloves, ginger and chillies and sauté for 3–5 minutes or until fragrant. Stir in the kurma powder and continue frying for about 5–7 minutes, until the oil separates out. Add the chicken and 250ml water. Bring to a simmer, then cook for about 25 minutes or until the chicken is tender.

Pour in the coconut milk, stirring, and slowly bring to the boil. Season with salt to taste and continue simmering gently over a low heat until the sauce has thickened.

Add the sliced onion and split chillies. Stir to combine, then remove from the heat and serve on a bed of rice.

CHICKEN LAHORI

LAHORI MURG MASALA

Lahore is the gastronomic capital of Pakistan and the street food there is real theatre; a treat for the eyes. Pakistani cuisine generally involves a more heavy-handed use of oil and spices than a lot of Indian cuisine and this is proper Pakistani Punjabi fare: hearty and hot. If you're preparing the dish in advance, then leave out the yoghurt and add it just before you reheat the dish for serving.

SERVES 4

5 tablespoons vegetable oil
2 black cardamom pods
4 green cardamom pods
1 teaspoon cumin seeds
2 bay leaves
3 onions, chopped
1 tablespoon Ginger-Garlic
Paste (see page 223)
2 teaspoons red chilli powder
2 tablespoons ground
coriander

$1/2$ teaspoon ground turmeric
4 green chillies, chopped
3 tomatoes, chopped
8 skinless chicken thighs,
2 tablespoons plain yoghurt
400ml chicken stock or water
2 tablespoons finely chopped
coriander
1 teaspoon Garam Masala
(see page 223)
salt

Heat the oil in a wok and sauté the whole spices with the bay leaves until they crackle. Add the onions and sauté until lightly browned. Add the ginger-garlic paste and sauté for a minute, stirring well, then add the ground spices (except the garam masala), the green chillies and the tomatoes. Cook for 5–8 minutes or until the tomatoes soften.

Add the chicken pieces with the yoghurt, stock and salt to taste, and mix in well. Simmer gently for 20–25 minutes, until the chicken is cooked. If the sauce is too thick, add more stock. Stir in the chopped coriander leaves and garam masala, then serve. Finish with an optional garnish of rose petals.

CHICKEN LAHORI

CHICKEN TIKKA MASALA

No one from the Indian subcontinent can take credit for this dish. Made and invented in the UK, I see this as a truly British curry. I have eaten hundreds of incarnations of this recipe and still can't decide which one should be deemed authentic. However, I created this recipe for my kids and feel it is authentic enough for me! You can prepare and cook the chicken tikka beforehand – it will keep for up to 3–4 days in the fridge.

SERVES 4

500g boneless chicken thighs or breasts, cut into 2.5cm pieces
2 tablespoons vegetable oil
2 cloves
1 black cardamom pod
1 bay leaf
1 onion, finely chopped
1 tablespoon finely chopped fresh ginger
1 teaspoon ground cumin
1 teaspoon ground coriander
$1/2$ teaspoon red chilli powder
1 teaspoon ground fenugreek
5 tablespoons Onion Masala Gravy (see page 226)
1 tomato, skinned, deseeded and diced
4 tablespoons Greek yoghurt
1 tablespoon mango chutney (liquid part only)
150ml coconut milk
100ml single cream
100ml chicken stock or water
$1/2$ teaspoon Garam Masala (see page 223)
2 tablespoons finely chopped coriander leaves
salt

For the marinade
200g yoghurt
1 tablespoon Ginger-Garlic Paste (see page 223)
1 teaspoon red chilli powder
1 teaspoon ground coriander
$1/2$ teaspoon Garam Masala (see page 223)
1 tablespoon vegetable or mustard oil
$1/2$ teaspoon fenugreek leaf powder
1 tablespoon lemon juice
$1/2$ tablespoon besan (chickpea flour)

Start by marinating the chicken. Mix all the ingredients for the marinade together in a shallow ovenproof dish, then add the chicken and set aside at room temperature for 1 hour to marinate. When ready, preheat the oven grill to high and grill the chicken pieces for 5–8 minutes, turning and basting it throughout the cooking, until the chicken is lightly charred all over but still moist.

Heat the oil in a wok and sauté the cloves, black cardamom and bay leaf for 1 minute, then add the onion and ginger. Sauté for about 5–7 minutes, until the onion is translucent, then add the chicken tikka and sauté for 2–3 minutes, just until the chicken is heated through. Add the ground spices and sauté the mixture for 2–3 minutes, then add the onion masala gravy, diced tomatoes and yoghurt. Stir well for 2–3 minutes, then add the mango chutney, coconut milk, single cream and stock. Stir the mixture well, bring to a simmer (do not boil or it will split) and simmer for 3–4 minutes, until you have a homogeneous mixture. Season to taste, then sprinkle over the garam masala and chopped coriander leaves. Serve with rice or bread.

CHICKEN WITH RICE

MACHBOUS ALA DAJAJ

This is a Middle Eastern version of an Indian biriyani. I like to use chicken breasts on the bone, each cut into 2 pieces, but if you prefer thighs then use them by all means; just do not mix thighs and breasts because breasts will be cooked before thighs and continuing to cook them will spoil the texture of the breasts.

SERVES 4

300g basmati rice
3 tablespoons ghee or vegetable oil
3 onions, finely chopped
1 tablespoon Baharat (Middle Eastern spice powder; see page 220)
1 teaspoon ground turmeric
4 medium chicken breasts, on the bone, with skin, each cut crossways into 2
300g tomatoes, skinned and chopped
3 cloves

½ teaspoon loomi (dried lime) powder or grated lime zest
a 5cm piece of cinnamon stick
4 green cardamom pods
¼ teaspoon black pepper
salt

To garnish
2 tablespoons finely chopped coriander leaves
2 tablespoons finely chopped parsley

Tip the rice into a sieve and rinse under the cold tap, then leave to soak in a bowl of cold water for 5–10 minutes. Drain.

Heat the ghee in a pan and fry the onions until lightly browned. Add the baharat powder and turmeric and stir for a couple of minutes, then add the chicken pieces and sauté for 3–4 minutes to brown them lightly. Add the tomatoes, cloves, loomi powder, cinnamon, cardamom pods, pepper and salt to taste. Stir to mix well. Pour in 300ml water and bring to the boil, then reduce to a simmer.

Add the rice. Bring back to the boil, then cover and leave to simmer very gently for 30–35 minutes or until the rice and chicken are cooked. Garnish with the coriander and parsley and serve with pickles.

JEERA CHICKEN

The Indian community in Kenya created this dish and they love it. I have been asked time and time again for the recipe, so I had to include it in my book – this is my version. A spicy onion salad would be a good accompaniment.

SERVES 4

2 tablespoons cumin seeds
2 tablespoons vegetable oil
½ teaspoon black peppercorns
4–5 green cardamom pods
2 green chillies, finely chopped
1 tablespoon finely chopped garlic
1 tablespoon finely chopped fresh ginger

1 teaspoon ground coriander
2 teaspoons ground cumin
8 skinless, boneless chicken thighs, each cut in half
4 tablespoons plain yoghurt
1 teaspoon Garam Masala (see page 223)
2 tablespoons chopped coriander leaves
salt

Toast 1 tablespoon of the cumin seeds in a dry pan, then crush them lightly. Set aside until required.

Heat the oil in a pan and sauté the remaining cumin seeds with the peppercorns and cardamom pods for 1–2 minutes, until fragrant. Add the chillies, garlic and ginger and sauté for a further 2 minutes. Stir in the ground spices and sauté for a minute, then add the chicken pieces and stir to coat with the spices. Cook over a medium heat until the chicken loses its raw look.

Add the yoghurt, garam masala, 100ml of water and salt to taste. Simmer gently for 12–15 minutes or until the chicken is cooked. Add the toasted crushed cumin seeds and chopped coriander and serve hot with bread or rice. Garnish with a few sprigs of coriander.

KENYAN JEERA CHICKEN

THAI GREEN CHICKEN CURRY

GREEN CHICKEN CURRY

Chef David Thompson – a very good friend of mine – is my huge inspiration for Thai food and this is one of his most celebrated recipes for green chicken curry that I have adapted to suit the UK according to the Thai produce that is available here. This is a hot curry!

SERVES 4

1 tablespoon vegetable oil
400g skinless, boneless chicken thighs, cut into 2.5cm pieces
300ml chicken stock
15–20 apple or pea aubergines, or 1 medium aubergine, cut into 2.5cm cubes
500ml coconut milk
fish sauce, to taste
2–4 kaffir lime leaves
2 red chillies, diagonally sliced
a handful of Thai basil leaves

For the spice paste
3 tablespoons chopped green (bird's eye) chilli (adjust quantity to suit your taste)
1 tablespoon chopped galangal
1/2 tablespoon chopped fresh ginger
2 tablespoons chopped lemon grass
1 tablespoon finely chopped kaffir lime leaves
1 tablespoon chopped coriander roots
1 teaspoon chopped fresh turmeric or 1/2 teaspoon ground turmeric
100g chopped red shallots
6 garlic cloves, chopped
1 teaspoon shrimp paste (optional)
10 white peppercorns
1/2 teaspoon coriander seeds, toasted and ground
1/2 teaspoon cumin seeds, toasted and ground
handful of basil leaves, preferably Thai
salt

Place all the spice paste ingredients in a blender and blend to a fine paste. Don't use too much salt as fish sauce is very salty.

Heat the oil in a wok and sauté the chicken pieces to seal and lightly colour, then remove with a slotted spoon and set aside until required.

Add 4 tablespoons of the curry paste to the wok and sauté until fragrant, then add the stock, aubergine, chicken and coconut milk. Bring to the boil, then simmer for 10–15 minutes until the chicken and aubergine are cooked. Season with fish sauce, then add the remaining ingredients. Bring to a simmer, then serve with rice. You can garnish with finely sliced red chillies and a few leaves of basil.

CHICKEN IN WHITE SAUCE

OPOR AYAM

This curry is made all over Indonesia and every region may have something extra or different of their own to add. The souring agent is a local herb called belimbing wuluh, but it is not available outside Indonesia. I have used lemon and lime in this recipe, but have seen a few recipes where rhubarb has been used instead. Tamarind water is another option but it will most likely darken the sauce a bit. The choice is yours.

SERVES 4

8 skinless chicken drumsticks
juice and zest of 1 lemon
1/2 teaspoon salt
3 tablespoons vegetable oil
600ml coconut milk
3 kaffir lime leaves
1 tablespoon lime juice
salt

For the spice paste
1 onion, finely chopped and fried in 1 tablespoon of vegetable oil until translucent, then cooled
3 garlic cloves, chopped
8–10 almonds, skins removed
1 teaspoon ground coriander
1/2 teaspoon ground cumin
1/2 teaspoon chopped galangal
1 green chilli, chopped
50ml coconut milk

Mix the chicken drumsticks with the lemon juice and zest and the salt and set aside to marinate for 1 hour.

Heat the oil in a frying pan and fry the drumsticks until sealed and lightly coloured. Remove and keep aside until required.

Blend all the spice paste ingredients in a blender to a fine paste. Place in a pan and simmer for 5–6 minutes to heat, then add the coconut milk. Bring to the boil, then add the marinated drumsticks, kaffir lime leaves and lime juice. Simmer for 10–15 minutes, until the chicken is cooked through. Serve hot with rice.

WHITE CHICKEN CURRY

KUKULU KURMA

The sweetness of the cashew nuts and coconut, which are the dominant flavours in this Sri Lankan korma, demonstrate the influence of the Muslim community there, as they are partial to sweetness. The nuts and coconut also act as thickening agents, producing a rich, hearty dish.

SERVES 4

3 tablespoons ghee or
  vegetable oil
a 2.5cm piece of cinnamon
  stick
2–3 green cardamom pods
1 stick lemongrass, bruised
2 onions, finely chopped
1 tablespoon grated ginger
800g skinless, boneless
  chicken thighs, cut into 2.5
  cm pieces
1 tablespoon ground
  coriander

1 tablespoon ground fennel
1 teaspoon ground black
  pepper
1 teaspoon Garam Masala
  (see page 223)
50g cashew nuts, soaked in
  lukewarm water for 1 hour
  then blended to a fine paste
500ml coconut milk
1 tablespoon lemon juice
1 tablespoon finely chopped
  coriander leaves
salt

Heat the oil in a pan and sauté the cinnamon, cardamom and lemongrass over a medium heat, until fragrant. Add the onion and ginger and sauté for 5–7 minutes, until the onion is translucent. Add the chicken pieces and sauté for a further 5–7 minutes to seal and lightly colour. Add all the ground spices and sauté for 1–2 minutes, until fragrant, then add the cashew paste. Mix well for a minute, then add the coconut milk, salt to taste and bring to the boil. Simmer gently for 10–12 minutes or until the chicken is cooked. Stir in the lime juice and chopped coriander and serve with rice.

STIR-FRIED CHICKEN

KADHAI MURG

This is a classic North Indian recipe. A kadhai (or karahi) is a deep pan, similar in shape to a wok but with two handles, that is used for stir-frying and stews. Here, it is used to stir-fry the chicken then a spicy but light sauce is made. Tomatoes and fenugreek leaves are the dominant ingredients and they're spiced with garlic, red chilli and coriander seeds. Some people like to add onions to the sauce as well – it's a personal choice and I prefer to leave them out.

SERVES 4

3 tablespoons vegetable oil or
  ghee
800g skinless chicken thighs
  and drumsticks
2 tablespoons Garlic Paste
  (see page 223)
4–5 long dried red chillies,
  pounded to a coarse
  powder
1 tablespoon coriander seeds,
  pounded to a coarse
  powder
10 large tomatoes, chopped

3–4 green chillies, chopped
4–5 tablespoons finely
  chopped fresh ginger
100g coriander leaves, finely
  chopped
1 tablespoon tomato paste
1 teaspoon Garam Masala
  (see page 223)
1 teaspoon ground kasoori
  methi (dried fenugreek
  leaves)
salt, to taste

Heat the oil in a wok, add the chicken pieces and sauté to seal and lightly colour, then remove with a slotted spoon and set aside until required.

Re-heat the oil, add the garlic, chilli and coriander seeds and sauté for a minute, then add the tomatoes. Mix well and cook over a medium heat for 20 minutes, until the tomatoes start to soften. Add the green chillies, half the ginger, the coriander leaves and salt.

Stir in the tomato paste and cook for 3–4 minutes. Add the chicken and gently bring to a simmer, then cook for 25–30 minutes, stirring occasionally, until the chicken is cooked. Check the chicken is cooked by piercing the thickest part near the bone with the tip of a knife; the juices should run clear. Add the garam masala and kasoori methi and cook for a further 2–3 minutes, then add the remaining ginger. Check the seasoning and serve with Indian bread or rice, with a garnish of coriander sprigs.

NORTH INDIAN STIR-FRIED CHICKEN

TRINIDADIAN CHICKEN CURRY

TRINIDADIAN CHICKEN CURRY

Caribbean people love chicken curry, and each island has its own uniquely spiced speciality. This recipe traditionally calls for Trinidadian curry powder, but I've used the more common Caribbean curry powder with extra whole spices to get the same effect.

SERVES 4

12 skinless, boneless chicken thighs
2 medium potatoes, peeled and cut into thick roundels
2 tablespoons Caribbean Curry Powder (see page 220)
1 teaspoon ground turmeric
2 tablespoons vegetable oil
a 2.5cm piece of cinnamon stick
1 star anise
1/2 teaspoon fenugreek seeds
1 dried red chilli
1 onion, finely chopped

400ml chicken stock or water

For the marinade
1 tablespoon mustard (English or Dijon)
1 teaspoon mixed freshly cracked black and red peppercorns
2 onions, chopped
1 large tomato, chopped
6–8 garlic cloves, chopped
8–10 sprigs of coriander, chopped
salt

Mix together all the ingredients for the marinade in a bowl. Season with salt to taste. Add the chicken and potatoes and mix well to coat, then leave in a cool place for 2 hours.

Mix the curry powder and turmeric with 4–5 tablespoons of water and set aside.

Heat the oil in a pan and sauté the whole spices and dried red chilli until lightly coloured. Add the onion and sauté, stirring well, until translucent. Add the curry powder mixture and cook, stirring, for a minute.

Add the chicken and potatoes with their marinade. Pour in the stock and stir well. Bring to the boil, then simmer for 15–20 minutes or until the chicken and potatoes are cooked. Adjust the seasoning and serve with rice.

SRI LANKAN CHICKEN CURRY

KUKULMAS KARIYA

Combining spices such as cumin, cinnamon and curry leaves with aromatics such as pandan leaves and lemongrass shows the versatility of Sri Lankan cuisine – they use ingredients from all over the Asian region. This recipe was inspired by Sri Lankan friends living in the UK, but I have adapted it to make it simpler to prepare and cook.

SERVES 4–6

2 tablespoons vegetable or rapeseed oil
1 teaspoon crushed black peppercorns
a 5cm piece of cinnamon stick
6–8 green cardamom pods, bruised
6–7 cloves
400g shallots or onions, thinly sliced
1 tablespoon finely chopped garlic
1 tablespoon finely chopped fresh ginger
1kg skinless, boneless chicken

thighs, each cut into 4 pieces
2 tablespoons Ceylon Curry Powder (see page 221)
1 teaspoon red chilli powder
1 teaspoon ground turmeric
200g tomatoes, chopped (fresh or canned)
2 sprigs of curry leaves (about 20 leaves)
1 large pandan leaf, cut into 4 pieces
2–3 green chillies, slit
1 lemongrass stalk, bruised
400ml coconut milk
1 tablespoon lime juice

Heat the oil in a pan and sauté the black peppers, cinnamon, cardamom and cloves for 2–3 minutes or until fragrant. Add the sliced shallots and sauté until lightly coloured. Add the chopped garlic and ginger and sauté until the raw smell of garlic disappears. Add the chicken pieces and sauté for 5–7 minutes to seal and lightly colour, then add the curry powder, red chilli and turmeric and sauté for 2–3 minutes, until fragrant, mixing well. Add the tomatoes, curry and pandan leaves, chillies, lemon grass and 200ml of water, bring to a simmer and simmer for 5–7 minutes, until the chicken is almost cooked. Add the coconut milk and bring to the boil then lower the heat and simmer for 3–4 minutes to thicken the sauce. Just before serving, add the lime juice and mix well.

MANGALOREAN CHICKEN CURRY

KORI GASI

Mangalore is a port city in the southern Indian state of Karnataka. Like much of the South, chillies, coconut, curry leaves and spices such as fenugreek, mustard seeds and fennel seeds are the main players in this state. However, it's the act of toasting the coconut that gives a distinctive flavour to the curries of this region – so don't skip this important step on the road to authenticity.

SERVES 4

250g grated fresh coconut or unsweetened desiccated coconut
4 tablespoons vegetable oil
6–7 dried red chillies
3 tablespoons coriander seeds
1/2 teaspoon fenugreek seeds
1/2 teaspoon black mustard seeds
a 5cm piece of cinnamon stick
1 teaspoon cumin seeds
1/4 teaspoon black peppercorns

3–4 cloves
1/2 teaspoon ground turmeric
2 teaspoons Tamarind Water (see page 228) or pulp
2 onions, chopped
2 tablespoons finely chopped fresh ginger
5 garlic cloves
500ml coconut milk
15 curry leaves
800g skinless, boneless chicken thighs, cut into 2.5cm cubes

Toast the grated coconut in a pan until lightly coloured, then set aside until required.

Heat 1 tablespoon of the oil in another pan and sauté the chillies, coriander seeds, fenugreek seeds, mustard seeds, cinnamon stick, cumin seeds, peppercorns and cloves, adding them in this order and sautéing for a minute after each addition. Set aside to cool.

Tip all the toasted spices, toasted coconut, turmeric, tamarind water, half the chopped onions, ginger and garlic into a blender and blitz into a fine paste. Add 100ml coconut milk and blend again.

Heat the remaining oil in a wok and sauté the remaining onions and the curry leaves until lightly coloured. Add the spice paste and cook for 5–6 minutes, then add the chicken and cook for a further 4–5 minutes. Add 250ml water and cook slowly for 25–30 minutes, until the chicken is cooked through. Add the remaining coconut milk and bring to the boil, then simmer for 2–3 minutes. Serve with rice.

PERANAKAN SPICED FRIED CHICKEN

INCHE KABIN

For centuries, South East Asia's riches have attracted foreign traders to the region. While many returned to their countries of origin, some remained behind, marrying locals. The Malay term 'peranakan', meaning 'locally born', has come to refer to the communities resulting from these culturally mixed marriages. The Peranakan Chinese, for example, are descendants of Chinese traders who settled in Melaka and around the coastal areas of Java and Sumatra, as early as the 14th century. This recipe demonstrates their influence on Malaysian cuisine – the use of the stir-fry and the salad leaves being deep-fried are techniques that have clearly come from China rather than being indigenous to Malaysia.

SERVES 4

8–13 skinless, boneless chicken thighs
oil for deep-frying
mixed salad leaves, to garnish
Spicy Water Spinach (see page 217), to serve

For the marinade
a 2.5cm piece of cinnamon stick
3–4 small dried red chillies

1 tablespoon coriander seeds
1 teaspoon cumin seeds
1 teaspoon fennel seeds
1/2 teaspoon black peppercorns
2 teaspoons ground turmeric
2 teaspoons palm sugar
5–8 shallots, chopped
150ml coconut milk
salt

For the marinade, grind the cinnamon, dried chillies, coriander, cumin, fennel, black peppercorns and turmeric in a coffee grinder or spice mill to make a fine powder.

Combine the spice powder with the palm sugar, shallots, coconut milk and some salt in a blender and blitz to a very fine paste.

Arrange the chicken pieces side by side in a dish and pour over the paste. Turn the chicken to coat. Cover and leave to marinate in a cool place for 2–3 hours.

Heat enough oil for deep-frying in a wok. When it is hot (160–180°C), deep-fry the chicken pieces a few at a time for 12–15 minutes, until cooked through, golden brown and crisp. As each batch is fried, remove to a baking tray lined with kitchen paper and keep hot in a low oven (150°C/Gas Mark 2). Fry the mixed salad leaves in the hot oil until crisp; drain on kitchen paper. Use to garnish the chicken and serve with the spicy water spinach.

MALAYSIAN PERANAKAN SPICED FRIED CHICKEN

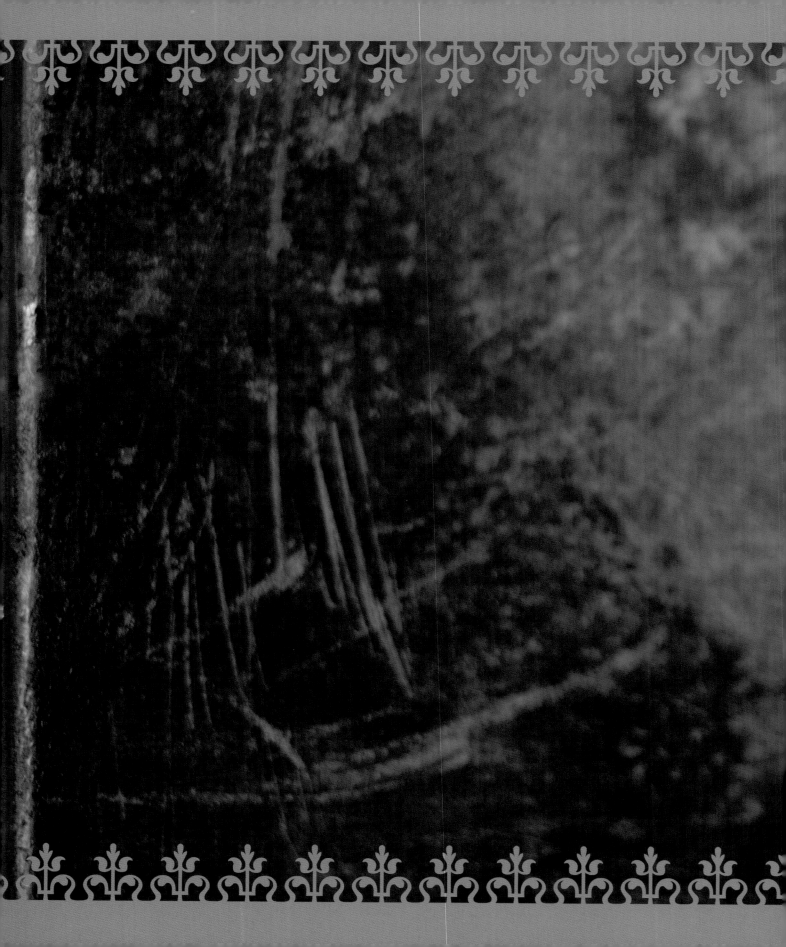

DUCK & GOOSE

DUCK AND POTATO CURRY

BEH THARE SIPYAN

In rice-producing countries, such as Burma, ducks are a common sight on the paddy fields and thus a widely available meat. Burmese cuisine reflects its range of regional influences. At a meal you might find a curry dish sitting alongside steamed dumplings, stir-fries and noodles – the idea being to help yourself to a little of each.

SERVES 4

400g duck breast, skin and fat removed, cut into 12–16 pieces
1 teaspoon ground turmeric
1 tablespoon fish sauce
100ml rapeseed or groundnut oil
2 potatoes, peeled and quartered
2 onions, pounded or very finely chopped to a rough paste
4 garlic cloves, finely chopped
3 dried red chillies, soaked in lukewarm water to soften and drained
1 teaspoon sweet paprika
300ml chicken stock or water
salt

In a bowl, toss the pieces of duck with the turmeric, fish sauce and some salt. Leave to marinate in a cool place for about 30 minutes or until required.

Heat the oil in a wok and sauté the potatoes over a high heat for 2–3 minutes, turning regularly to colour all sides. Remove to kitchen paper to drain. Reheat the oil and fry the duck pieces to brown them. Drain on kitchen paper.

Reheat the oil and sauté the onions, garlic and chillies for 15–20 minutes or until the onions are caramelised to a golden brown colour. Return the potatoes and duck to the wok and add the paprika and stock. Cover and simmer for 20–25 minutes or until the duck is perfectly cooked. The oil will probably be floating on the surface. If this bothers you, you can spoon it off. Serve with rice.

DUCK CURRY

HANSHER KALIA

This recipe reflects the Muslim influence on the food of Bangladesh – the Islamic Mughal Empire ruled most of India and Pakistan in the 16th and 17th centuries. This duck curry has a really good depth of spices. For a more modern presentation, you can choose to fry the duck pieces separate from the sauce, and serve on top of the sauce, as in the photo opposite.

SERVES 4–6

1 medium duck, with skin, cut into 16 pieces
3 onions, finely chopped
1 tablespoon Ginger-Garlic Paste (see page 223)
1 teaspoon red chilli powder
1 teaspoon ground cumin
1 teaspoon ground coriander
1 teaspoon curry powder
8–10 large cherry tomatoes, halved
2 tablespoons finely chopped coriander leaves
salt

For the garam masala paste
1 bay leaf
10 black peppercorns
a 5cm piece of cinnamon stick
6 green cardamom pods
4 cloves
1/4 teaspoon grated nutmeg
1 blade of mace
2 garlic cloves, peeled
1 tablespoon vegetable oil

Blend or pound all the ingredients for the garam masala with 50ml water to make a paste. Set aside until required.

Heat a non-stick pan and fry the duck pieces over a high heat (you won't need any oil as there will be lot of fat that will come out of the duck during cooking). When the skin is browned but the rest of the duck is still quite pink, remove the duck and set aside, reserving the fat. Leave the duck and brown all over if your prefer your duck to be medium.

Heat 3 tablespoons of the reserved fat in a separate pan and sauté the onions to colour lightly. Add the ginger-garlic paste and saute for 2–3 minutes to cook out the raw flavours, then add the garam masala paste and some salt. Cook, stirring, for a further 3–4 minutes or until fragrant.

Add the ground spices and stir to mix. Pour in about 750ml water. Bring to the boil, then cook on a low heat until the sauce has thickened. Add the tomatoes and chopped coriander a few minutes from the end. Serve the sauce onto serving plates, arranging the duck pieces on top and garnishing with a few salad leaves.

BANGLADESHI DUCK CURRY

SRI LANKAN DUCK CURRY

DUCK CURRY

THARA KARI

Duck is a common poultry that is used in everyday cooking in Sri Lanka – paddy fields and ducks go hand in hand. Arrack is a South East Asian liqueur, made from the fermented sap of coconut flowers. Alcohol is quite an unusual ingredient for this predominantly Buddhist island, however – it reflects a more Christian influence on the recipe.

SERVES 4–6

4 duck breasts, skin removed, diced
3 onions, finely chopped
2 tablespoons finely chopped garlic
2 tablespoons finely chopped ginger
a 2.5cm piece of cinnamon stick
1 star anise
1/2 teaspoon black pepper
1 pandan leaf
1 lemongrass stalk, bruised
2 tablespoons Ceylon Curry Powder (see page 221)
600ml coconut milk
3 tablespoons ghee or coconut oil
100ml arrack or whisky (optional)
1 tablespoon brown sugar
salt

Mix everything (except the ghee, arrack and sugar) together in a wok, seasoning with salt to taste. Simmer for 20–25 minutes or until the duck is cooked.

Remove the duck pieces from the sauce. Heat the ghee in a pan and sauté the duck until browned on all sides. Add the arrack, if using, and sugar, then pour the sauce on top and simmer for a further 10 minutes. Serve with rice and salad.

For a modern presentation, I like to pan-fry the duck separately and serve with the sauce, salad and rice alongside. To serve it this way (as in the photograph opposite), cook everything as above but omitting the duck. Then, heat a non-stick frying pan over a high heat until hot. Score the duck breast skin, season it with salt and add it to the pan, skin-side down (you won't need any oil as there will be lot of fat that will come out of the duck during cooking). Cook until the skin is brown and crisp but the rest of the duck is still quite pink, then flip the duck over and cook for another minute on the other side for rare meat, or 2–3 minutes for medium. Remove the duck and leave to rest for a few minutes, then slice and serve alongside the sauce, salad and rice.

DUCK BREAST WITH GREEN SAUCE

MASAK HIJAU

Some authentic versions of this dish can be very oily, but a little adaptation of Western methods and technique can turn it into a delectable modern recipe. Serve it with rice for tradition and a salad to complete the modern interpretation.

SERVES 4

3 kaffir lime leaves
4 spring onions, sliced
50g spinach leaves, shredded
200g fine green beans, cut into batons
4 duck breasts, with skin
sea salt

For the spice paste
1 onion, chopped
3–4 garlic cloves, peeled
4 green chillies, deseeded
1 tablespoon chopped fresh ginger
1 teaspoon chopped galangal
1/4 teaspoon ground turmeric
1 tablespoon chopped lemongrass
1 teaspoon terasi (dried shrimp paste; optional)
4 tablespoons Tamarind Water (see page 228) or lime juice
2 tablespoons vegetable or groundnut oil

Blend together all the ingredients for the spice paste to make a fine paste. Transfer the paste to a saucepan and simmer for 5 minutes. Add the kaffir lime leaves and 150ml water, then add the spring onions, spinach and green beans. Cook for 4–5 minutes, stirring occasionally, until the beans are just tender. Season to taste with salt, then remove from the heat. Set aside until required.

Score the duck skin in a criss-cross pattern and salt well. Place the breasts, skin-side down, in a non-stick pan and cook over a medium heat for 15–20 minutes. A lot of fat will be released during cooking; keep spooning this from the pan. When the skin is nice and crisp, turn the breasts over and cook for a further 2–3 minutes to sear.

Remove the duck breasts from the pan and leave to rest for 5 minutes. Meanwhile, reheat the sauce. Carve each duck breast into 5–6 pieces and serve by placing on top of the sauce.

DUCK CURRY WITH COCONUT

THARAVU KOOTAN

This mild curry from southern India reflects the a huge mix of cultures that can be found there, especially in Kerala. The large Syrian Christian and Muslim communities have been influential on the cuisine, adding some lovely splashes of colour and vibrancy to the dishes, as this recipe demonstrates.

SERVES 6

2 tablespoons vegetable oil
2 onions, sliced
1 tablespoon finely chopped fresh ginger
1 tablespoon finely chopped garlic
3 green chillies, slit
6 duck breasts, skin removed, cut into large dice
4 teaspoons white wine vinegar
500ml coconut milk
salt

For the spice paste
a 2.5cm piece of cinnamon stick

6 cloves
4 green cardamom pods
2 teaspoons ground coriander
1/2 teaspoon red chilli powder
1/2 teaspoon ground turmeric
1/2 teaspoon ground black pepper
2 tablespoons water

For the seasoning
1 teaspoon ghee or butter
1 teaspoon brown mustard seeds
4 shallots, chopped
12 curry leaves

To make the spice paste, tip all the ingredients into a blender and blend to a fine paste. Set aside until required.

Heat the oil in a pan, add the onions, ginger, garlic and green chillies and fry until the onion turns translucent. Add the duck, vinegar, salt, spice paste and 200ml water. Cover the pan and cook over a low heat for 8–10 minutes, until the duck is about half cooked. Add the coconut milk and simmer for a further 8–10 minutes, until the duck is completely cooked and the sauce thickens. If you like your duck quite pink then reduce the total cooking time to 12 minutes.

For the seasoning, heat the ghee in a separate pan, add the mustard seeds and cook until they pop. Add the remaining ingredients and sauté until the shallots turn light brown. Pour the seasoning over the duck curry and mix well. Serve with rice or bread.

DUCK JALFREZI

In the UK, the word 'jalfrezi' is commonly misunderstood to represent the heat level of a curry. In a typical British curry house, it's thought of as a 'medium heat' curry, sitting below what many British consider a 'very hot' curry, the vindaloo. In fact the word derives from from the Bengali word 'jhal', meaning 'spicy' and 'jalfrezi' is the term for the original dish in which cooked meats are stir-fried over a high heat with vegetables such as pepper and onion.

SERVES 4

3 tablespoons vegetable oil
4 duck breasts, cut into strips
1/2 teaspoon cumin seeds
1/2 teaspoon freshly ground black pepper
1 small knob of ginger, cut into very fine strips
1 onion, thickly sliced
4 green chillies, cut into very fine strips
1 teaspoon red chilli powder
1 tablespoon ground coriander
1/2 teaspoon ground turmeric

1 red and 1 green pepper, deseeded and cut into very fine strips
1/2 tablespoon tomato paste
4 tablespoons Onion Masala Gravy (see page 226)
70ml chicken stock or water
1/4 teaspoon Garam Masala (see page 223)
1 tablespoon lemon juice
2 tablespoons coriander leaves, to garnish
salt

Heat 1 tablespoon of the oil in a wok, add the sliced duck and stir-fry for 2–3 minutes to seal the meat. Remove to a plate and set aside until required.

Heat the remaining oil in the wok, add the cumin seeds, black pepper and ginger and sauté for 1–2 minutes, until the spices crackle. Add the onion and green chillies and sauté for 2–3 minutes, until the onion becomes translucent. Add the red chilli powder, ground coriander and turmeric and sauté for 1 minute. Add the duck, peppers, tomato paste and onion masala gravy. Loosen the mixture with the stock and stir-fry over a high heat for 4–5 minutes. Add the garam masala, lemon juice, some salt and chopped coriander. Mix well and serve garnished with coriander sprigs. Serve with Indian breads, such as naan or chapatti.

For a modern presentation, I like to pan-fry the duck separately (it's the chef in me!). To do this, heat a non-stick frying pan over a high heat until hot. Score the duck breast skin, season it with salt and add it to the pan, skin-side down. Cook until the skin is brown and crisp but the rest of the duck is still quite pink, then flip the duck over and cook for another minute on the other side for rare meat, or 2–3 minutes for medium. Remove the duck and leave to rest for a few minutes, then slice and serve on top of the onion and pepper.

BRITISH DUCK JALFREZI

GOOSE DOPIAZA

'Dopiaza' means to use onions twice in a dish, or as is sometimes understood: onions used in a double quantity in relation to the meat. In the UK, dopiaza became popular as it resembles a meat stew with a generous quantity of onions. Goose meat is a little unusual, but it works deliciously well with this sauce. Vegetables, seafood, chicken or lamb can be used instead.

SERVES 4

4 tablespoons vegetable oil
2 onions, one cut into 2.5cm dice, the other finely chopped
400g goose breast, skin removed, cut into 2.5cm dice
1 teaspoon cumin seeds
a 2.5cm piece of cassia or cinnamon stick
1/2 teaspoon cracked black peppercorns
1 teaspoon ground cumin
1 teaspoon ground turmeric
1 tablespoon ground coriander

1 teaspoon red chilli powder
1 tablespoon tomato paste
1 tomato, finely chopped
4–5 tablespoons chicken stock or water
1 tablespoon lemon juice
6 tablespoons Onion Masala Gravy (see page 226)
1/2 teaspoon ground fenugreek leaf
1/2 teaspoon Garam Masala (see page 223)
2 tablespoons finely chopped coriander leaves
salt

Heat the oil in a pan and sauté the diced onion until translucent, then remove with a slotted spoon and set aside until required.

Add the diced goose breast to the pan and cook over a high heat to seal and lightly colour. Remove and set aside until required.

Reheat the oil and sauté the cumin seeds, cinnamon and peppercorns until the spices sizzle. Add the finely chopped onion and sauté for 3–5 minutes until lightly coloured. Add the ground cumin, turmeric, coriander and red chilli powder and sauté for a minute to cook the spices. Add the tomato paste and chopped tomato and cook for 2–3 minutes, adding a little of the stock or water to loosen the sauce. Add the sautéed diced onions, the onion masala gravy and goose breast and cook over a medium heat for 8–10 minutes, until the goose is perfectly cooked. Add the fenugreek and garam masala and season with salt. Add the remaining stock or water to loosen the sauce and finish by adding the chopped coriander leaves. Serve with naan or chapattis.

DUCK IN WALNUT AND POMEGRANATE SAUCE

KHORESHE FESENJAN

Iranian food is quite sophisticated, with its use of basmati rice, choice meats and poultry, including venison and duck, spices like turmeric, cinnamon, saffron and sumac, nuts, dried mint leaves, ghee or butter for cooking and dried limes (loomi or limu omani) for flavour and souring. I have a lot of admiration for Iranian food because it has given so much to Indian cuisine. Tandoor ovens originally came from Iran. There they are made from iron, while in India they are traditionally made from clay. This luxurious dish is perfect for a festive meal in December when pomegranates are in season.

SERVES 4

1 duck (about 2.5kg), excess fat removed from the cavity
2 tablespoons ghee
2 onions, thinly sliced
2 carrots, cut into very fine strips
150ml pomegranate molasses, diluted with 250ml water
3 tablespoons brown sugar
a 5cm piece of cinnamon stick
1 tablespoon lime juice

a small pinch of saffron threads, soaked in warm water
1 teaspoon freshly crushed black peppercorns
200g walnuts, toasted then ground in a blender
salt

To garnish
100g pomegranate seeds
50g walnuts, toasted

In a heavy-bottomed pan, sear the duck on all sides to render the fat. Remove and keep aside until required. Tip the fat into a container and wipe the pan clean to prepare the sauce.

Heat the ghee in the pan and fry the onions until translucent. Add the carrot and sauté for a minute, then add the diluted pomegranate molasses, sugar, cinnamon, lime juice, saffron water, ground walnuts and salt to taste. Stir to mix well. Bring to the boil, then reduce to a simmer. Place the duck in the pan and simmer for 30–45 minutes or until the duck is cooked and the sauce is thick.

Lift out the duck and cut into serving pieces. Skim excess fat from the sauce, then check the seasoning, adjusting the tartness with lime juice and sugar. Garnish with the pomegranate seeds and walnuts and serve with rice.

BRITISH GOOSE DOPIAZA

SUMATRAN-STYLE GREEN CHILLI AND DUCK CURRY

GULAI ITIK

This is an amazing dish where the flavour of green chillies is the highlight. There are mild to extremely hot green chillies available, and you can use whichever you like, based on the tolerance of heat you have.

SERVES 4

1 tablespoon vegetable oil
400g duck breast, skin and fat removed, cut into 8 pieces
800ml hot water
2 tablespoons Tamarind Paste (see page 228)
1/2 teaspoon salt
1 teaspoon sugar
2 lemongrass stalks, lightly bruised at the bulb
4 green chillies, deseeded
4 kaffir lime leaves

For the spice paste
4 green chillies, deseeded
6 small shallots, chopped
1 teaspoon chopped galangal
4 macadamia nuts
3 garlic cloves, peeled
3 kaffir lime leaves
1 teaspoon ground turmeric
a 5cm piece of white lemongrass stalk, chopped
4 black peppercorns
4 tablespoons Tamarind Paste (see page 228)
2 tablespoons vegetable or groundnut oil
salt

Blend together all the ingredients for the spice paste, with salt to taste, to make a fine paste. Heat the vegetable oil in a large pan and sauté the paste for 3–5 minutes on a medium heat, until fragrant. Add the duck, water, tamarind paste, salt, sugar, lemongrass, green chillies and lime leaves. Bring to the boil, then simmer for 1 hour or until the duck is fully cooked and the sauce is reduced by half. Adjust the seasoning and serve with steamed rice.

KHMER DUCK CURRY

Cambodian curries are bit different from those made in the rest of Asia, in their unique use of sweet potatoes and their own mild chilli. For the best results, always make this spice paste fresh (freezing the paste is allowed).

SERVES 4

4 large duck breasts, with skin, each cut into 4 pieces
50ml vegetable oil
6 kaffir lime leaves
2 carrots, peeled and cut into 5mm roundels
300g sweet potatoes, peeled and sliced
2 small onions, peeled and quartered
4 tablespoons fish sauce
1 tablespoon palm or brown sugar
100g green beans, cut into 2.5cm pieces
1 long, thin aubergine, cut into roundels
600ml coconut milk

For the spice paste
4 star anise
a 2.5cm piece of cinnamon stick
1 teaspoon coriander seeds
4 tablespoons chopped coriander root
2 tablespoons grated orange zest
6–8 large dried chillies, soaked in lukewarm water to soften, drained and deseeded
1 teaspoon prahoc and kaapi (dried shrimp paste)
4 tablespoons Kroeung (Cambodian Spice Paste; see page 224)

First make the spice paste. Lightly toast the star anise, cinnamon stick and coriander seeds in a dry pan over a medium heat. Tip into a blender and blitz to make a fine powder. Add the remaining ingredients and blend to a fine paste.

Heat a frying pan and sear the duck breast pieces to seal and brown the meat and to render the fat. Remove from the pan and keep warm until required.

Heat the oil in a pan or wok over medium heat and sauté the spice paste until lightly browned. Reduce the heat and add the kaffir lime leaves, carrots, sweet potatoes, onions, fish sauce and sugar. Stir in 100ml water. Cook on a low heat for 10–12 minutes or until the vegetables are cooked.

Add the green beans, aubergine and duck pieces and cook for 5–7 minutes. Pour in the coconut milk and bring to the boil, then simmer for 2–3 minutes. Correct the seasoning with fish sauce and serve with jasmine rice.

CAMBODIAN KHMER DUCK CURRY

MALAYSIAN NONYA DUCK CURRY

NONYA DUCK CURRY

KARI ITIK

Members of the Peranakan community (see page 70) in Malaysia refer to themselves as 'baba', meaning 'gentleman', and 'nonya', meaning 'lady'. Nonya has now also come to describe the cuisine of this community, which combines Malay and Chinese ingredients and techniques.

SERVES 4

4 tablespoons vegetable oil
$^1/_2$ teaspoon ground turmeric
1 teaspoon ground coriander
4 tablespoons Tamarind
    Water (see page 228)
$1^1/_2$ teaspoons sugar
4–5 kaffir lime leaves
1 lemongrass stalk, bruised
70ml coconut milk
4–6 large cherry tomatoes
4 duck breasts, with skin
salt

coriander cress or coriander
    sprigs, to garnish

For the spice paste
1 lemongrass stalk, chopped
1 onion, chopped
3 garlic cloves, peeled
a small knob of fresh ginger,
    scraped
2 dried red chillies, soaked
    overnight and drained

Blend or pound together the ingredients for the spice paste to make a fine paste. Heat the oil in a wok and sauté the paste well until aromatic. Add the turmeric, ground coriander, tamarind juice, sugar, kaffir lime leaves, lemongrass and salt to taste. Sauté for 5–7 minutes or until the oil separates out from the spices. During cooking, gradually stir in 150ml water to keep the mixture moist. Add the coconut milk and cook, stirring, until the sauce thickens. Add the tomatoes, then remove from the heat and keep aside.

Score the duck skin in a criss-cross pattern and salt well. Place the breasts, skin-side down, in a non-stick frying pan and cook over a high heat to sear the skin until brown and render the fat. Continue cooking until the meat is light pink. Turn the breasts over and cook for a further 1–2 minutes. Allow the duck breasts to rest for 5–8 minutes, while you reheat the sauce. Serve the duck breasts with the sauce and rice, garnished with coriander cress.

GAME

VENISON WITH GREEN CHILLIES

KACHI MIRCH KA HIRAN

Simple and full of flavour, this spicy, gamey curry is wonderful for special occasions and celebrations. It is somehow ironic that so many wonderful game curries are no longer available to those in the Indian sub-continent since the banning of hunting, but at least the culinary tradition lives on in the recipes that have been handed down to us, amongst which this is one of my favourites.

SERVES 4–6

800g boneless venison haunch, cut into 2.5cm cubes

For the marinade
250g yoghurt
2 tablespoons coriander seeds, toasted and pounded to a powder
2 tablespoons chopped green chilli, pounded to a powder
1 tablespoon cumin seeds, toasted and pounded to a powder
1 teaspoon shahi jeera or caraway seeds, toasted and pounded to a powder
1 teaspoon black peppercorns, toasted and pounded to a powder
salt

For the sauce
150g ghee or vegetable oil
5–6 green cardamom pods
2 black cardamom pods
5 cloves
a 2.5cm piece of cinnamon stick
1 bay leaf
1 blade of mace
2 tablespoons finely chopped fresh ginger
5 green chillies, finely chopped
4 onions, thinly sliced
800ml chicken stock
a pinch of saffron
200ml single cream
1 teaspoon fennel powder

Mix together all the marinade ingredients. Add the cubed venison and leave to marinate in a cool place for 2 hours.

For the sauce, heat the ghee in a large pan and add the cardamom pods, cloves, cinnamon, bay leaf and mace and sauté over a medium heat for 1–2 minutes and as the spices crackle, add the ginger and green chilli. Stir for a minute, then add the sliced onions and sauté for 5–7 minutes, until translucent. Add the marinated venison meat with its marinade.

Add the stock and bring to the boil, then simmer over a very low heat for 30–40 minutes until the meat is cooked. Add the saffron and cream and mix well, then bring to a boil and adjust the seasoning. Sprinkle with the fennel powder and serve hot with rice or naan bread.

BLACK FOWL CURRY

KALU KUKULU MALUWA

In Sri Lanka, this is traditionally made with a wild jungle fowl that is related to pheasant. Chinese black chicken or guinea fowl work well as substitutes.

SERVES 4

2 tablespoons rapeseed oil
1 onion, finely chopped
12–15 curry leaves
a 5cm pandan leaf
a 2.5cm piece of cinnamon stick
4 cloves
4 green cardamom pods
1 teaspoon Garlic Paste (see page 223)
1 teaspoon Ginger Paste (see page 223)
1 teaspoon ground cumin
2 teaspoons ground coriander
1/2 teaspoon ground fennel
1/4 teaspoon ground turmeric

1 black chicken or guinea fowl, about 1kg, cut into 8 pieces on the bone
500ml coconut milk
1 teaspoon Tamarind Water (see page 228)
1/2 teaspoon freshly crushed black peppercorns
salt
2 green chillies, slit and sliced, to garnish

For the seasoning
1 teaspoon rapeseed oil
1/2 teaspoon mustard seeds
1/2 teaspoon dill seeds

Heat the oil in a wok and add the onion, curry leaves, pandan leaf, cinnamon, cloves, cardamom pods, and garlic and ginger pastes. Sauté for 3–4 minutes, stirring well. Stir in the ground cumin, coriander, fennel and turmeric. Sauté for a further 1–2 minutes, then add the chicken pieces. Cook, turning, until the chicken pieces are browned on all sides.

Add half the coconut milk with 50ml water and stir to mix. Bring to the boil, then simmer for 10 minutes. Add the tamarind water together with the remaining coconut milk and simmer for a further 10–12 minutes or until the chicken is cooked.

Meanwhile, prepare the seasoning. Heat the oil in a small pan and sauté the mustard and dill seeds until aromatic. Cool, then grind to a paste in a pestle and mortar.

Add the spice powder to the chicken and season with the pepper and salt to taste. Serve hot, garnished with the green chillies, and an optional red chilli for a striking hit of colour.

SRI LANKAN BLACK FOWL CURRY

THAI GUINEA FOWL CURRY

GUINEA FOWL CURRY

This recipe is inspired by a simple chicken curry from Chiang Mai in the north of Thailand.

SERVES 4

400g boneless guinea fowl thighs, cut into 2.5cm cubes
800ml chicken stock
100g shiitake mushrooms, sliced
12–15 leaves each of holy and Thai basil
2 heads of pak choi, leaves shredded
1 aubergine, diced
50g snake or green beans, cut into batons

For the spice paste
6 dried red chilies, deseeded, soaked for 1 hour and drained
2 stalks of lemon grass, chopped
3–4 red shallots, chopped
1 tablespoon chopped garlic
1 teaspoon shrimp paste
1 tablespoon vegetable oil
salt

Blend all the spice paste ingredients together to make a fine paste. Mix the guinea fowl with the paste and set aside in a cool place to marinate for 30 minutes.

Heat a wok and sauté the marinated guinea fowl for 2–3 minutes until fragrant. Add the stock and bring to the boil. Add all the remaining ingredients and simmer for 20–15 minutes, until cooked. Check the seasoning – the final result should be a salty, hot and slightly bitter curry. Serve with rice.

HARE RED CURRY

This Thai curry paste is one that builds the flavour and character of the dish. I have tried the recipe with beef, venison, pigeon, pork and it works just as well – it is such a versatile paste.

SERVES 4

2 tablespoons vegetable oil
500g boneless leg of hare, cut into 1cm cubes
2 tablespoons fish sauce
600ml coconut milk
1 tablespoon palm or brown sugar
4 kaffir lime leaves, torn
2 green chillies, sliced on the diagonal
a handful of Thai or holy basil leaves

For the spice paste
6 dried red chillies, deseeded, soaked for 1 hour and drained

2 stalks of lemon grass, chopped
1½ teaspoons kaffir lime (or ordinary lime) zest
3–4 red shallots, finely chopped
1 tablespoon chopped garlic
½ teaspoon kapi (dried shrimp paste)
1 teaspoon white peppercorns
1 tablespoon coriander seeds, toasted and ground
1 teaspoon cumin seeds, toasted and ground
½ nutmeg, grated and lightly toasted
5 cloves, toasted and ground
salt

Place all the paste ingredients in a blender and blend to a fine paste.

Heat the oil in a wok and sauté the paste for 3–4 minutes over a medium heat until fragrant. Add the hare and fish sauce and sauté for 2–3 minutes to seal, then add the coconut milk and simmer for 12–15 minutes, until the hare is cooked. Add the palm sugar, lime leaves, chillies and basil. Simmer for 2–3 minutes, check the seasoning and serve with rice.

MOUNTIE CHILLI

RABBIT IN CHILLI TOMATO SAUCE

ARNAB MASAK MERAH

Sudhir Ferris was my training mate at the Oberoi School of Hotel Management in India. After training he migrated to Canada and ditched the kitchens for a horse! He became a Mountie (a member of the Royal Canadian Mounted Police). When I stumbled upon this recipe, I thought of him. He probably cooks this for his unit and shows off his skills – because he was a very good chef and now a fabulous Mountie. Sudhir, this one is for you!

Rabbit is a little unusual in Malay cooking, but Masak Merah is a classic recipe that is served at banquets. I've use farmed rabbit for this dish, which is not as tough as wild rabbit and cooks in less time. If using wild rabbit the cooking time will be longer – over an hour at least. If you prefer, chicken or any other poultry can be used for this recipe instead. The tomatoes are added right at the end and are meant to be eaten raw so there's no need to try and heat them.

SERVES 4

2 tablespoons vegetable oil
500g minced bison or beef
2 onions, chopped
1 bay leaf
1 tablespoon chopped garlic
1 large red pepper, cored and finely chopped
1 large green pepper, cored and finely chopped
1/2 teaspoon ground allspice
1/2 teaspoon freshly ground black pepper
2 teaspoons cocoa powder
1 teaspoon ground cinnamon
1 teaspoon ground cumin
1 teaspoon ground coriander
1/2 teaspoon Garam Masala (see page 223)
1 teaspoon oregano leaves,

finely crushed or chopped
2 large tomatoes, chopped
500ml tomato passata or purée
400g red kidney beans, cooked
400g white or black beans, cooked
300ml stock or water
1 small green chilli, chopped
salt

To serve
thinly sliced spring onions
tortilla chips
black olives
sour cream
grated Cheddar cheese

SERVES 4

6 tablespoons vegetable oil
1 onion, finely chopped
1 tablespoon finely chopped garlic
1 tablespoon finely chopped fresh ginger
1 pandan leaf, tied into a knot
3 kaffir lime leaves
2 star anise
a 2.5cm piece of cinnamon bark

2 tablespoons Chilli Paste (see page 221)
1 tablespoon tomato paste
1 tablespoon soy sauce
2 tablespoons Tamarind Water (see page 228)
1 tablespoon palm sugar
1 rabbit, jointed into 6 pieces
8 large cherry tomatoes, halved

Heat the oil in a pan and sauté the bison over a medium heat until it crumbles and colours lightly. Add the onion, bay leaf and garlic and sauté for 3–5 minutes until the onion becomes translucent. Add the peppers, allspice, black pepper, cocoa powder, cinnamon, cumin, coriander, garam masala and oregano leaves. Add salt to taste and sauté for 2–3 minutes. Add the tomatoes, passata, all the beans, stock and green chilli. Mix well, bring to the boil, then simmer for 40–45 minutes until the meat is tender.

Serve with the spring onions, tortilla chips, olives, sour cream and cheese, or with rice.

Heat 2 tablespoons of the oil over a medium heat, add the rabbit pieces and brown lightly on all sides, then remove and set aside.

Heat the remaining oil in a pan and sauté the onion, ginger and garlic until lightly browned. Add the pandan leaf, lime leaves, star anise and cinnamon and cook, stirring, until the mixture turns light brown.

Add the chilli paste, tomato paste, soy sauce, tamarind juice, sugar and salt to taste. Cook for 6–8 minutes or until the oil separates out from the mixture.

Add the rabbit pieces and 100ml water. Bring to the boil, then simmer, stirring occasionally, for about 45 minutes, or until the rabbit is cooked. The timing may vary depending on how tough your rabbit is, but if it needs longer simply add more water and continue to simmer until the meat is tender and you have a thick sauce. Add the tomatoes, stir, then serve immediately.

RIGHT: MALAYSIAN RABBIT IN CHILLI TOMATO SAUCE

VENISON STEW

GULE DAGING RUSA

Venison is a little unusual in the Indonesian recipe repertoire as deer is not native to Indonesia, but this dish is too good to be missed. This dish can be made in advance and kept in the fridge for 3–4 days, but add the coconut milk only after you reheat the dish for serving.

SERVES 4

	For the spice paste
2 tablespoons vegetable oil	1 onion, chopped
1kg boneless venison haunch, cut into 2.5cm dice	3 garlic cloves, peeled
1 teaspoon palm or brown sugar	4–5 candlenuts or macadamia nuts
a 2.5cm piece of cinnamon stick	$\frac{1}{2}$ teaspoon red chilli powder
3 cloves	1 tablespoon finely chopped fresh ginger
1 bay leaf	$\frac{1}{4}$ teaspoon black pepper
100ml Tamarind Water (see page 228)	1 teaspoon chopped galangal
750ml coconut milk	$\frac{1}{2}$ teaspoon ground turmeric
salt	1 lemongrass stalk, chopped

Blend or pound together the ingredients for the spice paste to make a fine paste. Heat the oil in a wok and sauté the paste for 2–3 minutes.

Add the venison and stir-fry for 2–3 minutes to sear the meat. Add the rest of the ingredients except the coconut milk, seasoning with salt. Pour in 200ml water and stir well. Cover and cook on a low heat for 8–10 minutes or until the meat is tender.

Stir in the coconut milk and simmer gently for a couple of minutes to heat, then remove from the heat and serve.

PARTRIDGE CURRY

Orange-necked partridge is a common sight in the national wildlife parks of Cambodia. It is now a protected bird, however, so this curry is often made with chicken, duck or red-legged partridge imported from Europe.

SERVES 6

2 large potatoes, peeled and cut into 2.5cm dice	2 dried red chillies, soaked in lukewarm water to soften, drained and deseeded
oil for deep-frying	5 garlic cloves, chopped
1 tablespoon vegetable oil	2 medium shallots, chopped
750ml coconut milk	1 tablespoon chopped fresh galangal
3 oven-ready red-legged partridges, each cut into 4 pieces	a 5cm piece of cinnamon stick
1 onion, sliced into thin rings	2 star anise
2 tablespoons fish sauce	7–8 green cardamom pods
2 tablespoons palm or brown sugar	1 teaspoon grated nutmeg
5 kaffir lime leaves	1 teaspoon black peppercorns
salt	$\frac{1}{2}$ teaspoon coriander seeds
	1 teaspoon fennel seeds
For the paste	2 teaspoons prahoc or kaapi (dried shrimp paste)
2 tablespoons vegetable oil	100g coriander leaves, chopped
1 lemongrass stalk, sliced	$\frac{1}{4}$ teaspoon ground turmeric

First make the paste. Heat the oil in a wok and sauté all the ingredients, except the prahoc, chopped coriander and turmeric, for 3–5 minutes to release the flavours. Tip the mixture into a blender and add the shrimp paste, chopped coriander and turmeric with 200ml water and blend to a smooth paste. Set aside 250g of the paste; freeze the remainder for future use.

Blanch the potatoes in boiling water for 7–10 minutes or until just cooked. Drain and pat dry with kitchen paper. Heat enough oil for deep-frying in a wok or deep pan. When it is hot (180°C), deep-fry the potatoes until tender and golden brown. Drain on kitchen paper and keep aside until required.

Heat the vegetable oil in a heavy-based pan or pot and add half the coconut milk. Bring to the boil, then simmer for 2–3 minutes or until the oil separates out from the coconut milk. Add the spice paste and stir for 3–5 minutes, until fragrant.

Add the partridge and stir to coat with the sauce. Cook, stirring, for 2–3 minutes. Add the onion rings, fish sauce, sugar, kaffir lime leaves and salt to taste, and cook for 3–4 minutes. Pour in the remaining coconut milk and simmer for 20–25 minutes or until the partridge is cooked. Add the potatoes, stir to mix and bring to a simmer to reheat. Serve, garnished with pink pickled onions, if you wish, and with rice alongside.

CAMBODIAN PARTRIDGE CURRY

SINDHI HARE CURRY

SINDHI HARE CURRY

SEYALI JULNGLEE KHARGOSH

After the partition of India many Sindhis migrated to India from Pakistan and there are now groups scattered all over the country. Their contribution to Indian cuisine is huge and there are Sindhi dishes eaten everywhere. Onions tend to feature heavily in Sindhi cuisine, as they do here, made into a creamy purée that forms the base of the dish on which the other layers of flavour are built. I sauté the onions first so they don't turn bitter when blitzed. Shahi Jeera is a black seed, from the cumin family, commonly referred to as 'black cumin'. It is sometimes confused with nigella seeds (kalonji) but is in fact very different. The seeds have a smoky, earthy flavour and are worth seeking out from a good spice shop or online. I've suggested caraway seeds as an alternative, which is the best equivalent in terms of the flavour.

SERVES 4–6

3 hare legs, on the bone, cut into pieces or whole
200ml vegetable oil
8–10 onions, finely chopped
a 5cm piece of cassia or cinnamon stick
2 bay leaves
3 large black cardamom pods
1 blade of mace
1 teaspoon black peppercorns
6 cloves
50g fresh ginger, chopped
6 garlic cloves, chopped
2 tablespoons ground coriander
2 teaspoons ground cumin
1 teaspoon ground turmeric
2 teaspoons mild paprika or chilli powder
500g tomatoes, blended to a fine purée
1 teaspoon shahi jeera or caraway seeds, lightly toasted then ground to a powder
1 teaspoon ground green cardamom
spring onions, sliced on the diagonal, to garnish

For the marinade
200g coriander leaves
200g Greek yoghurt
3–4 green chillies, chopped
salt

For the marinade, blend the coriander leaves with the yoghurt to make a purée. Stir in the green chillies and salt to taste. Spread the marinade over the hare legs and leave to marinate in a cool place for 2 hours.

Heat 100ml of the oil in a pan and sauté the onions for about 5–7 minutes, until translucent, then blend them to a fine purée. Return the purée to the same pan and keep stirring to cook the purée over a low heat for 10–15 minutes to cook off any moisture.

Heat the remaining oil in another pan and sauté the cassia, bay leaves, mace, peppercorns and cloves until the spices crackle. Add the chopped ginger and garlic and sauté over a medium heat until lightly coloured. Add the coriander, cumin, turmeric and chilli powder and 50ml water and stir to mix well. Cook for 2–3 minutes, then add the onion purée and tomato purée and sauté for 5–8 minutes.

Add the marinated hare legs with their marinade and cook, covered, over a low heat for 45–60 minutes or until the meat is not quite cooked (prick it with the tip of a sharp knife; it should still be very pink). Stir every now and then to allow the mixture to cook evenly. Preheat the oven to 160°C/Gas Mark 3.

Check the seasoning and transfer the hare and all its sauce to an ovenproof dish. Cook for 1 hour, stirring every 15 minutes until the juices run clear when the thickest part of the meat is pierced with a sharp knife. Remove from the oven, sprinkle with the ground shahi jeera and cardamom and a few slices of spring onion and serve with naan.

PARTRIDGE COCONUT CURRY

AYAM HUTAN LEMAK

Rich in spice from lots of chilli and balanced with the cooling coconut milk, this curry needs the strong-flavoured meat to stand up to all the other ingredients fighting for attention. Try it with other game birds too.

SERVES 4

5 tablespoons vegetable oil
10 shallots, finely chopped
1 tablespoon finely chopped fresh ginger
1 tablespoon finely chopped garlic
2 lemongrass stalks (white part only), bruised
a small knob of galangal, bruised
6–8 kaffir lime leaves
1 tablespoon ground coriander
1 teaspoon ground turmeric
2 oven-ready red-legged partridges, each cut into 4

pieces
600ml chicken stock
600ml coconut milk
1 teaspoon ground white pepper
1 red onion, cut into rings
5 red bird's eye chillies
5 green chillies, slit
salt

To garnish
coriander cress or coriander sprigs
3 tablespoons Crispy Onions (see page 222)

Heat the oil in a pan and sauté the shallots with the ginger, garlic, lemongrass, galangal, lime leaves and ground coriander and turmeric for 5–6 minutes or until lightly coloured. Add the partridge pieces and cook, turning to coat with the spices and sear all over, for 2 minutes. Pour in the stock. Bring to a simmer and cook for 10–12 minutes or until the partridge is half cooked.

Add the coconut milk and season with the white pepper and salt to taste. Continue to simmer for 12–15 minutes or until the meat is cooked. Add the onion rings and all the chillies and cook for a further 2–3 minutes. Serve garnished with coriander cress and the crispy onions.

PIGEON STIR-FRIED WITH CHILLIES AND GINGER

BUMBU HIJAU MERPATI

The Banda islands in Indonesia were hugely important in the spice trade by virtue of the fact that up until the mid 19th century they were the only source of nutmeg and mace (the fleshy outer covering of the nutmeg, which is dried as a spice), both of which were hugely valued by the Europeans. This wonderfully easy Indonesian curry puts spices and fiery chillies to work with the strong flavour of pigeon meat – the result is, of course, delicious: a fantastic way of serving this game bird.

SERVES 4

4 skinless pigeon breasts, cut into strips
1 tablespoon lime juice
a small knob of fresh ginger, cut into very fine strips
1 tablespoon vegetable oil
2 green chillies, thinly sliced on the diagonal
1 red chilli, thinly sliced on the diagonal
1 lemongrass stalk, thinly sliced on the diagonal
coriander sprigs, to garnish

For the spice paste
4 green chillies
1 teaspoon black peppercorns
1 tablespoon chopped garlic
1 teaspoon chopped fresh ginger
a pinch of grated nutmeg
1 onion, chopped
2 tablespoons chopped macadamia nuts or candlenuts
2 tablespoons vegetable oil
2 tablespoons lime juice
salt

In a bowl, toss the pigeon breasts with the lime juice, ginger and some salt. Set aside in a cool place for 1 hour to marinate.

Blend or pound together all the ingredients for the spice paste, with salt to taste, to make a fine paste. Heat a wok and stir-fry the paste for 1–2 minutes, until fragrant. Add the oil to the wok followed by the sliced chillies and lemongrass, then add the marinated pigeon strips. Stir-fry on a high heat for 3–4 minutes or until the pigeon is cooked through; add 2–3 tablespoon of water if needed. Garnish with the coriander and an optional red chilli or two. Serve hot with rice.

INDONESIAN PIGEON STIR-FRIED WITH CHILLIES AND GINGER

SLOW-COOKED PARTRIDGE

DUM KA TITAR

Lucknow, the capital of the northern Indian state Utter Pradesh, is known for its creative cuisine. This is said to be on account of the royal patronage the region enjoyed; the royalty wanted to achieve a high level of finesse and artistry in cooking. There are stories that one ruler loved dishes that were made with lamb and saffron so he ordered his herd of lamb to be fed on a saffron diet to give the meat richer flavours. Lucknow is also said to be the creator of the now ubiquitous style of slow cooking in India – 'dum' cooking. The story goes that dum cooking was first used there in the late 18th century to provide a constant supply of food for the working populace employed in building the magnificent edifice, the Bara Imambara in Lucknow. Enormous containers were filled with rice, meat, vegetables and spices, and their lids were sealed with dough so that no air could escape and the contents would be kept beautifully moist. The meat would cook slowly in its own juices, without losing any of its succulent flavour and nutrients to the air. The slow cooking also ensured that food was available at all times. This recipe is simple – yet delivers amazing flavours.

SERVES 4

4 oven-ready grey-legged partridges, skin removed
30g Ginger-Garlic Paste (see page 233)
1 teaspoon salt
4 tablespoons vegetable oil
4 onions, thinly sliced
10g white poppy seeds, toasted
30g unsweetened desiccated coconut, toasted
20g chironji nuts or melon seeds, toasted
200g plain yoghurt
120g butter, melted
3–5 cloves
1 bay leaf
50g almonds, chopped
50g pistachios, chopped
a few saffron threads,

dissolved in 1 tablespoon milk
1 tablespoon kewra water (screw pine flower essence; optional)
800ml water or chicken stock
100g plain flour
1 tablespoon chopped coriander leaves, to garnish
3 tablespoons Crispy Onions (see page 222)

For the garam masala
1 teaspoon black pepper
1 black cardamom pod
6 green cardamom pods
a 2.5cm piece of cinnamon stick
1 blade of mace
1/2 nutmeg, grated

Mix the ginger-garlic paste with the salt, then rub all over the partridges and leave to marinate in a cool place for 1 hour.

Heat the oil in a pan and sauté the onions for about 5–7 minutes, until translucent, then blend them to a fine purée. Return the purée to the same pan and keep stirring to cook the purée over a low heat for 10–12 minutes to cook off any moisture.

For the garam masala, toast all the spices together in a pan. Leave to cool, then tip them into a pestle and mortar, spice grinder or coffee grinder and grind to a fine powder.

Blend the poppy seeds, desiccated coconut and chironji nuts or melon seeds with 30ml water to make a fine paste. Mix the onion paste, poppy seed paste and garam masala with all the remaining ingredients, except the coriander leaves, then add the marinated partridge. Place in a casserole with a tight-fitting lid and set aside to marinate for a further 30 minutes.

Preheat the oven to 170°C/Gas Mark 3.

Mix the flour with enough water to make a soft dough (about 75ml). Roll the dough into a long sausage shape. Put the lid on the casserole and seal the join with the dough sausage, pressing it into the join to make sure the pot is completely airtight. Alternatively you can wrap the top of the casserole with foil before covering it with the lid. Bake for 35–45 minutes, until the partridge is cooked. Remove the lid and seal and garnish with chopped coriander leaves and crispy cnions. Serve hot with bread or rice.

SPICY VENISON CURRY

VETTAYIRACHI PERALEN

There is a strong conservation ban on hunting deer in India and Bangladesh but here in the UK we can still enjoy these old recipes. This southern Indian curry showcases two popular ingredients from the region: curry leaves and mustard seeds. Their rustic aromas lend themselves well to strong-flavoured meats such as venison and wild boar.

SERVES 4

500g boneless venison fillet or haunch, diced
2 tablespoons white wine vinegar
1 tablespoon finely chopped fresh ginger
1 teaspoon ground turmeric
2 tablespoons rapeseed oil
1 large onion, chopped
3 garlic cloves, chopped
4 green chillies, slit
12 curry leaves
1 teaspoon black mustard seeds
1 teaspoon plain flour
1 teaspoon ground coriander
1 teaspoon black peppercorns, crushed
2 small tomatoes, diced
salt
coriander leaves, to garnish

Place the meat, vinegar, salt to taste and half the ginger and turmeric in a covered pan or pressure cooker with 250ml water for 25–30 minutes if using a pan or 10–12 minutes if using a pressure cooker. Strain the meat, reserving the stock, and set both aside until required.

Heat half the oil in a pan, add the onion, garlic, green chillies, curry leaves and remaining ginger and sauté for 5–7 minutes, until the onion becomes translucent. Set aside until required.

Heat the remaining oil in another pan and sauté the mustard seeds until they pop. Stir in the flour, ground coriander, peppercorns and remaining turmeric and sauté for a minute, then add the cooked venison. Cook for 3–4 minutes, then stir in the onion mixture. Pour in the reserved cooking stock and tomatoes and simmer until the sauce thickens. Garnish with coriander and serve with rice or bread.

SWAMP PARTRIDGE AND BAMBOO SHOOT CURRY

BHIL TITAR O BANSHER KOROL

Swamp partridge – variously called bhil titar, bun, jungli titar, kaihah, koera and koi on the Indian subcontinent – is a game bird found in swampy areas with high grass. It is roughly the size of a chicken and is a very handsome bird with chestnut plumage and a bright red throat. You won't be able to buy swamp partridge in the UK so either use four grey-legged partridges or two guinea fowl.

SERVES 4

4 tablespoons vegetable oil or ghee
4 oven-ready grey-legged partridges, skin removed, each cut into 4 pieces
4 onions, finely chopped
1 tablespoon Ginger-Garlic Paste (see page 223)
1 teaspoon ground turmeric
1 teaspoon red chilli powder
200ml chicken stock or water
1 x 225g can bamboo shoots, drained
400ml coconut milk
salt
coriander leaves, to garnish

Heat the oil in a pan and sauté the partridges to lightly brown all over. Remove and set aside until required.

Reheat the oil, then add the onions and sauté over a medium heat for 5 minutes or until lightly coloured. Add the ginger-garlic paste, turmeric, chilli powder and salt to taste. Sauté for 2–3 minutes to cook the spices, then pour in the stock. Return the partridge to the pan and simmer for about 20–25 minutes until cooked.

Add the bamboo shoots and coconut milk, bring back to a simmer and cook until the sauce thickens. Serve garnished with coriander leaves.

BANGLADESHI SWAMP PARTRIDGE AND BAMBOO SHOOT CURRY

(LEFT) TANZANIAN WILDEBEEST CURRY
(RIGHT) BANGLADESHI VENISON CURRY

TANZANIAN WILDEBEEST CURRY

The wildebeest, which inhabits the plains and open woodlands of Africa, is an antelope that looks like a cross between a horse, a deer and a cow. It is legally killed and its lean, protein-rich meat is used to make biltong. Its flavour is similar to venison. Exotic meats are available to buy from specialist butchers in the UK, particularly online, but venison haunch or beef fillet would make suitable substitutes.

SERVES 4

500g wildebeest haunch, cut into 2.5cm dice
4 tablespoons vegetable oil
2 onions, finely chopped
2 tomatoes, chopped
2 garlic cloves, chopped
3 tablespoons grated fresh ginger
1 tablespoon Malawi Curry Powder (see page 225)
seeds from 6 green cardamom pods
2 lemongrass stalks, bruised
500ml chicken or veal stock
2 sweet potatoes (unpeeled), cut into 1cm-thick slices
2 tablespoons olive or vegetable oil
300g plain yoghurt, whisked
2 small red chillies, sliced
1 tablespoon lime juice
1 tablespoon finely chopped coriander leaves
salt and pepper

Season the meat with salt and pepper. Heat 2 tablespoons of the vegetable oil in a pan and sear the meat for 3–5 minutes or until lightly browned. Remove and keep aside until required.

Add the remaining vegetable oil to the pan and fry the onions until light golden. Add the tomatoes, garlic, ginger, curry powder and salt to taste. Return the meat to the pan together with the lemongrass and stock. Bring to the boil, then simmer gently for 20–25 minutes until the meat is tender.

Meanwhile, blanch the sweet potatoes in boiling water for 7–10 minutes or until just cooked. Drain well. Heat the olive oil in a frying pan and fry the sweet potato slices until lightly browned and crisp.

Add the yoghurt and chillies to the meat pan and stir to mix. Heat through gently without boiling. Add the sweet potatoes and lime juice. Garnish with the chopped coriander and red chillies, if liked, and serve with rice.

VENISON CURRY

CHITAL HORIN GOTA MOSHLA

This recipe is another demonstration of the Indian style of slow cooking – 'dum' cooking (see page 113 for more about this), in which the cooking pot is sealed to prevent any moisture from escaping and keep the meat inside wonderfully juicy and tender. I've given you two options for how to seal the cooking pot. The dough method may be a little more work but it's still very quick to do – the dough can be made in seconds – and is definitely the more authentic version so I'd urge you to give it a try. The foil method works just as effectively.

SERVES 4–6

800g boneless venison haunch, cut into 2.5cm dice
250g plain yoghurt
200g ghee
8 dried red chillies (Kashmiri)
10 cloves
500g onions, thinly sliced
150g fresh ginger, finely sliced
150g garlic cloves, finely
sliced
100g plain flour
a pinch of saffron threads, soaked in 2 tablespoons warm milk
salt
spring onion, sliced on the diagonal, to garnish
coriander leaves, to garnish

Mix together all the ingredients, except the saffron and flour, in a casserole with a tight-fitting lid. Leave to marinate in a cool place for 2 hours.

If you want to cook the venison in the oven, preheat it to 160°C/Gas Mark 3. Mix the flour with enough water to make a soft dough (about 75ml). Roll the dough into a long sausage shape. Put the lid on the casserole and seal the join with the dough sausage, pressing it into the join to make sure the pot is completely airtight. Alternatively you can wrap the top of the casserole with foil before covering it with the lid. Place in the oven or on the lowest possible heat setting on the stove, and cook for 2$\frac{1}{2}$ hours.

Remove the dough seal and lid to check the meat – it should be cooked and tender. Pour in the saffron milk and mix, then garnish with the spring onion and coriander and serve with naan.

VENISON BHUNA

Bhuna is a cooking process where spices are fried in oil to extract the flavours, then meat is added and cooked in its own juices. It makes a delicious dish but with very little sauce. In the UK this dish has more sauce than the traditional version so I have used an onion masala gravy to fill out the original Indian version and have added red and green peppers to make it 'UK authentic'.

SERVES 4

4 tablespoons vegetable oil
1 small red and 1 small green pepper, cut into 2.5cm dice
1/2 teaspoon cumin seeds
2 green cardamom pods
1 bay leaf
1 dried red chilli
1 tablespoon finely chopped garlic
1 onion, finely chopped
600g venison haunch, cut into 2.5cm dice
1 teaspoon ground cumin
1 teaspoon ground turmeric
1 teaspoon ground coriander
1/2 teaspoon red chilli powder
4–5 tablespoons Onion Masala Gravy (see page 226)
100ml chicken stock or water
1/2 teaspoon ground Garam Masala (see page 223)
1/2 teaspoon fenugreek leaf powder
2 tablespoons finely chopped coriander leaves
salt

Heat 1 tablespoon of oil in a pan or wok and sauté the peppers, until softened, then remove and set aside. Wipe the pan or wok clean then heat the remaining oil and sauté the cumin seeds, cardamom, bay leaf, red chili and garlic. As the spices crackle, add the chopped onion and saute until the onion is light brown.

Add the venison and sauté over a high heat for 5–7 minutes to seal and lightly brown. Add the cumin, turmeric, coriander and red chilli powder. Sauté for 1 minute to cook the spices, then add the onion masala gravy and stock and season with salt. Cook over a low heat for 15–20 minutes until the meat is completely cooked. Add the sautéed peppers, garam masala and fenugreek, mix well, then add the chopped coriander and serve with naan or other Indian breads.

VENISON CURRY

GONA MAS THELDALA

Furred game, such as hare, wild boar and venison, plays an important role in Sri Lankan cuisine as it is part of the island's indigenous wildlife. The strong flavours in the game also stand up well to Sri Lankan spicing, which can be very hot. This is a dry curry so serve it with bread rather than rice, as one dish in a meal.

SERVES 4

2 tablespoons vegetable oil
1 small onion, finely chopped
1 pandan leaf, torn into small pieces
10–12 curry leaves
a 5cm piece of cinnamon stick
500g boneless venison haunch, cut into 2.5cm dice
1 tablespoon finely chopped fresh ginger
1 tablespoon finely chopped garlic
1 small mango, peeled and diced (optional)
1/2 teaspoon ground turmeric
2 tablespoons white wine vinegar
1 tablespoon crushed black peppercorns
20 pickled onions
5 green chillies, sliced
2 red chillies, sliced
3–4 tablespoons coconut milk
2 tablespoons grated fresh coconut or desiccated coconut
salt

Heat the oil in a wok and sauté the onion with the pandan leaf, curry leaves and cinnamon until lightly browned. Add the venison, ginger, garlic, mango, if using, turmeric and salt to taste and cook over a high heat, stirring well, for 5–8 minutes or until the meat is lightly browned. Add the vinegar, crushed peppercorns, pickled onions and chillies. Cook for 2–3 minutes, then add the coconut milk to moisten. Serve hot, sprinkled with the grated coconut.

SRI LANKAN VENISON CURRY

PAKISTANI VENISON HUNTER CURRY

VENISON HUNTER CURRY

SHIKAR KA GOSHT

I could happily fill a book with game-based curries and with venison in particular – I love its leanness and its subtle gamey flavour. The potatoes and pomegranate molasses give this dish a rich, slightly sweet character that mixes wonderfully with the aromas of fragrant spice and heat.

SERVES 4

800g boneless venison haunch, cut into 2.5cm dice
4 tablespoons vegetable oil or ghee
¼ teaspoon fenugreek seeds
1 teaspoon coriander seeds
1 teaspoon cumin seeds
2 black cardamom pods
a 2.5cm piece of cinnamon stick
2 dried red chillies
1 bay leaf
3 onions, finely chopped
1 tablespoon Ginger-Garlic Paste (see page 223)
1 tablespoon ground coriander
1 teaspoon red chilli powder
1 teaspoon Garam Masala (see page 223)
1 teaspoon pomegranate powder or dried pomegranate
2 sweet potatoes, peeled and cut into 2.5cm dice
3 tomatoes, chopped
1 tablespoon pomegranate molasses
2 tablespoons finely chopped coriander leaves
grated zest and juice of 1 lime
salt

Heat the oil in a pan and sauté the whole spices with the bay leaf until they begin to crackle. Add the chopped onions and sauté until lightly browned. Add the ginger-garlic paste and stir for 2–3 minutes to cook the paste well. Add the venison and brown on all sides over a medium heat, then add the ground spices, sweet potatoes and chopped tomatoes. Cover with a lid and cook gently for 10–15 minutes or until the venison and sweet potatoes are almost cooked, stirring occasionally

Add the pomegranate molasses and salt to taste and stir to mix. Simmer for a further 5 minutes. Stir in the chopped coriander, lime zest and juice, and serve with bread or rice.

WILD BOAR SATAY

SATE BABI HUTAN

Wild boar is the ancestor of the domesticated pig; it is a feisty animal. The tribal inhabitants of Borneo are great hunters and they eat everything they hunt, including wild boar. As you would expect, they have some interesting recipes for this meat. Pork makes a good substitute.

SERVES 4

800g boneless wild boar or pork fillet (tenderloin), cut into 2.5cm dice
oil for basting
1 tablespoon lime juice

For the spice paste
4–5 red chillies, chopped
1 tablespoon chopped fresh ginger
4 shallots or 1 onion, chopped
4 garlic cloves, peeled
2 tablespoons vegetable oil
2 tablespoons Tamarind Water (see page 228)
2 kaffir lime leaves, chopped
salt

To serve
1 lime, cut into wedges
cucumber slices
mint leaves

If you wish to use bamboo or wooden skewers, the night before, put 16 skewers in a bowl of water and leave to soak overnight. Blend or pound together the ingredients for the spice paste, with salt to taste, to make a fine paste. Toss the meat with the paste, then leave to marinate in a cool place for 1 hour.

Prepare a charcoal fire in the barbecue or preheat the grill to medium.

Thread the pieces of meat on to the soaked or metal skewers and cook over hot coals or under the grill, turning the satay to cook evenly. Baste with oil when you turn to keep the meat moist.

Drizzle the lime juice over the satay and serve with lime wedges, cucumber slices and mint sprigs.

WILD BOAR
WITH PEANUTS

SANGLIER À L'ARACHIDE

In most West African countries this dish would be made with wild or bush pig, which is much smaller than European wild boar, but wild boar is a reasonably close substitute, or you could use pork tenderloin. There are many ways to prepare the curry – this is my way. Try it with cassava chips or mash.

SERVES 4

3 tablespoons vegetable or groundnut oil
1kg boneless wild boar meat, cut into 2.5cm cubes
chicken stock or water
2 dried red chillies, cut into pieces
50g fresh ginger, thinly sliced
2 onions, chopped
1 tablespoon Malawi Curry Powder (see page 225)
250g smooth peanut butter
4 tomatoes, skinned and chopped
100g roasted peanuts
salt and pepper

Heat 2 tablespoons of the oil in a pan and sauté the cubes of meat until lightly browned all over. Pour in enough stock or water to cover. Bring to the boil, then simmer for about 10–12 minutes, until the meat is tender.

Meanwhile, heat the remaining oil in another pan and sauté the chillies and ginger for 1 minute, then add the onions and sauté for about 5–7 minutes, until translucent. Stir in the curry powder and season with salt and pepper.

Using a slotted spoon, lift the meat into the curry mixture. Stir the peanut butter into the meat cooking liquid, then add this to the curry with the tomatoes. Simmer for 2–3 minutes, stirring well. Serve garnished with the peanuts.

ZAMBIAN
GAZELLE CURRY

In land-locked Zambia antelopes such as gazelles provide good-quality meat, and a curry made with gazelle meat is very popular. Away from Africa, we can substitute springbok for the gazelle; this is easier to come by in the UK. Or you can use venison, goat, lamb or beef.

SERVES 4

4 tablespoons vegetable oil
800g springbok steak, venison haunch steak or beef fillet, cut into 2.5cm dice
1 teaspoon cumin seeds
1 bay leaf
1 dried red chilli
2 onions, finely chopped
1 tablespoon chopped garlic
1 tablespoon tomato paste
1/2 teaspoon red chilli powder or paprika
1/2 teaspoon ground turmeric
1/4 teaspoon ground cardamom
2 tablespoons raisins
250ml coconut milk
1 tablespoon unsweetened desiccated coconut, toasted
salt

Heat 1 tablespoon of the oil in a pan and sauté the gazelle meat to brown lightly. Remove from the pan and set aside until required.

Add the rest of the oil to the pan and heat, then add the cumin seeds, bay leaf and red chilli. When the spices crackle, add the onions and fry until translucent. Stir in the garlic.

Return the browned meat to the pan together with the tomato paste, red chilli powder, turmeric, cardamom and salt to taste. Stir well to mix, then sauté for 2–3 minutes. Add the raisins and coconut milk and simmer gently for 30–35 minutes or until the meat is cooked. This will be a thick, dry curry. Sprinkle over the toasted desiccated coconut and serve with rice or bread.

(LEFT)·AFRICAN WILD BOAR WITH PEANUTS
(RIGHT) ZAMBIAN GAZELLE CURRY

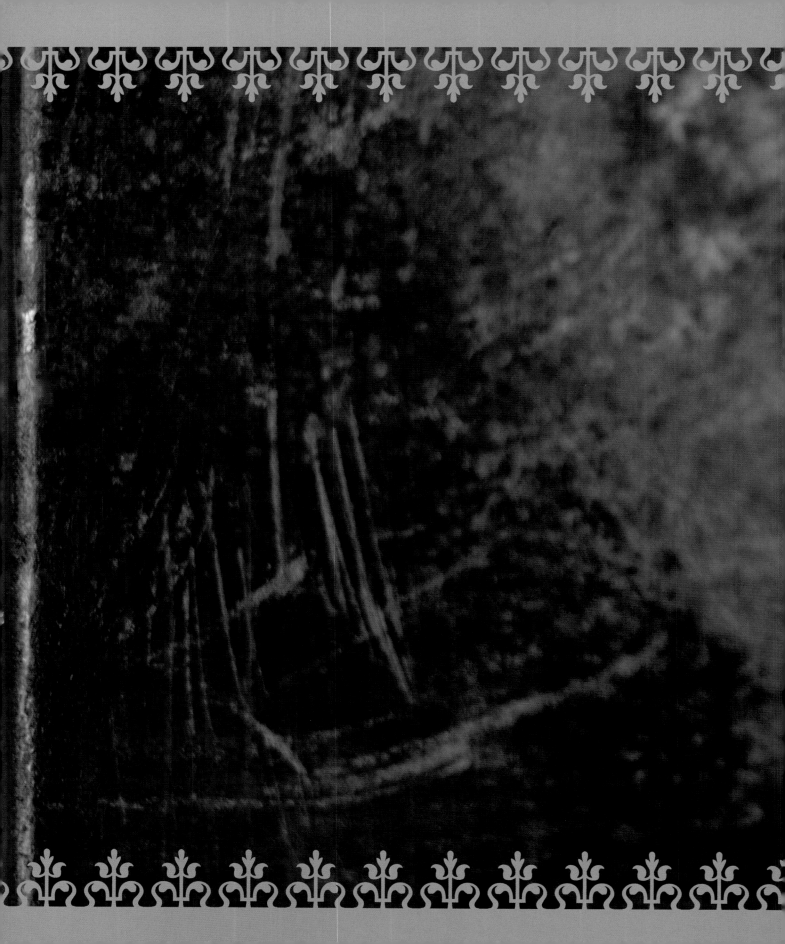

LAMB & GOAT

SOUTH AFRICAN BOBOTIE

BOBOTIE

There are many stories attached to this classic South African dish, in which minced lamb is mixed with fruit and spices then covered with a custard-like crust and baked in the oven. Some say that it came with the migrant workers from Indonesia, while others say it was the Dutch who brought it from Holland. Let's not fuss about it – whoever it was did a brilliant job! There are infinite versions of the recipe, even down to how it's cooked, so this one is my version. I've played with the spices until I think they're just right and have added nutmeg to the topping – nutmeg is such a wonderful partner for custard. I serve this with a mixed leaf salad with plenty of fresh mint.

SERVES 4

4 tablespoons vegetable oil
a 2.5cm piece of cinnamon stick
3 cloves
4–5 green cardamom pods
1 star anise
1 teaspoon cumin seeds
1 teaspoon fennel seeds
10 black peppercorns
2 bay leaves
2 onions, finely chopped
2 tablespoons Cape Malay Curry Powder (see page 220)
$1/2$ teaspoon ground turmeric
800g minced lamb
2 tomatoes, skinned and chopped
1 teaspoon brown sugar
1 large apple, peeled and grated
1 tablespoon grated lemon or

lime zest
100g sultanas or raisins, soaked in water to swell
3–4 kaffir lime leaves (optional)
2 tablespoons apricot jam or mango chutney
100g flaked almonds
1 egg
2 thick slices of white bread, soaked in 120ml milk
200ml milk
salt

For the crust
1 egg
150ml milk
$1/4$ teaspoon ground turmeric
freshly grated nutmeg, to taste

Preheat the oven to 180°C/Gas Mark 4. Heat the oil in a pan and sauté the whole spices and bay leaves until they begin to crackle. Add the chopped onion and sauté until lightly coloured. Stir in the curry powder and turmeric and sauté for a minute, then add the minced lamb and some salt. Cook, stirring, for 2–3 minutes to break up the meat. When it has lost its raw look, add the tomato, sugar, apple, lemon zest, sultanas and lime leaves, if using, and stir well. Cook for 3–5 minutes. Add the jam and continue to cook for 15–20 minutes, stirring, until the meat is almost cooked.

Remove from the heat. Add the egg, soaked bread, the extra milk and mix in well. Transfer the mixture to a well-greased baking dish and sprinkle the almonds on top. Bake for 30 minutes.

Meanwhile, whisk together the ingredients for the crust. Pour this evenly over the meat mixture and bake for a further 15–20 minutes or until the crust is set and lightly browned. Serve hot.

BRAISED MEAT WITH ROOT VEGETABLES

THARID

Tharid is an Emirati stew that is traditionally served over crisp, thin pieces of bread to soak up the vegetable and meat broth juices. The dish has been made famous as it is said to be one of the favourites of the Prophet Mohammed.

SERVES 4

3 tablespoons ghee or vegetable oil
3 onions, finely chopped
800g boneless stewing lamb or beef, cut into 2.5cm dice
2 teaspoons Baharat (Middle Eastern spice powder; see page 220)
1 teaspoon finely chopped garlic
400g tomatoes, skinned and chopped

1 tablespoon tomato paste
2 tablespoons finely chopped parsley
$1/2$ teaspoon crushed black pepper
a pinch of freshly grated nutmeg
2 potatoes, peeled and cut into 2.5cm dice
2 carrots, peeled and cut into 2.5cm dice
salt

Heat the ghee or oil in a pan and sauté the onions until translucent. Add the meat and sear until lightly browned. Add the baharat and garlic and stir well, then sauté for a further 2 minutes. Add the tomatoes, tomato paste, 1 tablespoon of the parsley, the pepper, nutmeg and salt to taste. Simmer for 40–45 minutes, covered, stirring occasionally.

Add the potatoes and carrots, with a little water if required, and cook for a further 30–45 minutes or until the meat and vegetables are perfectly cooked. Serve garnished with the remaining parsley.

GOAT GREEN CHILLI CURRY

KACHA MORICH PATHAR

As goat meat is so lean, marinating it for a few hours is a great way to ensure it doesn't dry out when it's cooked.

SERVES 4

800g boneless goat meat, cut into 2.5cm cubes
2 tablespoons Garlic Paste (see page 223)
200g plain yoghurt
100g ghee or vegetable oil
10–12 large red and green chillies, slit
salt

In a bowl, toss the goat with the garlic paste, yoghurt and some salt. Leave to marinate in a cool place for 2 hours to tenderise.

Heat the ghee or oil in a pan, add the goat, including its marinade, and the chillies and cook over a low heat for 30–35 minutes or until cooked and tender. Garnish with a selection of red and green chillies and serve with naan.

GOAT CURRY

In the 1800s, indentured labourers came to the Caribbean islands from the Indian states of Uttar Pradesh and Bihar. Being poor, their diet was based on pulses and sometimes fish; meat and poultry were kept for celebrations only. A goat curry was the sign of a big feast. Today their descendants keep up many cultural customs that have become obsolete in India.

SERVES 4

2kg leg of goat or lamb, with bone, cut into 2.5cm dice
2 tablespoons vegetable oil
3 onions, finely chopped
2 tablespoons finely chopped garlic
2 tablespoons Caribbean Curry Powder (see page 220)
500ml coconut milk
6–8 sprigs of thyme, leaves finely chopped
4 tablespoons finely chopped fresh ginger
4 tablespoons finely chopped chives
salt

For the marinade
2 tablespoons Caribbean Curry Powder (see page 220)
3–4 green chillies, or 1 deseeded Scotch bonnet chilli, chopped
2 tablespoons finely chopped garlic
2 tablespoons finely chopped fresh ginger
1 teaspoon ground allspice
a small bunch of chives, finely chopped
5–6 sprigs of thyme, leaves chopped
2 tablespoons vegetable oil

Mix together all the ingredients for the marinade in a bowl. Add the goat, mix well and leave in a cool place to marinate for 3–4 hours.

Heat the oil in a deep pan and sauté the onion with the garlic for 5–6 minutes or until lightly browned. Add the curry powder and sauté, stirring, for a minute, then add the marinated goat meat. Fry, stirring, for 8–10 minutes to brown the meat all over.

Add the coconut milk and 200ml water. Bring to the boil, then simmer gently for 40–50 minutes or until the meat is perfectly cooked. Correct the seasoning and stir in the thyme leaves, ginger and chives, then serve.

(LEFT) BANGLADESHI GOAT GREEN CHILLI CURRY
(RIGHT) CARIBBEAN GOAT CURRY

BUNNY CHOW

There are numerous stories about how this South African dish from Durban got its name. One tells how during the great depression of 1933, when whites and Chinese in the Durban area were suffering food shortages like everyone else, they discovered the cheapest food available was the vegetarian curry cooked by the Indian community. The concept of take-away was unknown then, but someone had the brilliant idea of filling a hollowed-out half loaf of bread with the curry to make it portable, with an edible eating utensil. Indians were known as 'bania', which means 'traders', and Chinese stir-fries had 'chow' at the end of their names, so the dish came to be called 'Bania Chow' and then 'Bunny Chow'. Durbanites are very proud of their Bunny Chow and its heritage. The version here is made with meat, but you can substitute red and white kidney beans.

SERVES 2–4

2 tablespoons vegetable oil
1/2 teaspoon cumin seeds
1/2 teaspoon fennel seeds
a 2.5cm piece of cinnamon stick
2 green cardamom pods
1 star anise
1 bay leaf
1 onion, finely chopped
2 tablespoons South African Curry Powder (see page 227)
2 tomatoes, chopped
1kg boneless leg of lamb or goat, cut into 2.5cm cubes
2 large potatoes, cut into 2.5cm cubes
1 tablespoon finely chopped fresh ginger
1 tablespoon finely chopped garlic
10–12 curry leaves
2 tablespoons finely chopped coriander leaves
2 tablespoons lime juice
2 loaves of bread, unsliced, each cut in half horizontally and most of the insides removed
salt

Heat the oil in a pan and sauté the whole spices and bay leaf until the spices sizzle. Add the onion and cook for 5–7 minutes until translucent. Stir in the curry powder and sauté for 1 minute, then add the tomatoes and stir to mix. Cook over a medium heat, stirring often, until you have a thick sauce.

Add the meat, potatoes, ginger, garlic, curry leaves and 200ml of water and season with salt. Simmer, stirring occasionally, for 40–50 minutes or until the meat and potatoes are tender, adding water if required. Stir in the chopped coriander and lime juice. To serve, spoon into the hollows in the bread and garnish with crisp-dried curry leaves, if you like.

LEFT: SOUTH AFRICAN BUNNY CHOW

FAMILY-STYLE GOAT CURRY

Goat is quite an unusual choice of meat in the UK and as a result you'll probably have to seek it out from a specialist butcher, however I'd urge you to give it a try. Goat meat has a richer flavour than lamb, pork or beef but it's also much lower in fat and high in protein so from a nutritional perspective it's a choice we should be embracing. Because it's so lean, goat needs to be cooked carefully with lots of moisture, over a very low heat, so that it doesn't dry out. If you prefer, you can use mutton or lamb.

SERVES 4–6

2 tablespoons coconut oil
2 cloves
a 2.5cm piece of cinnamon stick
4 green cardamom pods
1 lemongrass stalk, chopped
1kg leg of goat, mutton or lamb, with bone, cut into 2.5cm pieces
4 kaffir lime leaves
1 litre coconut milk
6 small round aubergines, cut in half lengthways
salt

For the spice powder
80g grated fresh coconut or desiccated coconut
2 teaspoons coriander seeds
1 teaspoon cumin seeds
5–8 macadamia nuts or 50g unsalted peanuts

For the spice paste
2 large onions, chopped
4 garlic cloves, peeled
4 large red chillies, deseeded
1 tablespoon chopped fresh ginger
1 teaspoon ground turmeric
a pinch of grated nutmeg
50ml coconut milk
2–3 tablespoons Tamarind Water (see page 228)

Toast the ingredients for the spice powder until lightly browned and aromatic. Cool, then grind to a fine powder. Set aside.

Blend together all the ingredients for the spice paste to make a fine paste. Keep aside.

Heat the coconut oil in a pan and sauté the cloves, cinnamon, cardamom pods and lemongrass for 2–3 minutes or until aromatic. Add the spice paste and sauté for 3–4 minutes, stirring well, then add the goat and stir for 10–12 minutes to lightly brown and coat the meat with spices. Add the toasted spice powder, lime leaves and cook, stirring, for a further 5 minutes.

Add half the coconut milk, 500ml water and salt to taste. Bring to the boil, then simmer for 30 minutes on a low heat.

Add the aubergines and the rest of the coconut milk. Continue simmering, stirring occasionally, until the meat is completely cooked. Check the seasoning and serve with rice.

ARMENIAN HARISSA

Not to be confused with the North African harissa sauce, this hearty dish is a spiced stew, common across the Middle East. It is traditionally served on the first day of the new year.

SERVES 4–6

300g wheat berries (whole-grain wheat), rinsed and soaked overnight
1kg boneless stewing lamb or beef, cut into 2.5cm dice
1 tablespoon freshly ground black pepper
100g butter or ghee
1 teaspoon ground cinnamon
1 teaspoon ground cumin
2 tablespoons finely chopped parsley
1 tablespoon lemon juice
salt

Put the wheat in a heavy-based pan with the soaking water. Bring to the boil, then simmer gently for 2 hours or until the grain is just tender.

Preheat the oven to 160°C/Gas Mark 3. Put the pieces of lamb or beef in a flameproof casserole with enough water to cover. Bring to the boil, then reduce to a gentle simmer and simmer for 15–20 minutes, skimming off the froth.

Add the grain to the casserole together with the cooking liquid. Season with the pepper and salt to taste. Cover and place in the oven and cook for 3 hours, stirring occasionally and adding water if required, to cook the grains and keep the meat moist.

Meanwhile, melt the butter in a small pan and stir in the cinnamon and cumin. Remove from the heat and add the parsley and lemon juice. Keep aside, then reheat just before serving.

At the end of the cooking time, the meat should be so tender it will break up easily when cut with a wooden spoon. Stir well to break up the pieces and mix to make a coarse purée. Ladle into soup plates and spoon over the reheated spicy butter.

GOAT CURRY

ELU MAS KARI

One of Sri Lanka's great culinary masterpieces. If you are not able to find goat meat, then feel free to substitute with lamb or mutton.

SERVES 4–6

800g leg of goat, with bone, cut into 2.5cm dice
3 tablespoons ghee or coconut oil
3 onions, finely chopped
1 tablespoon finely chopped garlic
1 tablespoon finely chopped fresh ginger
12–15 curry leaves
a 2.5cm piece of cinnamon stick
3 green cardamom pods, lightly bruised
2 green chillies, chopped
1/4 teaspoon black pepper
300ml vegetable or lamb stock
2 tomatoes, quartered
a few leaves of mint, to garnish

For the marinade
4 tablespoons Ceylon Curry Powder (see page 221)
1 teaspoon red chilli powder
1 teaspoon ground turmeric
1 tablespoon tomato paste
2 pandan leaves, torn into small pieces
1 lemongrass stalk, bruised
grated zest and juice of 1 lemon
4 tablespoons freshly grated coconut
100ml coconut milk
salt

Mix together all the ingredients for the marinade in a bowl with salt to taste. Add the goat and rub the marinade all over. Leave to marinate in a cool place for 30 minutes.

Heat the ghee or oil in a wok over a medium heat and sauté the onions with the garlic, ginger, curry leaves, cinnamon, cardamom, green chillies and black pepper until lightly coloured. Add the marinated goat and its marinade and sear the meat for 3–5 minutes, stirring. Add the stock and tomatoes and stir to mix. Bring to the boil, then simmer for 25–30 minutes over a low heat, until the goat is cooked. Garnish with the mint and serve with rice.

SRI LANKAN GOAT CURRY

IRAQI LAMBS' TROTTERS STEW

TASHREEB

Tashreeb is a best described as a poor man's dish fit for a king! It is a kind of rustic, hearty stew that would be served in the local cafés of various towns in Iraq. Local labourers will leave their homes before daybreak for morning prayers, then head straight to these cafés for their breakfast where they will devour a delicious chicken, beef, offal or even vegetarian tashreeb, soaking up the spicy gravy with pitta or khoubiz (a naan-like bread). And then they would head out for a long day's work! I wanted to try the authentic version and thought it would be an interesting way of serving offal, but if you prefer, you could use lamb shanks instead of the trotters and tripe – two shanks of about 350–500g will be enough to serve four.

SERVES 4

500g honeycomb or blanket tripe, washed and cut into 4cm square pieces

4 lambs' trotters, singed between the hooves to remove hair, washed and cleaned

150g dried chickpeas, soaked overnight and drained

2 loomi (dried limes), pierced all over with a fork, or thinly pared rind of 1 lime

1 garlic bulb, kept whole and loose outer skin removed

6–8 tablespoons ghee or vegetable oil

2 onions, finely chopped

400g tomatoes, skinned and chopped

1 tablespoon Baharat (Middle Eastern spice powder; see page 220)

1 tablespoon freshly crushed black pepper

2 tablespoons finely chopped parsley

salt

Combine the tripe, trotters and chickpeas in a large pot. Cover with water and bring to the boil, then drain off the water. Add fresh water to cover. Add the loomi and whole garlic bulb. Bring to a slow simmer, skimming as required.

Heat the ghee in a frying pan and fry the onions until translucent. Add the tomatoes and Baharat powder and cook, stirring frequently, for 7–10 minutes.

When the lamb mixture has been well skimmed and the liquid is clear, add the tomato mixture with the pepper and salt to taste. Cover and simmer for 3–4 hours or until the trotters and tripe are tender. Stir in the parsley.

If you wish, you can remove the meat from the trotters and put it back in the stew. Or serve as it is (on the bone) the traditional way. Serve with a flatbread such as khoubiz, naan or pitta.

KIDNEY AND LIVER CURRY

ERUMAS PEEGODU KARI

While the idea of eating liver might not at first sound very appetising, it has, for centuries, been prized as a delicacy and is still celebrated and lauded by many cuisines. Whether it's savoured by African hunters after a kill, pan-fried and served with caramelised onions in a British gastropub or mixed with truffles and cognac to make a fine French pâté de foie gras, there's no denying liver's wide appeal and versatility. This Sri Lankan curry would traditionally be made with goat's liver and kidneys, but lamb's liver and kidneys are easier to get hold of in the UK.

SERVES 4

400g lamb's liver, cleaned
200g lamb's kidneys, cleaned
1/2 teaspoon crushed black peppercorns
1 red onion, chopped
1 teaspoon ground turmeric
a 2.5cm piece of cinnamon stick
3 green chillies, sliced
1/4 teaspoon ground

cardamom
2 pandan leaves, cut into small pieces
3 tablespoons ghee or butter
3 white onions, chopped
500ml milk
100g cashew nuts, separated into halves
200g frozen peas, defrosted
salt

Blanch the liver and kidneys in boiling water for 5–7 minutes or until just cooked. Drain and cut into smaller pieces. Mix with the crushed black pepper, red onion, turmeric, cinnamon, green chillies, cardamom and pandan leaves. Keep aside until required.

Heat the ghee in a pan and sauté the chopped onions until lightly browned. Add the liver and kidney mixture and cook for 2–3 minutes, stirring well. Add the milk and cashew nuts. Bring to the boil, then simmer for 10–12 minutes. Add the peas and simmer for a further 3–4 minutes. Serve with rice.

KONKANI MUTTON CURRY

The Konkan region is a rugged section of the western Indian coastline. Alphonso mangoes are a common sight when exploring this region but there are many more elements to the cuisine of this beautiful, green and fertile belt. Konkan, or Malvan, food is heavily dominated by the use of coconut – fresh, dried and milk. It is also a very colourful cuisine, combining vibrant herbs and spices, as this recipe demonstrates.

SERVES 4

3 tablespoons vegetable oil
a 5cm piece of cinnamon stick
4 green cardamom pods
2 cloves
2 onions, chopped
1 tablespoon finely chopped fresh ginger
1 tablespoon finely chopped garlic
800g boneless leg or shoulder of mutton, cut into 2.5cm cubes
1/2 teaspoon ground turmeric
1 tablespoon ground coriander
1/2 teaspoon ground cumin
100g yoghurt, whisked

300ml lamb stock or water
1/2 teaspoon Garam Masala (see page 223)
1 tablespoon lime juice
salt

For the paste
400g coriander leaves
100g mint leaves
100g grated fresh coconut or unsweetened desiccated coconut
1 teaspoon mustard (French or English)
20 cashew nuts, lightly toasted
1 tablespoon lemon juice
1 tablespoon vegetable oil

Blend all the paste ingredients to a fine paste and set aside until required.

Heat the oil in a pan and sauté the cinnamon, cardamom and cloves until aromatic. Add the onions, ginger and garlic and sauté, stirring, for 10–15 minutes over a medium heat until the onions turn light brown in colour. Add the mutton, ground spices and salt. Sauté and stir for 4–5 minutes to seal the mutton, then add the yoghurt and stock and simmer for 30–40 minutes, covered, until the mutton is almost cooked – check by piercing it with the tip of a sharp knife; the knife should go in easily.

Add the paste and cook over a low heat for 10–12 minutes, then finish by adding the garam masala and lime juice. Serve hot with rice or bread.

LAMB CHOPS WITH SPINACH

CHAAMPAN DA SAAG GOSHT

There is a large farming community in the Punjab region of India and this is reflected in the locals' love of food from the land. Punjabi food is generally made up of strong and bold flavours and their use of spices is generous and liberal. This recipe for a typical Punjabi meat curry is a favourite of mine. It's packed with black cardamoms and cloves, both strong spices that really hold their own against the metallic flavour of the spinach and the lamb.

SERVES 4

1kg lamb chops, on the bone, trimmed

For the marinade
3 tablespoons finely chopped fresh ginger
2 tablespoons finely chopped green chillies
1 teaspoon ground cumin
3 tablespoons plain yoghurt
salt

For the garam masala
5 black cardamom pods
2 cloves
1/2 teaspoon black peppercorns
1/4 teaspoon grated nutmeg

For the sauce
2 tablespoons vegetable oil
1 tablespoon butter
a 5cm piece of cassia or cinnamon stick
1 bay leaf
4–6 black cardamom pods, lightly bruised
2–3 cloves
2 onions, finely chopped
1 tablespoon ground coriander
1 teaspoon ground cumin
2 tomatoes, chopped
1 tablespoon tomato paste
300ml lamb stock or water

For the spinach
3 tablespoons vegetable oil
2 tablespoons finely chopped garlic
1 tablespoon dried red chilli flakes
2 teaspoons cumin seeds
1kg baby spinach

Mix together all the ingredients for the marinade, rub all over the lamb chops and set aside in a cool place to marinate for 2 hours.

For the garam masala, toast all the spices in a pan until fragrant. Cool, then grind to a fine powder. Set aside until required.

For the sauce, heat the oil and butter in a pan and sauté the cassia, bay leaf, cardamom pods and cloves until the spices sizzle. Add the onions and sauté until lightly coloured. Add the ground coriander and cook for 2–3 minutes, then add the ground cumin and sauté for a further 2 minutes.

Add the marinated lamb and cook over a medium heat, stirring well, for 10–12 minutes until the yoghurt is absorbed. Increase the heat to high and sauté the lamb for 2–3 minutes, then add the tomatoes and tomato paste and cook for 2–3 minutes. Add the water or stock and salt to taste. Reduce the heat to low, cover and cook for 12–15 minutes, until the lamb is perfectly cooked.

Meanwhile, cook the spinach. Heat the oil in a wok and sauté the garlic, chilli and cumin seeds until the spices turn light brown. Add the spinach and quickly cook over a high heat to make them wilt. Season with salt and add to the lamb.

Mix the lamb and spinach together well and correct the seasoning. Sprinkle generously with the garam masala and some julienned red chilli and ginger, if you wish. Serve with roti or naan.

PUNJABI LAMB CHOPS WITH SPINACH

MOROCCAN LAMB TAGINE WITH APRICOTS AND SALTED ALMONDS

LAMB TAGINE WITH APRICOTS AND SALTED ALMONDS

TAGINE BIL MASHMASH

A tagine is a sweet and warmly spiced Moroccan stew in which meat and/or vegetables and pulses are slowly simmered. The dish's name comes from the pot in which it is cooked; a shallow, round clay dish with a cone-shaped lid. Cooking in a tagine gently moves the heat all around the pot so the steam rises, gets trapped in the conical lid and falls back into the stew as condensation, keeping it moist. The long, slow cooking, traditionally over embers, produces a rich, sticky stew that is meltingly tender. There are two main types of tagine: M'qualli, in which the meat is cooked in oil with saffron and ginger and the sauce turns yellow, and M'hammer, those cooked with olive oil or butter, cumin and paprika and the sauce is red. The recipe that follows is in line with M'qualli. Lamb and apricots are a lovely combination but goat, veal or beef can be used as well.

SERVES 4–6

1.5kg boneless shoulder of lamb, cut into chunks
1 tablespoon vegetable oil
1 large onion, finely chopped
4 garlic cloves, peeled
a 5cm piece of cinnamon stick
2 teaspoons Ras El Hanout (Moroccan spice powder; see page 227)
2 teaspoons ground ginger
1/2 teaspoon ground turmeric
a pinch of saffron threads
1 teaspoon freshly ground black pepper
50g unsalted butter, melted
1 litre lamb or vegetable stock
500g whole dried apricots, soaked in water to soften, then pitted
100g blanched almonds
50g salted butter
50ml honey
1 teaspoon ground cinnamon
salt

Toss the pieces of lamb with the oil, then sear in a hot frying pan over a high heat until browned on all sides. Remove from the heat.

In a flameproof tagine or casserole mix together the lamb, onion, garlic, cinnamon stick, ras el hanout, ginger, turmeric, saffron, pepper and melted unsalted butter. Add salt to taste. Cover and cook over a medium heat for 12–15 minutes. Pour in 750ml of the stock and continue cooking, covered, for 2 hours or until the meat is very tender.

Meanwhile, drain the apricots and cook in enough fresh water to cover for 30–40 minutes or until reduced to a nice pulp. Fry the almonds in the salted butter until lightly browned.

Add the apricots, nuts, honey, ground cinnamon and remaining stock to the lamb. Simmer for a further 10 minutes. Serve hot with couscous.

LAMB CHOPS WITH APRICOTS

JARDALOO CHAAPEN

The Parsee and Sindhi communities have exerted a profound influence on West Indian cuisine. Mixing fruit with meat is a technique that is used often in Iran so this recipe demonstrates the link between the cuisines of these two countries.

SERVES 4

100g dried apricots	seed
1 teaspoon white wine vinegar	2 tomatoes, chopped
3 tablespoons vegetable oil	800g lamb loin chops, with bone
a 5cm piece of cinnamon stick	1 teaspoon Garam Masala (see page 223)
2 onions, finely chopped	1/2 teaspoon freshly crushed black peppercorns
1 tablespoon Ginger-Garlic Paste (see page 223)	1 teaspoon palm sugar
1 teaspoon red chilli powder	salt
1 teaspoon ground cumin	

Soak the apricots overnight or for 8 hours in 200ml water with few drops of the vinegar.

Heat the oil in a wok and sauté the cinnamon stick with the chopped onions until golden brown in colour. Add the ginger-garlic paste and sauté for 2–3 minutes. Add the chilli powder and cumin and mix well. Add the tomatoes and cook for 4–5 minutes until the tomatoes soften.

Add the lamb, garam masala and pepper and stir for 3–6 minutes to seal the meat. Add salt to taste and 250ml water, bring to a simmer and cook slowly, covered, for 20–25 minutes until the meat is cooked. Add more water if required to moisten the meat.

Once the meat is cooked, add the remaining vinegar and drained apricots and simmer for 7–10 minutes. Remove and serve hot with rice or naan.

LAMBS' KIDNEYS AND TESTICLES MASALA

GURDA KAPOORA TAKA TAK

As in much of Asia, street food is a common sight in Pakistan, and the place to go to eat it in Lahore is Lakshmi Chowk. Chowk means 'centre' and this is undoubtedly the beating heart of the city – a bustling mass of streets lined with shops, restaurants and carts selling their wares. The food can be tantalising and challenging at the same time. While meat is a mainstay of the Muslim diet, the food sold on the stands needs to be cheap, so much of the meat sold is the cheaper cuts, particularly offal. The cooks are canny, however, so they use lots of spice and colour to make it appealing. As with all offal, make sure that the kidneys and testicles (fries) are as fresh as possible. If you'd prefer to leave out the fries, or can't get hold of them, simply double the quantity of kidneys.

SERVES 4

4 lambs' kidneys, cleaned and cut in half lengthways	1 tablespoon ground coriander
4 lambs' testicles (fries), cleaned and cut in half lengthways	1 teaspoon cumin seeds, toasted and ground
butter, for frying	1/4 teaspoon red chilli powder
3 tablespoons of Crispy Onions (optional, page 222), to garnish	1/4 teaspoon ground black pepper
	1/4 teaspoon Garam Masala (see page 223)
For the masala	1 tablespoon finely chopped fresh ginger
6 tablespoons ghee or butter	2 tablespoons finely chopped coriander leaves
2 tablespoons chopped garlic	1 teaspoon chaat masala (spice powder; see page 221)
1 tablespoon crushed dried red chilli	1 tablespoon lime juice
1 large onion, finely chopped	salt
1/4 teaspoon ground turmeric	

Melt some butter in a frying pan until foaming and fry the kidneys and testicles one after another for 1–2 minutes until sealed and lightly brown. Remove from the pan, sprinkle with a little salt and keep aside until required.

Wipe the frying pan with kitchen paper, then heat the ghee, add the garlic and crushed red chilli and sauté for a minute. Add the onion and sauté until lightly coloured. Stir in the ground spices and salt to taste, then sauté gently for 2 minutes, stirring well.

Add the kidneys and testicles and cook, stirring, for 12–15 minutes, moistening with a few tablespoons of water as needed to avoid burning. Add the ginger, chopped coriander, chaat masala and lime juice. Mix well. Garnish with the crispy onions if using, then serve with toasted bread slices or naan.

RIGHT: PAKISTANI LAMBS' KIDNEYS AND TESTICLES MASALA

PAKISTANI MEATBALL CURRY

MEATBALL CURRY

KOFTA KANDHARI

There are countless variations on the meatball (kofta) curry in Pakistan, among them Gushtaba, Yakhni and Keema Kofta. Gushtaba is a Kashmiri dish in which the meatballs (kofta) are simmered in a yoghurt-based sauce. For Yakhni Kofta the meatballs are cooked in a clear stock and eaten like a soup, and in Keema kofta they are cooked in a thick tomato-based sauce. This is my version of a meatball curry, which is based on a recipe originally from Kandahar that has found its way into Pakistan and then to a friend of mine's family, who gave it to me.

SERVES 4

For the kofta
500g minced lamb
50g cashew nuts
50g raisins, soaked in water to plump
4 tablespoons finely chopped mint leaves
3 green chillies, finely chopped
2 tablespoons finely chopped fresh ginger
1 tablespoon cumin seeds, lightly toasted and ground
1 teaspoon Garam Masala (see page 223)
1 teaspoon red chilli powder
500ml beef stock or water
salt

For the sauce
3 tablespoons vegetable oil
3 black cardamom pods, bruised
1/2 teaspoon black peppercorns
1 teaspoon cumin seeds
3–4 cloves
2 bay leaves
3 onions, finely chopped
1 tablespoon Ginger-Garlic Paste (see page 223)
1 tablespoon ground coriander
1 teaspoon ground turmeric
1 teaspoon red chilli powder
1/2 teaspoon Garam Masala (see page 223)
3 tomatoes, puréed whole
2 tablespoons finely chopped coriander leaves

Mix together all the ingredients (except the stock) for the kofta, seasoning with salt. Shape into golf-ball-sized meatballs. Heat the stock in a shallow pan and blanch the kofta, a few a time, for 3–5 minutes or until they are firm. As they are blanched, remove with a slotted spoon and keep aside. Reserve the stock for the gravy.

Heat the oil in a pan and sauté the whole spices with the bay leaves until they crackle. Add the onions and sauté until lightly browned. Add the ginger-garlic paste and stir for 2–3 minutes to cook the paste, then add all the ground spices, the puréed tomato and salt to taste. Simmer for 10–12 minutes.

Add the kofta and their blanching stock and simmer for 10–12 minutes or until the kofta are completely cooked. Correct the seasoning and add the chopped coriander. Serve with rice or bread.

LAMB CURRY

SEIKTHAR HIN

Burma is a predominantly Buddhist country and religion prohibits the killing of animals for consumption so meat is a rare and expensive commodity. The meat that is consumed is often from animals that have incurred a natural death; the animals are also likely to be older, which means the meat is tougher and the cooking time needs to be longer. This is a basic lamb curry that uses a cheaper cut of meat. It needs around an hour of cooking time to make the meat tender, but as with so many of the cheaper cuts, it's worth it. Lamb neck contains ribbons of fat running through it, which melt as it cooks, imparting all the delicious flavours into the sauce and potatoes.

SERVES 4

1kg lamb neck fillet, cut into 5cm pieces, or lamb ribs, cut into 5cm lengths and separated into individual ribs
1 teaspoon ground turmeric
1 tablespoon fish sauce
1 teaspoon red chilli powder
1 tablespoon ground cumin

2 tablespoons vegetable oil
2 onions, finely chopped
2 tablespoons white wine vinegar
1 litre lamb stock or water
2 medium potatoes, peeled and cut into wedges
salt

In a bowl, toss the meat with the turmeric, fish sauce, chilli powder, cumin and some salt. Mix thoroughly. Set aside until required.

Heat the oil in a pan and sauté the onions until lightly browned. Add the lamb and sear lightly to seal the meat. Add the vinegar and stock and bring to the boil, then simmer for 40 minutes. Add the potatoes and continue simmering gently for about 20 minutes or until the lamb and potatoes are tender. Serve hot with rice.

SINDHI MUTTON STEW

TEEWARN

Teewarn is a typical mutton stew made by the Sindhis. Some cooks add carrots, peas and potatoes, as I have, thus avoiding the need to prepare a separate vegetable dish. Served with bread this is truly a one-pot meal.

SERVES 4

2 carrots, cut into small dice
2 potatoes, peeled and cut into small dice
3 tablespoons vegetable oil
2 green cardamom pods
2 black cardamom pods
1 teaspoon cumin seeds
2 cloves
2 bay leaves
3 onions, finely chopped
1 tablespoon Ginger-Garlic Paste (see page 223)
1kg mutton chops
1 tablespoon ground coriander
1 teaspoon ground turmeric
1 teaspoon red chilli powder
3 tomatoes, finely chopped
100g plain yoghurt
1 tablespoon finely chopped fresh ginger
2 green chillies, thinly sliced
50g frozen peas, defrosted
1/2 teaspoon Garam Masala (see page 223)
1 tablespoon finely chopped coriander leaves
salt

Blanch the carrots and potatoes separately in boiling water for 3–4 minutes, until al dente. Drain and keep aside.

Heat the oil in a pan and sauté the whole spices with the bay leaves until they crackle. Add the onions and sauté until lightly browned. Add the ginger-garlic paste and cook, stirring, for 2 minutes, then add the mutton chops and cook, stirring constantly, for 10–12 minutes.

Add all the ground spices (except the garam masala), the blanched carrots and potatoes and the chopped tomatoes. Cook for 5–7 minutes or until the tomatoes break down to make a sauce, stirring occasionally.

Stir in the yoghurt, ginger, green chillies, peas and garam masala and simmer gently for 25–30 minutes, until the mutton is cooked. Garnish with the chopped coriander.

PUNJABI LAMB SHANK

NALLI GOSHT PUNJ-E-AAB

Lamb shank is quite a prized cut in northern India but it is used in various curries. The flavours in this recipe epitomise my home state.

SERVES 4

2 tablespoons Ginger-Garlic Paste (see page 223)
1 tablespoon mild sweet paprika or chilli powder
6 tablespoons vegetable oil
1 lamb shank, about 1.5kg, prepared
a 5cm piece of cassia or cinnamon bark
4–5 green cardamom pods
2–3 cloves
1 bay leaf
3 onions, thinly sliced
2 tablespoons finely chopped fresh ginger
1 tablespoon finely chopped garlic
4 green chillies, slit lengthwise
1 teaspoon ground turmeric
1 1/2 tablespoons ground coriander
2 teaspoons red chilli powder
1 tablespoon tomato paste
300ml lamb stock or water
10–12 plums, cut in half and stones removed
4 tablespoons finely chopped coriander leaves, plus a few extra sprigs to garnish
salt

In a bowl, mix together the ginger-garlic paste, sweet paprika, 2 tablespoons of the vegetable oil and salt to make a paste. Rub this paste liberally over the lamb shank and set aside in a cool place to marinate for 2 hours.

Heat a non-stick pan and seal the lamb shank over a high heat on all sides to lightly colour.

Heat the remaining oil in a pan and sauté the cinnamon, cardamom pods, cloves and bay leaf until the spices sizzle. Add the sliced onion and cook over a medium heat for 10–12 minutes or until lightly coloured. Add the chopped ginger, garlic and green chillies and sauté for a further 2–3 minutes.

Add the ground turmeric, coriander, chilli powder and tomato paste and moisten with 2–3 tablespoons of the stock, then add the seared lamb. Cover and cook over a low heat for 10 minutes, then add the plums and cook slowly, covered, for 10–12 minutes, until the plums soften. Add the remaining stock and half the coriander leaves, cover and simmer over a low heat for 30–40 minutes until the lamb is perfectly cooked. Serve garnished with the remaining chopped coriander leaves and sprigs.

RIGHT: PUNJABI LAMB SHANK

SUMATRAN LAMB KURMA

SUMATRAN LAMB KURMA

KAMBLING KURMA

The korma, or kurma, is thought to have originated in India (see page 46), but such is Asia's history that dishes have travelled and been adopted by other countries in the region, where they often take on a new life. So, while this seems to be an Indian-inspired recipe – probably south Indian because of the use of coconut – it is also characteristically Indonesian because of the lemongrass and as well as the coconut, which is also a much-loved ingredient there. Whatever its origins it all adds up to a fantastic korma.

SERVES 6

1kg lean, boneless, leg of lamb or mutton, cut into 2.5cm dice
6 tablespoons vegetable oil or ghee
6–8 shallots, finely chopped
4–6 garlic cloves, chopped
1 tablespoon finely chopped fresh ginger
2 teaspoons finely chopped lemongrass
a 5cm piece of cinnamon stick
1 star anise
2 bay leaves

400g potatoes, peeled and cut into 2.5cm dice
250ml coconut milk
salt

For the spice powder
$1/4$ teaspoon turmeric
1 teaspoon cumin seeds
1 teaspoon fennel seeds
1 tablespoon coriander seeds
4 green cardamom pods
4 cloves
10 black peppercorns

First make the spice powder. Lightly toast all the spices, one at a time, in a dry pan until fragrant. When they are cool, grind together to a fine powder in a spice mill or coffee grinder.

Mix together the lamb, spice powder and some salt in a bowl. Set aside in a cool place for 20 minutes.

Heat the oil or ghee in a pan and sauté the lamb for 4–5 minutes or until lightly browned. Use a slotted spoon to remove the lamb and set aside, then add the shallots to the pan and sauté for 5 minutes or until softened. Add the garlic, ginger and lemongrass and sauté for 2–3 minutes. Remove the mixture with the slotted spoon and keep aside.

Discard the oil left in the pan. Return the lamb and onion mixture to the pan and add the cinnamon stick, star anise, bay leaves and potatoes. Pour in enough hot water just to cover the ingredients. Bring to a boil over a high heat, then cover and simmer on the lowest possible heat for 45 minutes.

Remove the lid and add the coconut milk, topping up the liquid with a little hot water as well. Simmer, covered, for a further 15–20 minutes or until the lamb and potatoes are perfectly cooked. Adjust the seasoning and discard the cinnamon stick and bay leaves. Serve hot with rice.

MALAY LAMB CHOPS

KAMBING PANCUNGAN

The street food markets are colourful and very vibrant across Malaysia but more so in Kuala Lumpur. I came across a vendor in a night hawkers' market who was cooking beef kebabs with this marinade. I loved the marinade but thought it might work better with lamb: lamb chops are quicker and easier to cook (they can be kept pink and tender) and they have a more neutral flavour so they're a perfect canvas for the flavours of the marinade to shine.

SERVES 6

12 best end lamb chops, trimmed of any excess fat

For the marinade
4 garlic cloves, peeled
4 shallots, peeled
1 tablespoon sliced lemongrass
$1/4$ teaspoon finely chopped kaffir lime leaves
60ml light soy sauce
4 tablespoons tomato ketchup
2 tablespoons wine vinegar

$1/2$ teaspoon ground black pepper
4 tablespoons honey

For the mint dip
100g cucumber, peeled, halved and seeds removed
1 tablespoon chopped mint
1 tablespoon chopped parsley
1 tablespoon lemon juice
1 tablespoon Tabasco sauce
$1/2$ teaspoon salt, or to taste
120ml plain yoghurt

For the marinade, pound the garlic, shallots, lemongrass and lime leaves in a mortar to make a paste. Combine with the remaining marinade ingredients and 60ml water in a bowl, then place the lamb chops side by side in a flat dish and pour over the marinade, turning the chops coat them. Cover with cling film and leave to marinate in the fridge for at least 4 hours or preferably overnight.

To make the mint dip, chop the cucumber into fine pieces. Combine with the remaining dip ingredients in a bowl and lightly whisk together until well blended. Transfer to a serving bowl and chill until ready to serve.

Prepare a charcoal fire in the barbecue or preheat the grill to high. Barbecue or grill the chops for about 3–5 minutes on each side, until tender but still slightly pink in the middle, depending on how cooked you like your lamb. Keep brushing them with the marinade during cooking. Serve with the mint dip.

RANGOON MUTTON CURRY

SEIKTHAR HIN

India has had quite an influence on the cooking in Rangoon. There is an area that could be called the 'Indian Quarter' or 'Little India' – spice shops, street food stalls and all things Indian make up the scene here. Mutton is a common meat in India and it works well in braising recipes like this one. I have used boneless meat in this recipe – but do use the stewing pieces like neck or rib on the bone if you prefer.

SERVES 4

600g boneless mutton or leg of lamb, cut into 2.5cm cubes
1 teaspoon ground turmeric
4 tablespoons rapeseed or groundnut oil
1 tablespoon sugar
2 onions, finely chopped
6 garlic cloves, very finely chopped
1 tablespoon finely chopped fresh ginger
1 bay leaf

1 dried red chilli
a 5cm piece of cinnamon stick
150g plain yoghurt, whisked
400ml lamb stock or water
salt

For the spice powder
1 teaspoon cumin seeds
1 teaspoon coriander seeds
1/2 teaspoon mustard seeds
1 dried red chilli

In a bowl, toss the meat with the turmeric and some salt, then leave to marinate in a cool place for at least 1 hour.

Lightly toast all the spices for the spice powder. Cool, then grind to a fine powder.

Heat 2 tablespoons of the oil in a pan and add the sugar. When it caramelises lightly, add the marinated meat and cook until light brown on all over. Remove to a bowl and keep aside until required. Wipe the pan clean with kitchen paper.

Heat the remaining oil in the pan. Add the onions, garlic, ginger, bay leaf, dried chilli and cinnamon stick and cook until the onions are translucent. Add the spice powder and sauté for 2 minutes, then add the meat followed by the yoghurt and stock. Bring almost to the boil, then simmer for 45–50 minutes or until the meat is cooked and the sauce is thick. Correct the seasoning. You can garnish with a few crisp-fried curry leaves. Serve with rice.

MEAT COCONUT CURRY

ERACHI MAPPAS

Despite being born in northern India, I was a student in Chennai, and some of the strongest impressions I have of Keralan food date from that time. I often stayed with friends during the holidays and got to experience their families' cooking. As well as the spices, even the cooking methods in northern and southern Indian differ vastly. In the North the spices are cooked at the beginning and then the meat or vegetables are added, while in the South the spices are often added at the end. Here is a rich, coconutty, Keralan curry that takes me back to my student days.

SERVES 4

500g boneless lamb chump or beef rump, cut into 2.5cm cubes
1 teaspoon red chilli powder
1/2 teaspoon ground black pepper
1 1/2 teaspoons ground coriander
1 teaspoon ground turmeric
1/2 teaspoon ground cinnamon
2 cloves, ground
1/2 teaspoon ground fennel seeds
12–15 curry leaves
1 tablespoon finely chopped fresh ginger

1 tablespoon finely chopped garlic
3 green chillies, slit
2 onions, sliced
400ml coconut milk
salt

For seasoning
1 tablespoon coconut oil
1 teaspoon black mustard seeds
2 shallots, chopped
12 curry leaves
2 tomatoes, chopped

Place the meat in a pan and cover with 200ml water. Bring to boil then cover and simmer over a low heat for 10–15 minutes, until the meat is half cooked. Add all the remaining ingredients except the coconut milk to the pan and cook over a low heat for 20 minutes. Add the coconut milk and simmer for 3–5 minutes to finish cooking the meat.

In a separate pan, heat the oil and sauté the mustard seeds until they pop, then add the shallots and curry leaves. Cook gently until the shallots turn brown, then add the tomatoes. Stir this mixture into the meat and bring back to a simmer for a minute to heat through. Serve with rice or bread.

KERALAN MEAT COCONUT CURRY

PORK

HOT AND SOUR PORK

BABI ASAM PEDAS

Pork is not a very common meat in Indonesia, but people who do eat pork really exploit the flavours of the ingredients the country has to offer. In this recipe the heat from the chillies and ginger balanced with the sourness of the lime and tamarind demonstrates this skill at its best.

SERVES 4

600g pork fillet (tenderloin), cut into thin strips
6 tablespoons vegetable oil
1 tablespoon finely chopped fresh ginger
2 green chillies, thinly sliced
2 red chillies, thinly sliced
4–5 spring onions, thinly sliced on the diagonal
3 tablespoons dark soy sauce
10 cherry tomatoes, cut in half

2 tablespoons lime juice

For the marinade
100ml Tamarind Water (see page 228)
1 tablespoon finely chopped garlic
1 teaspoon red chilli powder
2 teaspoons cornflour
1 teaspoon finely chopped fresh ginger
salt

Mix together all the ingredients for the marinade, with salt to taste. Add the pork strips and toss to coat. Leave to marinate for 30–40 minutes.

Heat 4 tablespoons of the oil in a wok and fry the pork strips over a high heat until lightly browned. Remove with a slotted spoon and keep aside.

Pour the oil in the wok into a container to discard, then wipe the wok clean. Heat the remaining 2 tablespoons of oil in the wok and sauté the ginger, chillies and spring onions, until the onion is translucent. Add the pork strips then the soy sauce, tomatoes and lime juice. Stir-fry for 2–3 minutes and serve.

JAMAICAN GRILLED PORK CHOPS

The Jamaican way of cooking with spices has a unique style. Allspice berries, Scotch bonnet chillies and the use of thyme all add up to make this recipe very Jamaican! If you're not keen on a lot of heat, replace the Scotch bonnet chilli with green chilli for a milder level.

SERVES 4

8 thick pork chops
4 red apples, halved and cored
quartered limes, to serve

For the spice powder
1 teaspoon allspice berries
1 teaspoon black peppercorns
$1/2$ teaspoon grated nutmeg

For the spice paste
4 tablespoons Tamarind Water (see page 228)
2 tablespoons chopped fresh ginger
$1/2$ Scotch bonnet chilli, deseeded
2 tablespoons chopped garlic
2 teaspoons thyme leaves
1 tablespoon sugar
1 teaspoon salt
2 tablespoons vegetable oil

Combine the ingredients for the spice powder in a coffee grinder or spice mill and grind to a fine powder.

Using a food processor or a mortar and pestle, make a coarse paste from the ingredients for the spice paste. Mix the powder with the paste.

Rub the spice mixture all over the pork chops and apples. Set aside in a cool place for 2 hours.

Make a charcoal fire in a barbecue, letting it burn down to a medium heat, or preheat the grill to moderately high. Grill the chops for 20–25 minutes, turning halfway through the cooking time, until well browned; the centre will be light pink and juicy. Grill the apples for the final 2–3 minutes of the cooking time to colour on each side. Serve hot with a squeeze of lime juice.

JAMAICAN GRILLED PORK CHOPS

KERALAN PORK CURRY

KERALA PORK CURRY

PANNIYIRACHI KOOTAN

Some flavour combinations are universal, whatever the cuisine or method of cooking. Pork and apples are one such example and they're perfect partners in this recipe, which comes from the Syrian Christian community in Kerala.

SERVES 6–8

1kg boneless pork, cut into
    2.5 cm cubes
2 tablespoons rapeseed oil
3 large onions, chopped
3 tomatoes, chopped
2 tablespoons white wine
    vinegar
2 apples, peeled and pips
    removed, diced
salt

For the paste
1 teaspoon black mustard

seeds
a 5cm piece of cinnamon
    stick
4 tablespoons tamarind pulp
2 teaspoons ground turmeric
1 teaspoon ground black
    pepper
2 green chillies
12–15 cloves of garlic
2 tablespoons chopped fresh
    ginger
3 tablespoons raisins

To make the spice paste, tip all the ingredients into a blender and process until you have a fine, smooth paste. Add 50ml water, if necessary, to loosen the mixture a little.

Place the pork either in a pressure cooker or in a covered pan with 500ml water and cook for 7–10 minutes in the pressure cooker, or 25–30 minutes in the pan, until the pork is just undercooked, then strain and reserve the meat and stock.

Heat the oil in a pan and sauté the onion until translucent. Add the tomatoes and cook until they soften. Add the spice paste and sauté for 3–5 minutes, then add the cooked pork and cook until it is light brown. Add the reserved stock, vinegar, apples and 200ml water, and season with salt. Simmer over a low heat for 25–30 minutes, until the pork is completely cooked and the gravy has thickened. Garnish with crisp-fried curry leaves, if you wish, and serve hot with rice or bread.

PIG'S TROTTERS CURRY

In South East Asian countries, every part of the animal is used for food; this recipe is a great example.

SERVES 4

3 tablespoons palm sugar
1 litre pork or chicken stock
4 garlic cloves, finely chopped
2 red Thai chillies, chopped
2 tablespoons lime juice
4 tablespoons fish sauce
3 tablespoons chopped
    coriander roots
2 tablespoons unsalted
    peanuts, crushed
2 tablespoons soy sauce

4 pig's trotters, cleaned
4 spring onions, sliced on the
    diagonal
2 lemongrass stalks, bruised
30g fresh ginger, sliced
2 dried red chillies
4 star anise
a 2.5cm piece of cinnamon
    stick
4 hard-boiled eggs, peeled
coriander sprigs, to garnish

In a heavy pan, dissolve the sugar in 150ml water, then bring to the boil and boil until the mixture turns syrupy and brown. Remove from the heat and stir in the stock, garlic, Thai chillies, lime juice, fish sauce, coriander roots, peanuts and soy sauce.

Put the pan back on the heat and bring to a simmer. Add the pig's trotters, spring onions, lemongrass, ginger, dried red chillies, star anise and cinnamon. Bring to the boil, then simmer on a very low heat for 3–4 hours or until the meat is really tender.

Skim the fat off, then drop in the boiled eggs and simmer for a further 10–12 minutes until the eggs are heated through. Garnish with coriander sprigs and serve hot with jasmine rice.

PORK AND GREEN MANGO CURRY

WET THAR THAYET DHI HIN

For the Burmese, pork, mangoes and tea are three of the best things that nature has provided. This is a great recipe that uses two of those three, and the sour mango balances the rich pork perfectly. If you cannot get green mango, use a tangy cooking apple instead.

SERVES 4

2 onions, quartered
3 garlic cloves, peeled
2 dried red chillies
6 tablespoons groundnut oil
1/2 teaspoon ground turmeric
1 teaspoon belacan (dried shrimp paste), grated or broken into small pieces

400g pork shoulder, cut into 2.5cm cubes
1 medium unripe green mango, peeled, stoned and cut into very thin strips
300ml pork or vegetable stock or water
salt

Very finely chop the onions, garlic and red chillies together to make a coarse paste. Heat the oil in a pan and cook the onion paste slowly until it caramelises to a light brown colour. Add the turmeric and shrimp paste and stir through well.

Add the pork, mango, stock and some salt. Bring to the boil, then simmer gently for 45–50 minutes or until the pork is completely cooked and the liquid has reduced to a thick brown sauce. Correct the seasoning and serve with salad, rice and a side vegetable.

PORK AND BUTTERNUT SQUASH CURRY

You could make a vegetarian option of this wonderfully creamy curry, using vegetable marrow, courgettes, mushrooms and aubergines instead of the pork.

SERVES 4 (LARGE PORTIONS)

2 tablespoons vegetable oil
1 tablespoon finely chopped galangal
2 small red chillies, deseeded and sliced
3 shallots, finely sliced
2 tablespoons Kroeung (Cambodian spice paste; see page 224)
1/2 teaspoon ground turmeric
2 teaspoons mild curry powder
1 teaspoon ground fenugreek
1 teaspoon palm or brown sugar
500g pork loin, cut into

2.5cm dice
2 tablespoons tuk prahoc (diluted dried shrimp paste; see page 226) or fish sauce
800ml coconut milk
400g butternut squash, cut into 2.5cm dice
5 kaffir lime leaves
salt

To garnish
2 tablespoons chopped coriander leaves (optional)
leaves from a handful of mint sprigs (optional)

Heat the oil in a wok and sauté the galangal, chillies and shallots until fragrant. Add the spice paste and sauté until lightly coloured. Stir in the turmeric, curry powder, fenugreek and sugar, then add the pork pieces and mix in well. Sauté until lightly browned all over.

Add the tuk prahoc and pour in the coconut milk. Bring to the boil, then reduce to a simmer. Add the squash and cook for 20–25 minutes or until the pork and squash are cooked and the sauce has reduced.

Season to taste with salt and garnish with chopped coriander and mint leaves, if using.

CAMBODIAN PORK AND BUTTERNUT SQUASH CURRY

PORK BASIL STIR FRY

Based on a traditional stir-fry recipe, this dish is really hot! The paste can be made and cooked in advance and can be used as and when required. Store it in an airtight container in the fridge for 3–4 days or in ice cube trays in the freezer for 3–4 months.

SERVES 4

6–8 tablespoons vegetable oil or rendered pork fat
400g pork loin, cut into 2.5cm cubes
200ml pork or vegetable stock
1 teaspoon sugar
3–4 tablespoons fish sauce
100g snake or green beans, cut into batons and blanched
1 small knob of ginger, shredded
4–6 kaffir lime leaves, torn
3–4 long red chillies, sliced
a handful of holy basil leaves

For the spice paste
10 dried long red chillies, soaked in lukewarm water to soften and drained
3 tablespoons chopped galangal
2 tablespoons chopped fresh ginger
2 stalks of lemongrass, chopped
6 garlic cloves, chopped
3–4 tablespoons chopped coriander root
1 tablespoon kapi (dried shrimp paste; optional)
salt

Place all the paste ingredients in a blender and blend to a fine paste.

Heat the oil in a wok and sauté the paste over a medium heat for 2–3 minutes until fragrant. Add the pork and sauté for 4–5 minutes, then add a little of the stock to moisten. Add the sugar and fish sauce and cook for 20–25 minutes – keep moistening with stock until the pork is completely cooked. Add the beans, ginger, lime leaves, chillies and basil and stir to mix well. Serve with noodles or rice.

SPICY PORK MINCE SATAY

PEDAS SATE BABI

This recipe really works well on the barbecue. You could cook the satay under the grill, but it does come alive when cooked over charcoal. I've suggested making single, finger-like meatballs for each skewer but you could make smaller balls and put several on each skewer, then remove them and serve them as canapés with cocktail sticks.

SERVES 4

1kg minced pork (leg or fillet)
100g fresh pork fat
1 teaspoon sambal olek (chilli paste; see page 227)
4 garlic cloves, peeled
1 tablespoon chopped fresh ginger
1 tablespoon ground coriander
2 teaspoons ground cumin
100g mint leaves
1 teaspoon brown sugar

1 lemongrass stalk
4 kaffir lime leaves
2 tablespoons lime juice or white wine vinegar
1 egg
2 tablespoons freshly grated or desiccated coconut
salt
2 tablespoons vegetable oil, for basting
2 tablespoons lime juice, to serve

If you wish to use wooden skewers, the night before, put about 20 bamboo skewers in a bowl of water and leave to soak overnight.

Mince all the ingredients together, seasoning with salt to taste. If you don't have a meat mincer, use a food processor and pulse until minced. Divide into 20 portions. Shape into balls, then place each ball on a skewer and flatten each out so that they're more like fingers.

Prepare a charcoal fire, or preheat the grill to high. Cook the satay, basting with the oil, and cooking on all sides for about 10–12 minutes, until brown. Serve hot drizzled with the lime juice.

THAI PORK BASIL STIR FRY

YELLOW PORK CURRY

CARI THIT LON SAN

You could also use the cheaper, tough cuts of meat in this recipe, which lend themselves to the long, slow cooking time – the result will be just as wonderful. This dish could be described as Vietnam's take on comfort food.

SERVES 4–6

2 tablespoons vegetable oil
200g spring onions, finely chopped
5 garlic cloves, finely chopped
2 tablespoons finely chopped fresh ginger
1.5kg pork loin, cut into strips
1 teaspoon ground turmeric
1 tablespoon ground cumin
1 tablespoon ground coriander

1 teaspoon crushed black peppercorns
1 teaspoon paprika
1 teaspoon ground cinnamon
1 tablespoon red chilli powder
2 tablespoons fish sauce
200g sweet potatoes, peeled and diced
600ml coconut milk
1 large aubergine, cubed
stock or water, if needed

Heat the oil in a pan and cook the spring onions, garlic and ginger until fragrant. Add the pork and ground spices and mix well, then cook, stirring, until the pieces of pork are lightly browned. Add the fish sauce and cook on medium heat for 30 minutes, stirring occasionally.

Add the sweet potatoes and coconut milk and simmer, stirring, over a medium heat for 3–5 minutes, then add the aubergine and continue to simmer for 20 minutes. Add a little stock or water if the sauce is too thick, then simmer for a further 5 minutes or until the meat is tender and juicy.

PORK CURRY

URUMAS KARI

For this Sri Lankan curry, choose a cut of pork that has some fat, such as shoulder – fat is the carrier of flavours. This is a spicy one!

SERVES 4

600g pork chops
2 tablespoons vegetable oil
2 red onions, thinly sliced
1 tablespoon finely chopped fresh ginger
1 tablespoon finely chopped garlic
1 star anise
a 2.5cm piece of cinnamon stick
$1/4$ teaspoon black pepper
1 lemongrass stalk, bruised
2 green chillies, sliced
10–15 curry leaves
200ml chicken stock

150ml coconut milk
salt

For the marinade
4 tablespoons Ceylon Curry Powder (see page 221)
1 teaspoon red chilli powder
3 tablespoons Tamarind Water (see page 228) or lemon juice
1 tablespoon tomato paste
1 tablespoon finely chopped fresh ginger

Mix together all the ingredients for the marinade in a bowl. Add the pork and rub the marinade all over the meat. Set aside for about 30 minutes.

Heat the oil in a pan and sauté the onions with the ginger, garlic, cinnamon, star anise, black pepper, lemongrass, chillies and curry leaves for 2–3 minutes or until lightly coloured. Add the pork with its marinade and stir, then lightly brown the meat over a medium heat. Add the stock and salt to taste. Bring to the boil, then simmer for 20–25 minutes or until the pork is tender.

Add the coconut milk, stir well and continue simmering until the sauce thickens and the pork is completely cooked. Serve hot with rice.

SRI LANKAN PORK CURRY

BURMESE TAMARIND PORK RIBS

TAMARIND PORK RIBS

MAGYI WETNANYO HIN

Burmese cuisine uses all the parts of the animal to avoid waste, however there isn't much meat on the spare ribs I've used in this recipe so you need quite a large quantity to feed four people.

SERVES 4

2 large onions, roughly chopped
6 garlic cloves, chopped
3 dried red chillies, soaked in lukewarm water to soften and drained
100ml rapeseed oil
1/2 teaspoon ground turmeric
1 tablespoon belacan (dried shrimp paste), broken into small pieces

1kg pork spare ribs, cut into 4cm pieces
150ml pork or vegetable stock or water
4–5 tablespoons Tamarind Water (see page 228)
2 spring onions, thinly sliced
2 red chillies, thinly sliced on the diagonal
salt

In a mortar and pestle, crush the onions, garlic and chillies together to make a coarse paste.

Heat the oil in a wok and sauté the onion paste gently for 10–15 minutes or until caramelised to a light brown colour. Add the turmeric and belacan and stir through. Add the pork and stock and bring to the boil, then simmer very gently, covered, for 30–40 minutes or until the pork is cooked. Add more stock or water during the cooking, if required.

Add the tamarind and cook for a further 10–15 minutes to thicken the gravy. The pork should be tender enough to fall apart when tested with a fork. Correct the seasoning. Garnish with the spring onions and red chillies, and serve.

SPICY PORK

SHIKAR BHAJI

For Christians in Bangladesh, Christmas Day, or Burro Din, is a day for friends, family and feasting. Before the day, the meat shops of Dhaka's Kowran Bazaar market are busy preparing hams, sausages and cold beef in brine. The traditional Bengali Christmas dinner is called Prem Bhoj, or a feast of love! This pork curry is a common dish during the holiday period.

SERVES 4

1kg pork shoulder, cut into 2.5 cm cubes
3 red onions, quartered
70ml malt vinegar
1 tablespoon brown sugar
4 tablespoons mustard oil
1 teaspoon cumin seeds
1 large red onion, finely chopped
2 green chillies, sliced on the

diagonal
2 red chillies, sliced on the diagonal
1 teaspoon freshly ground black pepper
2 spring onions, thinly sliced
2 sprigs of coriander leaves
1 tablespoon fresh lime juice
salt

In a bowl, toss the pork with the quartered onions, vinegar, sugar and some salt. Cover tightly and leave to marinate overnight in the refrigerator.

Tip the pork mixture into a pot and add enough water to cover. Bring to the boil, then simmer for 45 minutes or until the meat is cooked. Drain and discard the liquid. Set the pork and onions aside until required.

Heat the oil in a wok and sauté the cumin seeds. When they crackle, add the chopped onion and sauté until light brown. Add the pork pieces and turn up the heat to high. Add the green and red chillies and the black pepper, and sauté until the pork is well browned. Mix in the spring onions and coriander and sprinkle with the lime juice, then serve.

PORK KAPITAN

This curry came to life in the 16th century when the Chinese first started trading and settling in what is now Malaysia. The 'Kapitan' was the Chinese captain of a ship – the intermediary between the local rulers and the Chinese – and this recipe was created for him by his Malay cooks. Traditionally made with chicken, it is a true fusion of Chinese and Malay cooking both in terms of the ingredients and the techniques used.

SERVES 4–6

2 teaspoons groundnut oil
a 2.5cm piece of cinnamon
 stick
1kg pork shoulder, cut into
 2.5cm cubes
400ml coconut milk
250ml chicken stock
1 tablespoon palm sugar
1 tablespoon tamarind pulp
 or a piece of dried asam
 gelugur
salt and pepper

For the paste
6 dried red chillies, soaked in
 hot water for 20 minutes
6 shallots, chopped

5 garlic cloves, chopped
1 tablespoon chopped fresh
 ginger
2 teaspoons chopped fresh
 turmeric root or $^1/_2$
 teaspoon ground turmeric
2 teaspoons Chinese five-
 spice powder
$^1/_2$ teaspoon belacan (dried
 shrimp paste)
$^1/_2$ teaspoon salt

To garnish
coriander sprigs
1 red onion, sliced
red chillies

Using a pestle and mortar or a food processor, pound or blend together all the paste ingredients into a semi-smooth paste.

Heat the oil in a large pan over a medium heat. Fry the curry paste with the cinnamon stick for 1–2 minutes or until fragrant. Add the pork and fry for 1–2 minutes. Pour in the coconut milk and stock and add the sugar, tamarind and some salt and pepper. Stir, then bring to a simmer. Reduce the heat to low, cover and leave to simmer gently for $1^1/_2$ hours or until the pork is tender.

Serve over rice garnished with a the coriander sprigs, red onion and red chillies.

BEEF

BEEF AND AUBERGINE CURRY

KEING SAIKO

Recipes often used to suggest that you salt aubergines before cooking them, supposedly to remove their bitter flavour. This really isn't necessary nowadays as aubergines have been cultivated so that they are less bitter. I really love aubergines, but if you don't, simply substitute pumpkin or a squash.

SERVES 4

4 tablespoons vegetable oil
400ml coconut milk
1 teaspoon kaapi or prahoc (dried shrimp paste)
900g boneless sirloin steak, cut into 5cm strips
3 tablespoons fish sauce
2 tablespoons sugar
300ml beef stock or water
300g pea aubergines or regular aubergine, cut into 2.5cm cubes
salt

fresh Thai basil leaves, to garnish

For the paste
2 medium dried red chillies
1 lemongrass stalk, chopped
2 large shallots, chopped
2 teaspoons grated galangal
6–7 kaffir lime leaves, deveined
1/4 teaspoon ground turmeric
3 tablespoons chopped coriander root or stalks

Blend all the ingredients for the paste with 250ml water to make a fine paste.

Heat 3 tablespoons of the oil in a wok with half the coconut milk and bring to a simmer. Add the spice paste and kaapi and cook for 7–10 minutes or until the sauce thickens and looks shiny.

Stir in the beef strips and simmer gently for 5–6 minutes or until the beef is about half cooked. Add the fish sauce, sugar, remaining coconut milk, stock and salt to taste. Bring to the boil, then simmer for 15–20 minutes or until the meat is perfectly cooked.

In a separate pan, heat the remaining oil and sauté the aubergines for 5–7 minutes. Stir into the curry and simmer for 2 minutes. Garnish with basil leaves and serve with rice.

BEEF AND PLANTAIN STEW

NDIZI NA NYAMA

If you cannot get plantains (ndizi in Swahili) to make this spicy East African stew, you can use firm, under-ripe bananas. The stew can also be made without the meat.

SERVES 4

400g beef topside, cut into 2.5cm dice
1/2 teaspoon black pepper
1/2 teaspoon East African Curry Powder (see page 222)
1 teaspoon red chilli powder
3 tablespoons vegetable oil
2 onions, finely chopped
1 bay leaf

2 tomatoes, chopped
1 tablespoon tomato paste
6 plantains, peeled and sliced
200ml coconut milk
salt
coriander sprigs, to garnish (optional)
mint leaves, to garnish (optional)

Combine the beef, black pepper, curry powder, chilli powder, salt to taste and enough water to cover in a pot. Bring to the boil, then simmer for 15–20 minutes, until the beef is cooked.

Meanwhile, heat the oil in a pan and sauté the onions with the bay leaf until lightly coloured. Add the tomatoes and tomato paste and stir well, then cook gently for a further 10–15 minutes.

Add the plantains to the meat and simmer for 10 minutes or until the plantains are tender. Add the tomato mixture to the beef together with the coconut milk and stir to mix, then simmer for a further 10 minutes. Taste and adjust the seasoning, then garnish with the coriander and mint, if using, and serve with rice.

AFRICAN BEEF AND PLANTAIN STEW

BRITISH BEEF BALTI

BEEF BALTI

When I came to the UK in 1994, baltis were the 'happening' thing and 'balti houses' were opening up all over Britain. I had a close look at the balti recipe and came to the conclusion that it is a British phenomenon and had nothing to do with an Indian recipe. The word 'balti' refers to the pot in which the curry is cooked and there are various theories as to where this name came from, ranging from its meaning – a 'bucket' in Hindi and Portuguese – to Baltistan, the region in north Pakistan in which the dish is sometimes said to have originated. But in fact the balti recipe was made in the UK for the UK – end of story!

SERVES 4

4 tablespoons vegetable oil
1 green pepper, cut into very thin strips, with a little reserved to garnish
1 teaspoon fennel seeds
1 black cardamom pod, lightly bruised
a 5cm piece of cassia or cinnamon stick
1 bay leaf
1 onion, thinly sliced
1 tablespoon Ginger-Garlic paste (see page 223)
600g beef fillet, cut into 2.5cm cubes

3–4 green chillies, thinly sliced
1 teaspoon ground cumin
1 tablespoon ground coriander
1/2 teaspoon red chilli powder
1 tomato, chopped
5 tablespoons Onion Masala Gravy (see page 226)
100ml beef stock or water
1/2 teaspoon ground fenugreek
1/2 teaspoon Garam Masala (see page 223)
salt

Heat 1 tablespoon of the oil in a frying pan and lightly sauté the pepper strips over a medium heat until lightly seared but still crunchy, then set aside.

Heat the remaining oil in a separate pan and sauté the fennel seeds, cardamom, cassia and bay leaf. As soon as the spices sizzle, add the sliced onion and sauté for 3–5 minutes or until lightly coloured. Add the ginger-garlic paste and sauté for 2–3 minutes, until the raw garlic smell goes away, then add the beef. Sauté the meat for 5–8 minutes over a high heat to seal and lightly colour, then add the green chillies, cumin, coriander and red chilli powder. Cook for 2–3 minutes, then add the tomatoes, onion masala, salt and stock. Simmer for 10–12 minutes to cook the meat well. Add the fenugreek, garam masala and sautéed pepper. Stir for 2–3 minutes, then add the chopped coriander leaves. Garnish with the remaining strips of green pepper and serve with naan or rice.

CHILLI-FRIED BEEF

DENGDENG PEDAS

Here's a really hot and fiery recipe! It uses both red chilli powder and fresh green chillies, and ginger and spring onions add to the punch. For some extra colour, you could add diced tomatoes.

SERVES 4

700g beef topside or skirt steak, cut into thin strips
2 tablespoons vegetable oil
1 teaspoon freshly ground black pepper
2 tablespoons finely chopped fresh ginger
1 tablespoon ground coriander
1/2 teaspoon red chilli powder
1 tablespoon lemon juice

salt

For the stir-fry
2 tablespoons vegetable oil
4 garlic cloves, sliced
2 onions, thinly sliced
2 green chillies, thinly sliced
2 tablespoons lime juice
4 spring onions, thinly sliced on the diagonal

In a dish or plastic food bag, toss the beef strips with 1 tablespoon of the oil, the pepper, ginger, coriander, chilli powder, lemon juice and salt to taste. Leave to marinate in a cool place for 1 hour.

Heat the remaining oil in a wok and sauté the beef strips very quickly over a high heat until lightly browned. Remove and keep warm until required.

Wipe the wok, then heat the oil for the stir-fry and sauté the garlic and onion over a high heat until lightly browned. Return the beef strips to the wok with the chillies, lime juice, spring onions and salt to taste. Sauté for 2–3 minutes, to heat through, then serve hot.

BEEF CURRY

HARAK MAS CURRY

As a major stop on both the spice and silk routes, Sri Lanka's cuisine inevitably reflects its history and draws influences from a rich and diverse range of religions and cultures. The Portuguese and Dutch colonial influences are evident in this recipe through the use of garlic and vinegar, which would have been traded for spices.

SERVES 4

800g beef stewing steak, cut
  into dice
3 tablespoons vegetable oil
2 onions, finely chopped
2–3 green cardamom pods
1 teaspoon mustard seeds
10 curry leaves
2 cloves
a 2.5cm piece of cinnamon
  stick
2 strips of pandan leaves
3 ripe tomatoes, chopped
2 fresh red chillies, sliced
150ml beef stock
150ml coconut milk

For the marinade
1 tablespoon white wine
  vinegar
1 tablespoon finely chopped
  garlic
1 tablespoon finely chopped
  fresh ginger
2 tablespoons Ceylon Curry
  Powder (see page 221)
1 teaspoon red chilli powder
1/2 teaspoon crushed black
  pepper
salt

Mix together all the ingredients for the marinade in a bowl. Add the beef and mix well, then leave in a cool place for 30 minutes.

Heat the oil in a pan and sauté the onions with the cardamom, mustard seeds, curry leaves, cloves, cinnamon and pandan leaves until lightly coloured. Add the beef, tomatoes, red chillies and stock and mix well. Bring to the boil, then simmer for 30 minutes or until the beef is almost cooked. Stir in the coconut milk and simmer for 2–3 minutes to heat through. Check the seasoning, then serve.

BEEF CURRY WITH PEANUTS

SARAMAN

It is difficult to make the spice paste for this recipe in a smaller quantity so I've suggested you freeze half of it. It freezes well and is great paired with duck, lamb, venison and pork as well. Stock up on the other basic storecupboard ingredients – the coconut milk and peanuts – and you've got a ready-made curry on standby, an easy meal that's perfect for a lazy weekend meal, just left to simmer away while you sit back and relax.

SERVES 6–8

1kg beef topside, cut into
  2.5cm cubes
3 tablespoons Ginger Paste
  (see page 223)
4 tablespoons vegetable oil
1 litre coconut milk
1 teaspoon kaapi (dried
  shrimp paste)
5 tablespoons sugar
4 tablespoons fish sauce
4 tablespoons Tamarind
  Water (see page 228)
200g roasted unsalted peanuts
salt

For the paste
3 tablespoons vegetable oil
3 dried red chillies
1 tablespoons finely chopped
  galangal
6 garlic cloves, sliced
3 large shallots, chopped
a 5cm piece of cinnamon stick
3 star anise
20 green cardamom pods
1 nutmeg, grated
2–3 blades of mace
2 lemongrass stalks, chopped
100g coriander leaves,
  chopped
1/2 teaspoon ground turmeric

In a bowl, rub together the beef and ginger paste, then leave to marinate in a cool place for 30 minutes.

To make the paste, heat the oil in a wok and sauté the chillies, galangal, garlic, shallots, cinnamon stick, star anise, cardamom, nutmeg, mace and lemongrass for 5–6 minutes or until fragrant. Tip into a blender and add the chopped coriander, turmeric and 300ml water. Blend to a smooth paste. Divide in half and freeze one half for future use. Keep the remainder (about 100g) aside until needed.

Heat the oil in a large pan and add one-third of the coconut milk. Bring to the boil, then simmer for 3–4 minutes. Add the spice paste, shrimp paste and marinated beef. Cook gently, stirring occasionally, for about 10 minutes. Add the remaining coconut milk, the sugar, fish sauce, tamarind water, peanuts and salt to taste. Cook on a low heat for 1–1½ hours or until the beef is well cooked and tender.

If the sauce is too thick, add beef stock or water. Check the seasoning. Serve with rice or bread.

RIGHT: CAMBODIAN BEEF CURRY WITH PEANUTS

AFRICAN BEEF MATORI

BEEF MITORI

East African dishes are notable for the presence of certain ingredients – bananas, peanuts and potatoes being the most common. This curry, in which beef is marinated with garlic and chillies and then fried and stewed with potatoes and bananas is a classic example of the region's cuisine.

SERVES 4

500g boneless stewing beef, cut into 2.5cm dice
3 potatoes, peeled and quartered
300ml beef stock
2 tablespoons vegetable oil
2 onions, chopped
3 tomatoes, skinned and chopped
4 ripe bananas, sliced
300ml coconut milk

salt and pepper

For the marinade
2 tablespoons finely chopped garlic
2 tablespoons finely chopped red chilli
1 tablespoon East African Curry Powder (see page 222)
4 tablespoons vegetable oil

Mix together the ingredients for the marinade in a bowl, seasoning with salt to taste. Add the beef and turn to coat, then leave in a cool place to marinate for 30 minutes.

Meanwhile, blanch the potatoes in boiling water for 7–10 minutes, until just cooked. Drain and set aside.

Heat a wok and fry the marinated beef pieces until browned all over. Add the stock and bring to the boil, then simmer for 30–40 minutes or until the beef is cooked.

In a separate pan, heat the oil and sauté the onions until translucent. Add the potatoes, tomatoes and most of the banana (reserve a few slices for serving), then add the beef with its stock. Stir to mix and adjust the seasoning with salt and pepper. Add the coconut milk and simmer until the potatoes are cooked. To serve, scatter a few of the reserved banana slices over and accompany with rice.

BEEF IN PEPPER SAUCE

BEEF DENGENG

The Sarawak region of Malaysia on the island of Borneo is famous for producing a very fragrant variety of peppercorn. The strong flavours of beef and pepper work really well together and need little else to make a beautiful dish.

SERVES 2

400g lean beef, such as rump or fillet, cut into thin strips
120ml thick soy sauce
1 tablespoon crushed black peppercorns
6 tablespoons groundnut or vegetable oil
1 red onion, sliced

1 tablespoon green peppercorns (bottled)
2 tablespoons Chilli Paste, or to taste (see page 221; optional)
1 teaspoon sugar (optional)
salt
mixed salad, to serve

Put the beef into a bowl. Add half the soy sauce and the crushed black pepper. Mix well and set aside to marinate for 30 minutes.

Heat half the oil in a wok or large frying pan. When smoking hot, add the marinated beef and sauté for 1–2 minutes or until well browned. Remove the beef from the pan and set aside.

Clean the pan and reheat. When hot, add the remaining oil followed by the onion. Sauté for 1 minute. Add the green pepper and stir-fry for another minute. Add the remaining soy sauce and stir in, then mix in the chilli paste and 2 tablespoons of water followed by the sugar, if using. Finally, add salt to taste. When the sauce begins to boil and has thickened, add the beef and mix well. When the beef is piping hot, serve immediately, with salad.

TRIPE CURRY

AHMAIOU HIN

There's no doubt that tripe isn't the most popular of cuts of meat, in part because it has a reputation for having a pungent smell and a chewy texture. But cook it slowly to tenderise it and pair with spices and it can be transformed. Like this one, many recipes will suggest blanching the tripe first, as this helps to remove the aromas and to kill off any lingering microbes.

SERVES 4

500g honeycomb tripe, cleaned, cut into 5 x 2.5cm pieces
2 tablespoons vegetable oil
1 onion, finely chopped
1 tablespoon finely chopped garlic
1/2 teaspoon red chilli powder
1/2 teaspoon ground cumin
1/2 teaspoon ground turmeric
800ml beef stock
2 spring onions, thinly sliced on the diagonal
salt

Blanch the tripe pieces in boiling water for 15 minutes; drain, rinse and set aside until required.

Heat the oil in a pan and sauté the onion and garlic with the chilli powder until the onion softens. Add the cumin, turmeric, tripe and some salt, and cook, stirring, for 2–3 minutes. Pour in the stock and bring to the boil, then simmer for 1–1 1/2 hours or until the tripe is tender and the gravy has reduced to about 100ml. Garnish with the spring onions and serve.

BEEF SKEWERS

This easy recipe is classic street food in Vietnam. Serve with a salad of lettuce leaves, sliced cucumber, beansprouts, holy basil, mint leaves and coriander leaves.

SERVE 4

800g fillet of beef, cut into 2.5cm dice
1 large pineapple, peeled, cored and cut into 2.5cm dice
3 tablespoons toasted sesame seeds
3 spring onions, diagonally sliced

For the marinade
3 tablespoons finely chopped garlic
2 red chillies, chopped
1 lemongrass stalk, finely chopped

1 teaspoon caster sugar
1 tablespoon fish sauce
1 tablespoon thick soy sauce
2 teaspoons rice wine vinegar
1 teaspoon sesame seeds
1 tablespoon vegetable oil

For the nuoc cham (dipping sauce)
2 teaspoons caster sugar
1 red chilli
2 garlic cloves, peeled
juice of 1 lime
1 tablespoon rice wine vinegar
2 tablespoon fish sauce

The night before, put 12–15 bamboo or wooden skewers in a bowl of water and leave to soak overnight.

Whisk together all the ingredients for the marinade in a bowl. Mix in the beef and pineapple and leave to marinate in a cool place for 1 hour.

Meanwhile, make the nuoc cham. In a bowl whisk the sugar with 100ml boiling water to dissolve. Pound the chilli with the garlic to make a paste, then mix with the sugar water. Stir in the lime juice, vinegar and fish sauce.

Prepare a charcoal fire in a barbecue or preheat the grill to high. Thread the beef and pineapple dice alternately on the soaked skewers. Grill for 2–3 minutes on each side, basting with the marinade when you turn the skewers.

Arrange the skewers on a platter and sprinkle with the toasted sesame seeds and spring onions. Serve with a salad and the nuoc cham.

VIETNAMESE BEEF SKEWERS

SRI LANKAN LIVER CURRY

LIVER CURRY

PEEGODU KARI

Sri Lankans enjoy offal and are masters at spicing offal curries. This recipe is a little unusual in that the liver is boiled first and then cooked again in the sauce but this keeps it beautifully soft and moist. Cardamom and fennel are added to balance the liver's bitter flavour.

SERVES 4

500g calf's liver, sliced
3 tablespoons white wine vinegar
1/2 teaspoon black peppercorns
3 green cardamom pods, bruised
1 cinnamon stick
3 cloves
1 tablespoon lime juice
1/4 teaspoon red chilli powder
1 teaspoon sweet paprika
1 teaspoon ground fennel
1 teaspoon ground coriander
1 teaspoon ground cumin

salt
salad leaves, to garnish

For the sauce
2 tablespoons ghee
1 onion, finely chopped
4 garlic cloves, finely chopped
1 tablespoon finely chopped fresh ginger
10 curry leaves
1 lemongrass stalk
300ml coconut milk
2 tablespoons finely chopped dill leaves

Put the liver in a pan and add the vinegar, peppercorns, salt to taste and water to cover. Bring to a simmer and cook for 5–8 minutes or until the liver is firm. Drain. When the liver is cool, remove the membrane (cow's and calf's liver has a thin transparent membrane that needs removing before or after cooking) and cut into 1cm dice.

In a bowl, toss the liver dice with the cardamom, cinnamon, cloves, lime juice, chilli powder, paprika, fennel, coriander and cumin. Leave to marinate in a cool place for 30 minutes.

Heat the ghee in a pan and sauté the onion with the garlic, ginger, curry leaves and lemongrass until lightly coloured. Add the marinated liver with its marinade and the coconut milk. Simmer for 10–12 minutes, until the sauce has reduced and thickened. Stir in the chopped dill leaves, garnish with the salad leaves and serve with rice.

BEEF MINCE MASALA

BADE KA KHEEMA MASALA

Mince as you've probably never had it before! I love this dish for its simplicity, ease, aromatic flavours and for the boiled egg that finishes off the dish so perfectly!

SERVES 4

6 tablespoons vegetable oil
4 green cardamom pods
1 black cardamom pod
1 teaspoon cumin seeds
2 cloves
2 bay leaves
2 green chillies, chopped
2 tablespoons finely chopped fresh ginger
3 onions, finely chopped
600g minced beef fillet
3 tomatoes, finely chopped
2 tablespoons plain yoghurt
1 tablespoon Ginger-Garlic Paste (see page 223)

1 teaspoon red chilli powder
1 tablespoon ground coriander
1/2 teaspoon ground turmeric
200ml beef stock or water
200g frozen peas, thawed and drained
2 hard-boiled eggs, chopped
2 tablespoons finely coriander leaves
1/2 teaspoon Garam Masala (see page 223)
salt

Heat the oil in a pan and sauté the whole spices with the bay leaves for a minute. Add the green chillies, ginger and onions and sauté until the onions are lightly browned. Add the minced beef and salt to taste, and sauté for 4–5 minutes, then add the chopped tomatoes, yoghurt, ginger-garlic paste and ground spices. Cook gently for 15–20 minutes or until the oil separates out.

Add the stock and peas and cook for a further 10 minutes. Sprinkle over the chopped eggs, chopped coriander and garam masala, and serve with bread or rice.

BEEF RENDANG

DAGING RENDANG

Rendangs are cooked in Malaysia, Indonesia, Brunei, the Philippines, Thailand and Singapore so the potential for argument over the best and most 'authentic' recipe is huge; even within Malaysia each region will have numerous versions of its own. To complicate matters further there are wet and dry versions. My Chicken Rendang (see page 67) is wet, whereas this beef version is much drier – the sauce is thick and just coats the meat. However it's served, a rendang is luxurious, sweet, spicy and rich. Here's my version of this classic dish.

SERVES 4

2 shallots, peeled
1 lemongrass stalk
2 garlic cloves, peeled
2 tablespoons chopped fresh ginger
2 tablespoons vegetable oil
2 tablespoons Chilli Paste, or to taste (see page 221; optional)
1 teaspoon salt

400g beef fillet, cubed
1 kaffir lime leaf
2 teaspoons ground turmeric
200ml coconut milk
1 teaspoon palm sugar or muscovado sugar
1 tablespoon kerisik (toasted ground coconut; see page 224)

Pound or blend together the shallots, lemongrass, garlic and ginger. Heat the oil in a heavy saucepan over a medium heat, add the shallot mixture and cook until fragrant, dry and golden brown, stirring often.

Stir in as much of the chilli paste as wished (or none at all) and salt. Add the beef and turn up the heat slightly. Brown the beef cubes on all sides, stirring to coat well with the seasoning mixture.

Add the lime leaf and turmeric. Continue cooking and stirring until the beef is tender and the any juices or liquid have dried up.

Add the coconut milk, which should cover the beef. Stir well to mix, then cook until the mixture thickens and begins to brown. Add the sugar, then stir in the kerisik. Serve with steamed rice.

MALAY BEEF CURRY

DAGING CURRY

An opulently rich curry from Malaysia. The fillet of beef is expensive of course, but more than worth the cost as the resulting curry is complex, satisfying and very special. The cashew nut paste provides an extra and unexpected dimension to the dish.

SERVES 4

2 tablespoons vegetable oil or ghee
500g beef fillet, cut into 5cm cubes
2 onions, thinly sliced
a 10cm cinnamon stick
100g cashew nuts, soaked in lukewarm water for 1 hour then blended to a smooth paste
1 tablespoon Ginger-Garlic Paste (see page 223)

1½ tablespoons Malaysian Meat Curry Powder (see page 225)
chilli powder, to taste
a few saffron threads, soaked in 50ml warm water
250ml plain yoghurt, whisked
2 tomatoes, quartered
salt
2 tablespoons finely chopped coriander leaves, to garnish

Heat the oil in a wok, add the beef and brown well over a medium heat. Remove from the wok with a slotted spoon and set aside.

Add a little more oil to the wok, if needed, then add the onions with the cinnamon stick. Stir-fry until the onions are translucent. Add the cashew nut paste and ginger-garlic paste, together with the meat curry powder and chilli powder. Stir-fry until quite toasted and oil starts to ooze out. Take care not to let the mixture burn.

Return the browned beef to the wok and season with salt. Stir well to coat the cubes of meat evenly. Add the saffron water plus enough additional water to come 2.5cm above the meat. Bring to the boil, then reduce the heat to low and cover the wok. Simmer, stirring occasionally, for 30–45 minutes or until the beef is tender. Add a little water if the curry starts to look dry during cooking.

When the meat is almost cooked, add the yoghurt and tomatoes. Continue simmering gently, covered, until heated through. Garnish with the chopped coriander, a green chilli, if you wish, and serve with bread or rice.

MALAYSIAN BEEF CURRY

THAI MUSSAMAN BEEF CURRY

MUSSAMAN BEEF CURRY

This is quite a unique curry among Thai curries in that its spicing is more akin to Arabic and Indian curries. There is a heavy emphasis on dry spices, rather than fresh aromatics, which is a sign of the Muslim origins of the dish – it is said to have been brought to Thailand by Indian Muslim traders. Given its Muslim roots the dish is most traditionally made with beef (never with pork), but it is a very versatile recipe that can easily be prepared with other meats.

SERVES 4

3 tablespoons oil, plus extra for deep frying
4 potatoes, cut into chunks
500g beef flank, cut into 2.5cm cubes
1 litre coconut milk
1 knob of ginger, peeled and cut into very fine strips
6–8 green cardamom pods
100g roasted peanuts
2 bay leaves
4 tablespoons palm sugar
3 tablespoons fish sauce
6 tablespoons Tamarind Water (see page 228)
15–18 pickled onions, skinned and lightly fried to colour
1/2 a ripe pineapple, juiced
coriander sprigs, to garnish

For the spice paste
10–12 long dried red chilies, soaked in lukewarm water to soften and drained
8–10 red shallots, chopped
6 garlic cloves, chopped
3 tablespoons chopped galangal
1 tablespoon chopped fresh ginger
2 stalks of lemongrass, chopped
3 tablespoons chopped coriander roots
200g grated fresh coconut or unsweetened desiccated coconut, toasted
salt

For the spice powder
2 tablespoons coriander seeds
1 tablespoon cumin seeds
4–5 cloves
1/2 a nutmeg, freshly grated
2 blades of mace
a 5cm piece of cinnamon stick
70g roasted peanuts
10 green cardamom pods
3 bay leaves

Heat enough oil for deep-frying in a large, deep pan. When it is hot (170–180°C), add the potatoes and deep-fry until a light golden colour. Drain on kitchen paper and set aside until required.

Deep-fry the cubes of beef until sealed and coloured, then drain on kitchen paper and set aside until required.

For the spice paste, sauté all the ingredients in a dry wok until lightly browned. For the spice powder, toast each spice separately, then whiz them all together in a blender to a fine powder, then sieve. Mix the paste mixture and spice powder together, then whiz in a blender to make a fine paste and set aside until required.

Pour the coconut milk into a wok and bring to the boil, then reduce to a simmer and add the beef and ginger. Cook for 3–5 minutes over a low heat. Add the cardamom, peanuts and bay leaves and simmer for 10 minutes, then add the potatoes and onions.

Heat the 3 tablespoons of oil in a pan, add the spice paste and sauté, stirring regularly, until fragrant and it slowly starts to darken. Take care not to let it burn. When the paste is oily, hot and sizzling, season with the sugar. As the sugar begins to caramelise, add the fish sauce and tamarind water. The balance of sweet, sour and salty has to be tested by tasting.

Add the cooked paste to the beef and stir well. Stir in the pineapple juice and check the seasoning for the final time. Garnish with coriander sprigs and serve with rice.

BEEF WITH WHOLE GARLIC

LOSHUN MANGSHO

The garlic in this recipe is used like new potatoes – just rinsed with water and cooked in its wafer-thin skin. The soft garlic pulp is squeezed out of the skin of the cloves as you eat the dish: it is deliciously mild and sweet.

SERVES 4–6

4 tablespoons mustard oil
8 green cardamom pods
a 5cm piece of cinnamon stick
5 cloves
1 blade of mace
2 onions, thinly sliced
1 tablespoon Ginger-Garlic Paste (see page 223)
1 teaspoon ground cumin
1 teaspoon red chilli powder
1/2 teaspoon ground turmeric
2 teaspoons ground coriander
800g beef rump steak, cut into 2.5cm dice
4–5 small heads of garlic (whole), thick skin removed and rinsed
salt
coriander sprigs, to garnish

Heat the oil in a pan and sauté the whole spices until fragrant. Add the onions and sauté until translucent. Add the ginger-garlic paste and stir well, then sauté for 2 minutes or until fragrant. Add all the ground spices and stir for a minute to cook them.

Add the beef, garlic, some salt and enough water to cover the meat. Bring to the boil, then cook on a low heat, stirring occasionally, for 30–40 minutes or until the beef and garlic are completely tender and cooked. Serve garnished with coriander sprigs.

PARADISE BEEF CURRY

Allspice is not, as its name implies, a mixture of several spices. In fact, it is the dried fruit of a Caribbean tree, also called the Jamaica pepper or pimento, and it is one of the most important ingredients in Caribbean cuisine. Perhaps most commonly used in Jamaica, in jerk seasoning, its flavour is reminiscent of cinnamon, cloves and nutmeg. Try this easy island recipe and discover it for yourself.

SERVES 4

3 tablespoons vegetable oil
1 star anise
a 2.5cm piece of cinnamon stick
1 teaspoon cumin seeds
1 teaspoon fennel seeds
1/2 teaspoon fenugreek seeds
1/2 teaspoon mustard seeds
2 bay leaves
2 onions, thinly sliced
2 tablespoons Caribbean Curry Powder (see page 220)
1/2 teaspoon ground allspice
1/2 teaspoon ground turmeric
1 teaspoon cracked black peppercorns
1 tablespoon Ginger-Garlic Paste (see page 223)
800g beef fillet, cut into 2.5cm dice
500g carrots, peeled and cut into roundels
500g sweet potatoes, cut into dice
3 tomatoes, finely chopped
600ml beef stock or water
800ml coconut milk
2 tablespoons finely chopped coriander leaves
salt

Heat the oil in a frying pan over a medium heat and sauté the whole spices with the bay leaves for a minute or until they begin to crackle. Add the sliced onions and sauté until translucent. Add the curry powder, ground spices, pepper and ginger-garlic paste and sauté for 2–3 minutes, stirring well.

Add the beef, carrots and sweet potatoes. Season with salt and mix well. Add the chopped tomatoes and cook, stirring, for 2–3 minutes, then pour in the stock and coconut milk. Simmer for 30–35 minutes or until the meat and vegetables are cooked. Sprinkle with chopped coriander and serve with rice.

(LEFT) BANGLADESHI BEEF WITH WHOLE GARLIC
(RIGHT) CARIBBEAN PARADISE BEEF CURRY

BEEF

STIR-FRIED BEEF CURRY

AHMAITHAR KEBAT KYAW

This is a slightly unusual curry, with Muslim influences – Muslims from the Arab world who have migrated and settled in India and the Far East like to make kebabs then turn them into a curry. Grilling or barbecuing the beef first gives an extra punch of flavour.

SERVES 4

60g skirt steak, cut into 2.5cm cubes
1 tablespoon finely chopped garlic
1/2 teaspoon ground turmeric
2 tablespoon ground cumin
1 teaspoon red chilli powder
1 tablespoon lemon juice
2 tablespoons grated fresh ginger
1/2 teaspoon Garam Masala

(see page 223)
5 tablespoons vegetable oil
2 onions, sliced
1/2 teaspoon Burmese curry powder
2 medium tomatoes, sliced
2 tablespoons chopped coriander leaves
1 teaspoon lime juice
salt

In a bowl, toss the pieces of beef with the garlic, turmeric, cumin, chilli powder, lemon juice, ginger, garam masala, 1 tablespoon of the oil and some salt. Thread the beef pieces on to metal skewers and set aside to tenderise for 1 hour.

Preheat the grill to high or prepare a charcoal fire in a barbecue. Either grill or barbecue the meat to brown it well on all sides. Remove and baste with 2 tablespoons of the oil, then take the beef off the skewers and keep warm.

Heat the remaining oil in a wok over a medium heat and sauté the onions until translucent. Add the curry powder and sauté for a minute, stirring well, then add the tomatoes and browned beef pieces. Cook, stirring, for 3–4 minutes or until the tomatoes soften. Add the chopped coriander and lime juice, and serve hot.

SUMATRAN BUFFALO RENDANG

This is the third rendang recipe in this book, which perhaps goes to show how widespread and debatable a recipe it can be. The Beef Rendang on page 180 is Malaysian but in Indonesia, the dish is often made with buffalo, which is tougher than beef so needs a much longer cooking time. Buffalo meat can be difficult to come by in Europe, but stewing beef works well.

SERVES 4–6

6 shallots or 2 onions, peeled
4 garlic cloves, peeled
1 tablespoon grated fresh ginger
1 teaspoon ground turmeric
1 tablespoon red chilli powder
1 tablespoon finely chopped galangal

1 tablespoon finely chopped lemongrass
1kg boneless buffalo or beef brisket or other stewing beef, cut into 5cm dice
1 bay leaf
2 litres coconut milk
salt

Blend or pound together the shallots or onions, garlic, ginger, turmeric, chilli powder, galangal and lemongrass. Mix this paste with the beef, bay leaf, coconut milk and some salt in a wok. Bring just to the boil, then bubble on a low heat, stirring occasionally, for 60–70 minutes or until all the sauce has been absorbed and the meat is tender with a good brown colour. Serve with rice, cucumber and chillies.

YEMENI BEEF SHANKS

HOR'EE

Yemeni food can be hot and spicy but there is always a coolant with or after the meal in the form of yoghurt or sour milk. Yemenis are also huge bread enthusiasts and their local breads, which are numerous and varied, complete the Yemeni meal experience. The Yemeni types of bread range from simple flatbreads and their dense pitta breads, to sweeter, more pastry-like offerings. I'll leave it to you to decide what best to serve to accompany this curry.

SERVES 4–6

2kg beef shin (foreshank), with bone, cut into 5–7.5cm pieces
3 medium onions, peeled and quartered
6 garlic cloves, peeled
400g tomatoes, skinned and chopped
2 teaspoons hawayij (Yemeni Spice Mix; see page 223)
3–4 dried red chillies
1/2 teaspoon crushed black pepper
salt

Place the meat in a pot, cover with cold water and bring to the boil, then reduce to a simmer and skim off as much of the froth as you can. Once the froth clears add the onions, garlic, tomatoes, hawayij, chillies, pepper and salt to taste.

Cover and simmer for 3–4 hours or until the meat is tender and the liquid reduced to a thick sauce. Serve hot with breads.

BISON MEATBALL CURRY

Bison is a low-fat, full-flavoured meat and is a great choice for curry as its strong flavour holds up well against the spices and isn't masked by them. As it's so lean, bison meat does have the potential to dry out easily, which is why meatballs are a perfect vehicle for it as they're cooked in so much liquid. Here the meatballs are blanched in stock then gently simmered in the spicy tomato sauce which leaves them juicy, tender and packed with full of spicy flavour.

SERVES 4

For the meatballs
500g minced bison
100g breadcrumbs
1 tablespoon chopped garlic
1 tablespoon finely chopped coriander leaves
1/2 teaspoon red chilli powder
1 teaspoon toasted ground cumin
1 litre beef stock

For the sauce
2 tablespoons vegetable oil
1/2 teaspoon cumin seeds
2 cloves
2 green cardamom pods
1 bay leaf
1 tablespoon finely chopped garlic
2 onions, finely chopped
1 teaspoon red chilli powder
1 teaspoon ground turmeric
1 tablespoon ground coriander
1/2 teaspoon Garam Masala (see page 223)
2 tomatoes, chopped
300ml coconut milk
salt
coriander sprigs, to garnish

Mix together all the ingredients for the meatballs (except the stock) in a large bowl, then shape the mixture into balls a little smaller than golf balls. Bring the stock to the boil in a large pan, then add the meatballs and cook for 5 minutes to blanch, then remove and set aside.

To make the sauce, heat the oil in a pan and sauté the cumin seeds, cloves, cardamom pods and bay leaf until the spices crackle. Add the chopped garlic and sauté to colour lightly, then add the chopped onions. Stir and cook over a low heat until the onions turn light brown.

Add the chilli powder, turmeric, coriander and garam masala and mix well. Add the chopped tomatoes and cook for 5–7 minutes to soften the tomatoes. Add the coconut milk and bring to a simmer, then add the meatballs. Simmer for a further 5 minutes, then garnish with coriander sprigs and serve with rice.

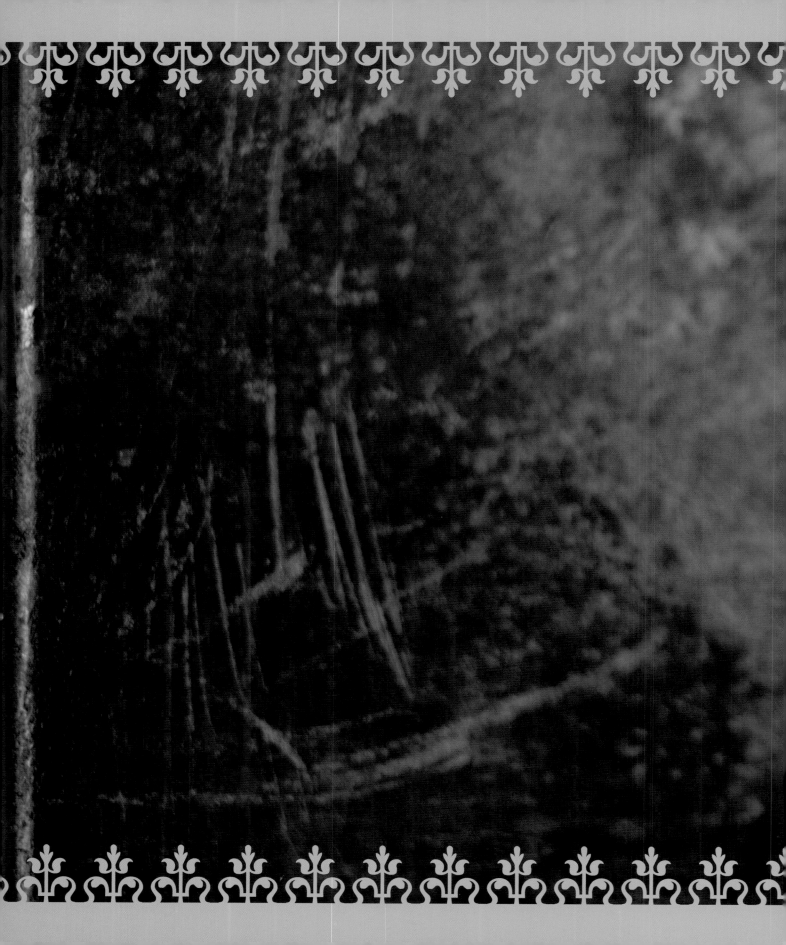

VEGETABLES

AUBERGINE CURRY

WAMBATU MOJU

This is really a kind of pickle that is served with various Sri Lankan curries as an accompaniment or side dish. I find the pickle flavour works very well with crisp food – try it with poppadums or even plain crisp pitta bread. It is a great relish.

SERVES 4 (AS A SIDE DISH)

500g aubergines, cut into
    2.5cm cubes
1/2 teaspoon ground turmeric
oil for deep-frying
10–12 dried anchovies
1 small red onion, thinly
    sliced
2 tablespoons vegetable oil
10 curry leaves
2 red chillies, slit
2 green chillies, slit
salt

For the spice paste
3 garlic cloves, peeled
1 tablespoon finely chopped
    fresh ginger
1 teaspoon mustard seeds
1 tablespoon Ceylon Curry
    Powder (see page 221)
    or ground coriander
3 tablespoons white wine
    vinegar
2 tablespoons sugar
salt

Sprinkle the aubergine with the turmeric and season with salt and set aside.

Blend or pound together the ingredients for the spice paste until fine and set aside.

Heat enough oil for deep-frying in a wok. When it is hot (160–180°C), deep-fry the aubergines until light brown, then the anchovies until crisp, then the onion until lightly coloured. As each batch is fried, remove to kitchen paper to drain.

Heat the vegetable oil in a pan and sauté the curry leaves and chillies until lightly cooked. Add the spice paste and cook, stirring, until fragrant. Add all the deep-fried ingredients and stir to mix well, then cook for a further 3–4 minutes. Remove from the heat. Serve at room temperature. This can be kept in an airtight container in the fridge for up to 2 weeks.

AUBERGINE AND BEAN CURRY

Asians love aubergines – perhaps because they have quite a neutral flavour so are like a blank canvas, or a sponge, absorbing all the wonderful aromatics and spices that this region's cuisines throw at it.

SERVES 4

2 tablespoons vegetable or
    rapeseed oil
4 garlic cloves, very finely
    chopped
2 shallots, thinly sliced
2 dried red chillies
3 tablespoons Kroeung
    (Cambodian spice paste;
    see page 224)
1 tablespoon tuk prahoc (see
    page 226) or fish sauce
1 tablespoon palm sugar
2–3 aubergines (about 400g),

    cut into 2.5cm cubes
6 kaffir lime leaves
500ml coconut milk
300ml vegetable or chicken
    stock
a bunch of Thai basil leaves
salt and black pepper

To serve
2 limes, cut in half
1 small red onion, sliced into
    rings

Heat the oil in a wok or pan and sauté the garlic, shallots and red chillies for 2–3 minutes or until lightly coloured. Stir in the kroeung, shrimp paste and palm sugar. Cook for a further 2–3 minutes or until the mixture darkens.

Add the aubergines and lime leaves followed by the coconut milk and stock. Bring to the boil, then simmer gently for 20 minutes or until the aubergines are cooked. Stir in the basil leaves and correct the seasoning. Serve with the lime wedges, onion rings and jasmine rice.

CAMBODIAN AUBERGINE AND BEAN CURRY

SWAHILI AUBERGINE CURRY

A wonderfully comforting curry from East Africa that's easy to prepare and is packed with gently spiced vegetables amongst which aubergine is definitely the star. A perfect light supper or lunch dish.

SERVES 4

2 potatoes, peeled and cut into 1cm dice
4 tablespoons ghee or vegetable oil
2 onions, finely chopped
4 aubergines, cut into 2.5cm dice
1 tablespoon finely chopped garlic
1 teaspoon Malawi Curry

Powder (see page 225)
1/4 teaspoon red chilli powder
3 tomatoes, chopped
1 tablespoon finely chopped fresh ginger
1 tablespoon finely chopped coriander leaves
1 tablespoon lime juice
salt

Blanch the potatoes in boiling water for 7–10 minutes, or until just cooked. Drain.

Heat the ghee in a pan over a medium heat and sauté the onions until lightly browned. Add the potatoes, aubergines, garlic, curry powder, chilli powder and salt to taste. Sauté for 2–3 minutes, stirring to mix well.

Add the tomatoes and 250ml water. Bring to a simmer, then cook gently until the aubergine are very tender. Correct the seasoning and stir in the ginger, chopped coriander and lime juice. Serve with bread or rice.

AUBERGINES FRIED IN SOY-LIME SAUCE

SOY LEMAK

On my trip round Malaysia I was invited to cook with Celine Marbeck, an accomplished Malaysian cook of Portuguese-Dutch ancestry. She is an active promoter of Cristang cuisine and has written several books on the subject. The Cristang are an ethnic community in Malaysia whose origins can be traced to the first European settlers in Asia. The cuisine pulls together elements from their cultural mix to bring out the best of East and West. This recipe is a version of a dish that I cooked with her.

SERVES 2

2 small aubergines
1 teaspoon fine salt
1 teaspoon freshly ground pepper
1 teaspoon finely chopped garlic
1 tablespoon plain flour
oil for deep-frying
1 1/2 tablespoons groundnut or vegetable oil
2 red chillies, sliced

1 large onion, sliced into rings
1 teaspoon chopped coriander, to garnish

For the sauce
2 teaspoons thick soy sauce
2 teaspoons lime juice
1 teaspoon sugar
1 heaped teaspoon cornflour
salt

Cut the aubergines in half lengthways and score the white flesh, being careful not to cut through the skin. Season with the salt, pepper and garlic, then dust all over with the flour. Heat enough oil for deep-frying in a wok. When it is hot (about 180°C), deep-fry the aubergines, turning regularly, for 4–5 minutes or until tender and light golden brown. (If the garlic starts to burn, reduce the heat slightly.) Remove and drain on kitchen paper. Keep hot.

In a bowl, mix together the sauce ingredients with 4 tablespoons of water and salt to taste. Set aside.

Heat the 1 1/2 tablespoons oil in a new pan and sauté the chillies and sliced onion over a medium heat, until they start to soften. Pour in the sauce ingredients, stir to mix and bring to a simmer. Taste and adjust the seasoning. Add another 4 tablespoons of water to loosen the sauce. Pour the sauce over the fried aubergines and serve immediately.

BAMBOO SHOOT CURRY

MYIT SIPYAN

Asia is the home of bamboo; it is used in Asian cuisines in various forms – fermented, pickled, curried, fried among others. This is a side dish preparation that has influences from India and the Far East. Fresh bamboo that is prepared for cooking is the best – but outside Asia canned bamboo shoots is the best alternative.

SERVES 4 (AS A SIDE DISH)

1 onion, chopped
1 tablespoon finely chopped garlic
1 tablespoon grated fresh ginger
3 tablespoons rapeseed oil
$1/4$ teaspoon ground turmeric
$1/4$ teaspoon red chilli powder
a handful of dried shrimps, soaked in hot water to rehydrate
3 green chillies, sliced
3 large tomatoes, chopped
2 x 225g cans whole bamboo shoots, drained and sliced
1 tablespoon fish sauce

Heat the oil in a wok and sauté the onion, ginger and garlic for 5–7 minutes over a medium heat, until translucent. Add the turmeric, red chilli powder and dried shrimps and cook for 2–3 minutes until fragrant.

Add the green chillies, tomatoes, bamboo shoots and 200ml water. Bring to the boil, then simmer for 10–15 minutes or until the gravy thickens. Correct the seasoning with the fish sauce and serve with jasmine rice.

GREEN LEAVES WITH COCONUT

MALLUNG

A mallung is a side dish in a Sri Lankan meal, and two or three mallung might be served. Many types of leafy green vegetable would be used to make this dish; here in the UK greens like spinach, cabbage, chard and kale are good substitutes for the Sri Lankan leaves.

SERVES 4–6 (AS A SIDE DISH)

500g leafy greens (see above), shredded
1 onion, finely chopped
2 green chillies, slit
$1/2$ teaspoon ground turmeric
5–6 curry leaves
$1/2$ teaspoon freshly crushed black peppercorns
2 teaspoons dried shrimp, pounded to a powder
2 tablespoons lemon juice
3 tablespoons freshly grated coconut or unsweetened desiccated coconut
3–4 tablespoons coconut milk
salt

Heat a non-stick frying pan or wok and add all the ingredients except the grated coconut. Season with salt. Cook, stirring, over a medium heat for 3–5 minutes or until the greens are tender. Add the grated coconut and stir to mix, then serve hot.

PAKISTANI SPICED BEETROOT

SPICED BEETROOT

CHUKUNDER KI SUBJI

Pakistan is predominantly a meat-eating country and the use of vegetables to make a main dish is not so common, but they're very inventive with their accompaniments. This recipe is a little unusual and can be served with bread and pickles to bulk it out for a light lunch.

SERVES 4–6 (AS A SIDE DISH)

500g beetroot, peeled and cut into batons
1 small onion, finely chopped
$1/4$ teaspoon ground turmeric
1 teaspoon red chilli powder

3 tablespoons vegetable oil
3 green chillies, thinly sliced
salt
coriander leaves, finely chopped, to garnish

Place the beetroot, onion, turmeric, chilli powder, salt to taste and 100ml water in a pan and cook over a low heat for 10–12 minutes or until the beetroot is tender. Add the oil and green chillies and cook over a medium heat for a further 5 minutes or until all the water has evaporated. Garnish with the coriander and serve with bread and pickles or as a side dish.

BUTTER BEAN CURRY

PEIGYEE HIN

Beans and lentils are a common food for the Burmese, particularly monks. As most of the monasteries have only the food that is donated to them, they have to be very creative with humble ingredients when preparing their meals. This is a simple recipe that can be made with most types of dried beans or lentils.

SERVES 4

3 tablespoons vegetable oil
1 onion, finely chopped
$1/2$ teaspoon ground turmeric
1 x 400g can butter beans, drained and rinsed

300ml vegetable stock or water
5–6 spring onions, thinly sliced
salt

Heat the oil in a wok over a medium heat and sauté the onion until translucent. Add the turmeric powder and sauté for a minute, stirring well. Add the butter beans, stock and salt to taste. Bring to the boil, then simmer for 10 minutes, until the beans are heated through. Garnish with the sliced spring onions and serve.

BUTTERNUT SQUASH CURRY

WATTAKA KARI

Powdered or crushed Maldive fish is a traditional flavouring in Sri Lanka. It is a type of sun-dried tuna, similar to the Japanese bonito flakes. It adds a depth of flavour to dishes, but don't worry if you can't get hold of it; the dish will still taste delicious.

SERVES 4–6 (AS A SIDE DISH)

500g butternut squash, peeled and cut into 2.5cm cubes
1 tablespoon sugar
1 onion, thinly sliced
2 green chillies, slit
a pinch of ground saffron
10 curry leaves
1/2 teaspoon fenugreek seeds
2 teaspoons Maldive fish or bonito flakes (optional)
a 2.5cm piece of cinnamon stick
1/2 teaspoon ground turmeric
300ml coconut milk
salt

For the paste
5 garlic cloves, peeled
1 tablespoon mustard seeds
1 teaspoon black peppercorns
4 tablespoons grated fresh coconut or unsweetened desiccated coconut
1/4 teaspoon Ceylon Curry Powder (see page 221; optional)
100ml coconut milk

Blend together the ingredients for the paste to make a fine paste. Keep aside until needed.

Put the butternut squash and all the remaining ingredients in a pan. Add 200ml water and salt to taste. Bring to the boil, then simmer gently for 20 minutes or until the squash is almost cooked.

Add the paste and simmer for a further 5–6 minutes or until the squash is tender. Serve with a rice-based meal.

BROAD BEANS AND AUBERGINE

SHEEM BEGUN CHORCHORI

In Bangladesh, the beans (sheem) used to make this recipe are flat beans – they look a little like broad beans but are half the size and there's no need to peel them. As these are not readily available here in the UK, I have used broad beans, which work equally well.

SERVES 4

2 medium potatoes, peeled and cut into 2.5cm cubes
2 tablespoons mustard oil or vegetable oil
1/2 teaspoon Panch Phoran (see page 226)
2 green chillies, slit
150g broad beans, peeled and skinned
2 aubergines, cut into 2.5cm cubes
1 onion, thinly sliced
1 teaspoon ground turmeric
1/2 teaspoon red chilli powder
salt

Blanch the potatoes in boiling water for 7–10 minutes, until just cooked. Drain.

Heat the oil in a wok and sauté the panch phoran with the green chillies until they splutter. Add the broad beans, potatoes and aubergines with some salt and sauté for 5 minutes.

Add the onion. Mix the turmeric and chilli powder with 50ml water and pour into the pan. Stir to mix, then cook gently for a further 5–8 minutes or until all the vegetables are cooked. Add a little more water during the cooking, if required. Serve hot.

BANGLADESHI BROAD BEANS AND AUBERGINE

SOUTH INDIAN CABBAGE PORIYAL

CABBAGE PORIYAL

MUTTAKOS PORIYAL

This salad-like vegetable preparation from south India makes a great accompaniment to a spicy meal – it's fresh and light and balances out the spice well.

SERVES 4 (AS A SIDE DISH)

2 green chillies, slit
500g green or Savoy cabbage, chopped into small pieces
100g frozen peas, defrosted
2 tablespoons freshly grated coconut or unsweetened desiccated coconut
salt

For the seasoning
2 teaspoons coconut or vegetable oil
1 teaspoon black mustard seeds
1 teaspoon cumin seeds
1 teaspoon black gram daal
1 dried red chilli
1/4 teaspoon ground asafoetida
10–12 curry leaves

Heat the oil in a wok, then add all the seasoning ingredients. When the mustard seeds begin to splutter, add the green chillies. Sauté for 1 minute, then add the cabbage and peas and salt to taste. Cook over a high heat until the cabbage wilts and softens. Add the grated coconut and serve hot.

CAULIFLOWER CASHEW CURRY

PUKOSU CADJU KARI

The marriage of cashew nuts and cauliflower with peas in a coconut-milk-based sauce makes for a very satisfying and quite rich side dish, just lifted at the end by the hit of lemon juice.

SERVES 4

200g cashew nuts
400g cauliflower florets
2 tablespoons vegetable oil
1 onion, chopped
1 large green chilli, slit
1 pandan leaf, tied into a knot
10 curry leaves
1 teaspoon mustard seeds
2 garlic cloves, finely chopped
a 2.5cm piece of cinnamon stick
1/2 teaspoon ground turmeric
11/2 tablespoons Ceylon Curry Powder (see page 221)
300ml coconut milk
100g frozen peas, defrosted
1 tablespoon lemon juice
salt

Lightly toast the cashews in a dry frying pan then immediately turn out on to a plate to stop the cooking, otherwise they will continue to cook in the heat of the pan.

Blanch the cauliflower florets in a pan of boiling water for 3–5 minutes or until just cooked. Drain and keep aside until needed.

Heat the oil in a pan and sauté the onion with the green chilli, pandan leaf, curry leaves, mustard seeds, garlic and cinnamon stick until light golden. Add the blanched cauliflower, cashew nuts, turmeric, curry powder and salt to taste. Stir for a couple of minutes, then pour in the coconut milk and bring to a simmer. Add the peas. Simmer for 2–3 minutes, then stir in the lemon juice and serve with rice.

COURGETTES WITH POPPY SEEDS

JINGE POSTO

The gourd or Cucurbitaceae family is quite large and includes courgettes, squashes, pumpkins, melons and cucumbers. On the Indian sub-continent there are numerous types of squash available, as there are in the UK. I've chosen to use courgettes for this recipe but you could try experimenting with your preferred types of squash. The spicing is simple but it's just enough to complement the gentle flavour of the vegetable.

SERVES 4–6

2 tablespoons vegetable oil
$^1/_4$ teaspoon mustard seeds
1 dried red chilli
1 onion, finely sliced
2 fresh red chillies, chopped
5–6 medium courgettes, cut into 2.5cm cubes
$^1/_4$ teaspoon ground turmeric
$^1/_4$ teaspoon Chilli Paste (see page 221)
2 tablespoons white poppy seeds, soaked in lukewarm water to soften, then ground to a paste
salt
1 tablespoon finely chopped coriander leaves, to garnish

Heat the oil in a wok over a medium heat and sauté the mustard seeds with the dried red chili for a minute. Add the onion, fresh red chillies and courgettes and sauté for 2 minutes. Add the turmeric, chilli paste and some salt and stir to mix. Sauté for a minute, then add the poppy paste and cook on a low heat until the courgettes are tender. Serve garnished with the coriander.

CHICKPEA CURRY

KADALA PARUPPU MALLUNG

I have used chickpeas here, but broad beans, red kidney beans, butter beans or any other pulse could be used in this dish, and you can replace the dried pulses with canned.

SERVES 4

400g dried chickpeas, soaked overnight
2 tablespoons vegetable oil
1 onion, finely chopped
a 2.5cm piece of cinnamon stick
2 green chillies, sliced
10–12 curry leaves
2 tomatoes, chopped
2 tablespoons dried shrimps, crushed or powdered
2 tablespoons finely chopped coriander leaves
1 tablespoon lime juice
salt

1 red chilli, to garnish (optional)

For the coconut paste
4 garlic cloves, peeled
1 tablespoon chopped fresh ginger
1 teaspoon mustard seeds, soaked in warm water for 2 hours to soften
2 tablespoons coconut milk
6 tablespoons grated fresh coconut or unsweetened desiccated coconut

Drain the chickpeas and put them in a pan with fresh cold water to cover generously. Bring to the boil and boil for 10 minutes, then simmer for 60–90 minutes until the chickpeas are tender. Drain well.

Blend or pound together the coconut paste ingredients.

Heat the oil in a pan and sauté the onion with the cinnamon stick, green chillies and curry leaves until lightly coloured. Add the tomatoes with salt to taste, stir well and cook until they start to break down. Add the chickpeas, dried shrimps and chopped coriander. Simmer, stirring frequently, for 5–8 minutes or until the chickpeas are hot. Stir in the coconut paste and cook for a further 3–5 minutes. Add the lime juice and garnish with the red chilli, if using, and serve.

RIGHT: SRI LANKAN CHICKPEA CURRY

EGG CURRY

DIMER KARI

This recipe is based on a dish my mother used to make for us as children. The combination of fried potatoes – golden and crusty on the outside and soft on the inside – with eggs is my sort of comfort food, and brings back happy childhood memories. This would make a great brunch dish, served with lots of toast or Indian breads to mop up the spiced tomato sauce.

SERVES 4

4 large chicken or duck eggs	1/2 teaspoon ground turmeric
4 small potatoes, peeled and quartered	1/2 teaspoon red chilli powder
3 tablespoons vegetable oil	2 teaspoons Ginger-Garlic Paste (see page 223)
1 bay leaf	2 medium tomatoes, chopped
2 green cardamom pods	300ml chicken stock or water
2 cloves	1 tablespoon finely chopped coriander leaves
a 2.5cm piece of cinnamon stick	1/4 teaspoon Garam Masala (see page 223)
5 black peppercorns	salt
1 onion, thinly sliced	

Hard-boil the eggs, then peel them and cut in half. Set aside.

Blanch the potatoes for 7–10 minutes or until just cooked; drain and pat dry. Heat 1 tablespoon of the oil in a pan over a medium heat and fry the potatoes until tender, crusty and well browned.

Heat the remaining oil in a pan and sauté the bay leaf and whole spices for a minute or until they splutter. Add the onion and sauté until tender and light brown. Add the turmeric, chilli powder and ginger-garlic paste and sauté for 3–4 minutes; sprinkle with a little water to prevent the mixture from burning. Mix in the chopped tomatoes and cook on a low heat for 5–8 minutes.

Add the stock and salt to taste. Bring to the boil, then reduce to a simmer. Add the eggs and potatoes. Reduce the heat further and leave to cook for 3–5 minutes or until the sauce thickens. Sprinkle with the chopped coriander and garam, and serve hot with rice or bread.

FIDDLEHEAD CURRY

GULAI PAKU

Fiddleheads are young, unfurled fern leaves that are used as a vegetable but they are only found in North America and the rain forests of the Far East. Fresh fiddleheads aren't available in the UK, but with you can find frozen or bottled ones. Very young French beans can be substituted in this dish, and it's good made with vegetables like courgettes, cauliflower, broccoli and pumpkin too.

SERVES 4 (AS A SIDE DISH)

800ml coconut milk	1 teaspoon chopped fresh ginger
3 tablespoons Tamarind Water (see page 228)	1/2 teaspoon chopped galangal
500g fresh or frozen fiddleheads (defrosted if frozen) or 600g bottled fiddleheads	4–5 candlenuts or macadamia nuts
	2 teaspoons ground coriander
	1 teaspoon ground turmeric
	2 kaffir lime leaves
For the spice paste	1 tablespoon chopped lemongrass
1 teaspoon Sambal Olek (chilli paste; see page 227)	4–5 tablespoons coconut milk
1 onion, chopped	salt
3 garlic cloves, peeled	

Blend all the ingredients for the spice paste, with salt to taste, to make a fine paste. Heat a wok, add the spice paste and cook for 5–7 minutes, stirring, until fragrant. Add the coconut milk and tamarind water and stir well. Bring to the boil, then simmer for 20–25 minutes or until the sauce is thick enough to coat the back of a spoon.

Add the fiddleheads (or other vegetables) and simmer for 7–10 minutes until tender and perfectly cooked. Serve hot.

LEFT: BANGLADESHI EGG CURRY

FIDDLEHEADS PORIYAL

A poriyal is typically a dish made by sautéeing shredded vegetables with spices, including mustard seeds. It makes a wonderfully light and fragrant addition to an Indian meal; providing a good balance to some of the richer curries. I sometimes turn this into more of a warm salad by leaving it to cool slightly and then stirring in a pinch of sugar and a squeeze of lime juice just before serving.

SERVES 4 (AS A SIDE DISH)

1 teaspoon vegetable oil
1 tablespoon butter
1 tablespoon finely chopped garlic
1 small green chilli, chopped
1/2 teaspoon cumin seeds
1/4 teaspoon black mustard seeds

1/2 teaspoon sesame seeds
1 onion, finely chopped
5–6 curry leaves, chopped
500g fresh or frozen fiddleheads (defrosted if frozen) or 600g bottled fiddleheads
salt

Blanch the fiddleheads by plunging them into boiling water for 1 minute, until tender. Drain.

Heat the oil and butter in a pan. Add the chopped garlic and chilli and sauté until lightly coloured. Add the cumin, mustard and sesame seeds; when they crackle, add the chopped onion and curry leaves. Sauté until the onion turns translucent, then add the fiddleheads and season with salt. Sauté for 3–4 minutes until they soften a little but remain crunchy. Serve hot.

LAOTIAN TOFU CURRY

It is often thought that landlocked Laos has the same cuisine as its Thai neighbour. But while the country has undoubtedly borrowed ingredients and techniques from its neighbours, including China, Vietnam and Cambodia, as well as Thailand, it does have its own style. As a foreigner one of the most striking differences you will notice if you visit Laos, is the ubiquitous sticky rice. For unlike their neighbours, who favour steamed rice, sticky rice is served at every meal. Diners take a handful of the rice, roll it into balls and either dip it into the sauces or condiments or eat it plain. The other notable feature is the Laotian love of the raw and typically at least one dish of raw greens will be served at every meal. Serve this Laotian curry as the locals would, with fresh greens alongside, and perhaps some sticky rice.

SERVES 4 (AS A SIDE DISH)

250g tofu, cut into 3cm cubes
oil for deep-frying
2 tablespoons vegetable oil
1 onion, sliced
1 teaspoon finely chopped galangal
5 lemongrass stalks, bruised and made into a knot
5 kaffir lime leaves
2 tablespoons curry powder
1 teaspoon red chilli powder
1 large potato, peeled and cut into 3cm cubes
20 button mushrooms, quartered
100g pumpkin flesh, cut into

3cm cubes
1 aubergine, cut into 3cm cubes
100g green beans
1 1/2 teaspoons soy bean paste
1 1/2 teaspoons oyster sauce
1 tablespoon fish sauce
1 teaspoon sugar
250ml coconut milk
10 slices canned bamboo shoots
1 1/2 teaspoons lime juice
12–15 basil leaves, chopped
salt and pepper
12 pink pickled onions, to garnish

Heat enough oil for deep-frying in a wok. When it is hot (170–180°C), deep-fry the tofu for 2–3 minutes or until light golden. Drain on kitchen paper and set aside.

Heat the oil in a wok and sauté the onion with the galangal, lemongrass and kaffir lime leaves over a high heat for 3 minutes or until the onion is golden brown. Reduce the heat, then stir in the curry powder and chilli powder. If the mixture is very dry add a little cold water.

Add all the vegetables (except the bamboo shoots) and stir to mix, then add the soy bean paste, oyster sauce, fish sauce, sugar and coconut milk. If the sauce is very thick, stir in a little water. Cover and simmer for 3–5 minutes over a medium heat.

Stir the vegetables, then add the tofu and bamboo shoots. Cover again and simmer for a further 3–5 minutes. Stir in the lime juice and basil and season with salt and pepper. Garnish with the pickled onions and serve hot with rice.

LAOTIAN TOFU CURRY

CARIBBEAN MANGO CURRY

MANGO CURRY

AAM CURRIE

In the Caribbean, mango is often used as a vegetable and to make condiments, like this one. This recipe is adapted from Kumar Mahabir's Caribbean East Indian Recipes, an amazing book in which the author has put together recipes that have been handed down through at least four generations of Caribbean Indians. These old recipes are in danger of becoming obsolete yet so often they're the best, and I love discovering them.

SERVES 4 (AS A SIDE DISH)

2 tablespoons vegetable oil
1 teaspoon cumin seeds
4 garlic cloves
4 teaspoons Caribbean Curry Powder (see page 220)
1 teaspoon ground cumin
1 tablespoon ground coriander
1 teaspoon crushed black pepper

6 semi-ripe mangoes, peeled and cut into 2.5cm dice
200g brown sugar
1.5 litres vegetable stock or water
salt
coriander leaves, very finely chopped
chives, very finely chopped

Heat the oil in a pan and briefly sauté the cumin seeds and garlic until the seeds are fragrant. Add the curry powder, cumin, coriander, pepper and salt to taste and stir well. Add the mango and sauté, stirring, to coat with the spices. Stir in the sugar, then add the stock and simmer gently until the mangoes are soft and pulpy. Garnish with a little of the coriander and chives and serve hot.

INDONESIAN VEGETABLE CURRY

VEGETARIAN SAYUR LODEH

Sayur Lodeh is a popular dish all over Indonesia. Vegetables are simmered in coconut milk to make a delicious, comforting soup. I find it pretty addictive!

SERVES 4

225g firm tofu, cut into 4 pieces
oil for deep-frying
5–6 tablespoons vegetable oil
75g green beans, trimmed and cut into 3cm strips
100g aubergine, sliced
50g carrot, diced
100g cabbage, cut into 3cm squares
125–150ml coconut milk
3/4 teaspoon mild curry powder (optional)

1 teaspoon sugar, or to taste
1/2 teaspoon salt, or to taste

For the spice paste
6 dried chillies, chopped
3 lemongrass stalks, chopped
25–30g galangal, chopped
a thumb-sized piece of fresh turmeric, chopped
2–3 candlenuts or macadamia nuts, chopped
1 1/2 teaspoons vegetarian telasi or belacan

Blend or pound all the ingredients for the spice paste to make a fine paste. (It can be made in advance and kept refrigerated for 7–10 days.)

Heat enough oil for deep-frying in a wok. When it is hot (170–180°C), deep-fry the tofu for 2–3 minutes or until light golden. Drain on kitchen paper and set aside.

Heat the vegetable oil in a wok or frying pan. Add the paste and fry for 10 minutes or until thickened and fragrant. Add the vegetables, tofu, coconut milk and 250–300ml water. Stir well. Bring to the boil, then simmer for 15 minutes or until all the vegetables are tender. Season with curry powder (if using), salt and sugar to taste. Serve hot with rice or bread.

MIXED VEGETABLE CURRY

HINTHEESONE KALA HIN

This Burmese dish is also known as 'chettiar curry' because it used to be the food of Burmese farmers who worked for chettiars – rich landlords who had come from South India and made Burma their home.

SERVES 4

100g yellow split peas, cooked until al dente
2 tablespoons vegetable oil
1 teaspoon cumin seeds
1 onion, thinly sliced
1/2 teaspoon ground turmeric
1 teaspoon ground cumin
1 tablespoon ground coriander
1 teaspoon red chilli powder
1 bay leaf
1 tablespoon Tamarind Water (see page 228)
1 small mooli, peeled and cut into 5mm slices
2 small, thin aubergines, cut into 5mm slices
100g orange or yellow Asian pumpkin flesh, cut into 2.5cm cubes
2 medium potatoes, peeled and sliced
2 carrots, sliced
1 litre vegetable stock or water
salt
1 tablespoon chopped coriander leaves, to garnish

Place the yellow split peas in a pan of cold water, bring to the boil and simmer for 15–20 minutes, until al dente.

Heat the oil in a large pan and sauté the cumin seeds. As they splutter, add the sliced onion and sauté over a medium heat until translucent. Add the ground spices, bay leaf and cooked split peas. Stir for a couple of minutes, then add the tamarind water and all the vegetables. Stir-fry for 2–3 minutes.

Pour in the stock and bring to the boil, then simmer on a low heat for 7–10 minutes, until all the vegetables are cooked. Garnish with chopped coriander and serve with rice.

MOOLI CURRY

MULOR GHUNTO

A mooli is a type of large, white radish, which is milder in flavour – less peppery – than most radishes, and can be cooked or eaten raw. In Bangladesh it is used as a vegetable accompaniment and as a salad ingredient. The Bengali variety of mooli is a little spicier than its European equivalent. Spices such as cumin, mustard and fennel work really well with mooli as they complement the pepper.

SERVES 4 (AS A SIDE DISH)

2 tablespoons vegetable oil
1 dried red chilli
1 teaspoon cumin seeds
3 medium mooli, scraped and cut into 2.5 cm cubes
2 medium potatoes, peeled and cut into 2.5 cm cubes
1/2 teaspoon ground turmeric
1/2 teaspoon chilli powder
1 tablespoon ground fennel seed
100g frozen peas, defrosted
50ml vegetable stock or water
sugar to taste
1/2 teaspoon Garam Masala (see page 223)
salt
1 tablespoon finely chopped coriander leaves, to garnish

Blanch the potatoes and mooli separately in boiling water for 7–10 minutes each, until just cooked. Drain and keep aside until required.

Heat the oil in a pan and sauté the dried red chili and cumin seeds. When they splutter, add the mooli and potatoes. Sauté for 2–3 minutes, then add all the ground spices, except the garam masala, and stir to mix. Add the peas and stock. Simmer on a low heat for about 5 minutes, until the vegetables are tender.

Add sugar and salt to taste and sprinkle with the garam masala. Serve garnished with coriander.

RIGHT: BANGLADESHI MOOLI CURRY

INDONESIAN POTATO RENDANG

POTATO RENDANG

RENDANG KENTANG

This recipe is slightly different from the meat and poultry rendang recipes I've included in this book (see pages 67, 180 and 186) but it just goes to emphasise how many variations there are. I like to use Jersey Royal potatoes, but feel free to use any variety – just cut big potatoes into large dice.

SERVES 4–6

700ml coconut milk
a few sprigs of Thai basil, plus extra to garnish
500g Jersey Royal potatoes, cut into thin wedges
salt

For the spice paste
1 thick lemongrass stalk, hard parts removed and thinly sliced
3–4 shallots, chopped
2 garlic cloves, peeled
5 small red Thai chillies
1 teaspoon ground turmeric
1 tablespoon finely chopped fresh ginger
1½ teaspoons finely chopped galangal
a few kaffir lime leaves

Blend or pound the ingredients for the spice paste, with 2–3 tablespoons water, to make a fine paste. Pour the coconut milk into a wok and bring to the boil. Add the spice paste and some 3–4 Thai basil sprigs and cook, stirring occasionally, until the mixture has reduced by half.

Add the potatoes and some salt. Cook for 30–40 minutes or until the potatoes are very tender, stirring well, until the mixture has thickened. Serve garnished with chopped Thai basil.

NEW POTATOES

NOTUN AALU BHAJI

This humble side dish may seem a little simple but it never fails to put a smile on my face. Perhaps it's nostalgia as it's an East Indian preparation that reminds me of my childhood, but new potatoes are so delicious, especially if freshly harvested, so really they need little to accompany them.

SERVES 4 (AS A SIDE DISH)

1 tablespoon mustard oil or vegetable oil
500g new potatoes, scrubbed and cut into very fine strips
¼ teaspoon ground turmeric (optional)
salt
1 tablespoon finely chopped coriander leaves, to garnish

Heat the oil in a wok and sauté the potatoes with the turmeric and salt to taste over a medium heat for 5–7 minutes, stirring. Then reduce the heat and cook until tender. Sprinkle with chopped coriander and serve.

PANEER LABABDAR

Paneer cheese is the vegetarian 'meat' in India. Indians love paneer in every form. This is one of those classic dishes for which the exact recipe and combination of flavours is heavily disputed among home cooks and chefs. For me it needs to have cumin, tomatoes, kasoori methi and cream so here's my version.

SERVES 4

3 tablespoons vegetable oil
1 teaspoon cumin seeds
2 onions, chopped
4 tomatoes, puréed
1/2 teaspoon red chili powder
1/2 teaspoon ground cumin
1/2 teaspoon Garam Masala (see page 223)
1 tablespoon kasoori methi (dried fenugreek leaves)
2 tablespoons unsalted butter
400g paneer, cut into 2.5cm dice
100ml single cream
2 tablespoons finely chopped coriander
small knob of ginger, cut into very fine strips
salt

Heat the oil in a pan. Add the cumin seeds and stir as they crackle, then add the chopped onions and sauté over a medium heat, until light brown in colour. Add the puréed tomatoes and bring to the boil, then simmer for 10 minutes. Add the red chilli, cumin, garam masala and kasoori methi and stir to mix well. Simmer for 2–3 minutes then add the butter and salt to taste. Add the paneer and simmer for 5–7 minutes, then add 50ml water if required to loosen the sauce. Add the cream and simmer gently without boiling for 2–3 minutes. Top with the coriander and ginger and serve hot.

PUMPKIN CURRY

KADOO KA SALAN

Asian pumpkin is available at Asian grocers and some supermarkets, but you can easily apply this recipe to any type of pumpkin or squash.

SERVES 4 (AS A SIDE DISH)

3 tablespoons vegetable oil
1 teaspoon cumin seeds
1/4 teaspoon nigella seeds
1 onion, finely chopped
1 tablespoon finely chopped fresh ginger
1/2 teaspoon ground turmeric
1 teaspoon red chilli powder
1 teaspoon ground coriander
3 tomatoes, chopped
500g yellow Asian pumpkin, peeled and cut into 2.5cm dice
1 teaspoon Garam Masala (see page 223)
2 green chillies, sliced
1 tablespoon lime juice
2 tablespoons finely chopped coriander leaves
salt

Heat the oil in a pan and sauté the cumin and nigella seeds. When they start to pop add the onion and sauté until lightly browned. Add the ginger, ground spices and salt to taste. Stir for a minute, then add the tomatoes and cook until they turn mushy.

Add the diced pumpkin, cover and cook for 8–10 minutes, until tender. Add the garam masala, chillies, lime juice and chopped coriander, mix well and serve.

RIGHT: PAKISTANI PUMPKIN CURRY

PUMPKIN WITH CHICKPEAS

KUMROR CHOKHA

The Bengali spice mix panch phoran (see page 226) works really well with the sweet flavour of pumpkin, and the ginger brings out the peppery notes in the dish. You could use a 400g can of chickpeas in place of the dried chickpeas to make this a really quick and easy dish to throw together midweek.

SERVES 4

70g dried chickpeas, soaked overnight, or 1 x 400g can chickpeas, drained and rinsed
3 tablespoons vegetable oil
1 bay leaf
2 dried red chillies
1/2 teaspoon panch phoran (Bengal spice mix; see page 226)
a pinch of asafoetida
300g yellow Asian pumpkin flesh, diced
2 small potatoes, peeled and diced
1/2 teaspoon ground turmeric
1 teaspoon ground cumin
1 tablespoon ground coriander
1 green chilli, chopped
1 tablespoon finely chopped fresh ginger
1 tablespoon ghee
2 tablespoons sugar
1 teaspoon Garam Masala (see page 223) powder
salt

Drain the soaked chickpeas and put them in a pan with fresh cold water to cover generously. Bring to the boil and boil for 10 minutes, then simmer for 60–90 minutes until the chickpeas are tender. Drain and keep aside until needed.

Heat the oil in a wok and stir-fry the bay leaf, red chillies, panch phoran and asafoetida until the spluttering stops. Add the pumpkin and potatoes and sauté for a further 5 minutes.

Add the ground spices and the green chilli and ginger mixed with 100ml water. Stir well. Add the chickpeas and simmer gently for 2–3 minutes or until all the vegetables are cooked and the excess liquid has evaporated. If using canned chickpeas you'll need to simmer for a little longer – about 10 minutes, to heat the chickpeas through.

Mix in the ghee, sugar and salt to taste. Sprinkle over the garam masala, mix and serve immediately with rice or bread.

SAVOY CABBAGE WITH COCONUT

This simple recipe has lots of punch from spices like galangal and chillies, but with a good cooling effect from the coconut milk. You can adapt the recipe to use all kinds of vegetables, such as green beans, potatoes and various greens.

SERVES 4 (AS A SIDE DISH)

2 tablespoons vegetable oil
2 banana shallots or 1 onion, thinly sliced
1 tablespoon finely chopped garlic
2 small red chillies, thinly sliced diagonally
1 teaspoon galangal powder
500g savoy cabbage leaves, cut into 2.5cm square pieces or shredded
200ml coconut milk
1 teaspoon sugar
6–8 ripe cherry tomatoes, cut in half
salt
coriander sprigs, to garnish

Heat the oil in a wok and sauté the shallots with the garlic, chillies and galangal powder over a medium heat for about 5–7 minutes, until the shallots are translucent. Add the cabbage and sauté for 2–3 minutes or until it begins to wilts.

Add the coconut milk, sugar, tomatoes and salt to taste and stir well. Bring to the boil, then lower the heat and simmer for 3–5 minutes or until the sauce begins to thicken. Serve hot, garnished with coriander sprigs.

SPINACH AND LENTIL CURRY

SINDHI SAI BHAJI

My friend Ash Deswani's mum shared this recipe with me. Ash's family is from the province of Sindh in Pakistan and this recipe, a kind of creamy, comforting vegetable and lentil mash, is a classic dish found all over the province.

SERVES 4–6

150g channa dal
3 teaspoons dry kasoori methi (fenugreek leaves)
2–3 tablespoons vegetable oil
$1/2$ onion, roughly chopped
$1/4$ teaspoon hing (asafoetida)
2 tablespoons grated fresh ginger
$1^1/2$ teaspoons garlic paste or 3 garlic cloves, chopped
3 green chillies, finely chopped
100g spinach leaves
100g potato, cut into 2.5cm cubes
1 small carrot, chopped
3 tomatoes, finely chopped
1 teaspoon ground turmeric
salt

Soak the chana dal in a bowl of water for about 30 minutes. Place the kasoori methi in a sieve and run cold water over them, then set aside.

Heat the oil in a large heavy-based pan. Add the onion and sauté for 2 minutes.

Meanwhile, rinse the soaked dal in a sieve under running cold water.

Add the hing, ginger, garlic and chillies to the pan and stir for a few seconds. Add the drained chana dal, spinach, potato, carrot and tomatoes and stir well. Add the turmeric, salt to taste and 1 litre of water. Cover the pan with a tight lid. Bring to boil on a high heat, then cook on a low heat for about 30 minutes, until the dal, potatoes and carrots are well cooked. Using a potato masher or a hand blender, mash the mixture very briefly but make sure the mixture does not become a paste – the consistency should be thick but not runny. Serve hot with rice.

SINDHI CURRY

SINDHI KADHI

Kadhi is a combination of vegetables thickened with gram flour – it is a kind of stew. There are many a versions of kadhi in India and Pakistan and each region has their own way of making it – this is the Sindhi version. This dish can be cooked a day in advance to allow the flavours to mature. Store it overnight in the fridge and bring to the boil again before serving.

SERVES 4–6

3–4 tablespoons vegetable oil
2 teaspoons cumin seeds
2 teaspoons fenugreek seeds
6–8 curry leaves
$1/4$ teaspoon asafoetida
2 tablespoons grated fresh ginger
3 green chillies, finely chopped
6 heaped tablespoons gram flour (besan)
1 teaspoon ground turmeric
1 tablespoon tamarind paste (readymade)
2 teaspoons jaggery or sugar
10–12 whole cluster beans (guar) or green beans, topped and tailed
6–8 moringa (moringa oleifera, shevaga ki faliyan), 7.5cm long (optional)
6–8 whole okra, topped and tailed
1 potato, cut into 2.5cm cubes
3 tablespoons finely chopped fresh coriander
salt

Heat the oil in a large heavy-bottomed pan. Add the cumin and fenugreek seeds and curry leaves and stir until the seeds crackle. Add the asafoetida, ginger and chillies and stir for a few seconds. Add half the gram flour and stir for 2–3 minutes. Add 700ml water and continue stirring until the mixture forms a smooth paste. Add the turmeric, tamarind paste and salt and continue to stir.

Meanwhile, mix the remaining the gram flour in a jug with 700ml water. Stir until there are no lumps, then add to the pan and bring to the boil (leave a ladle in the pan so that the liquid doesn't boil over – the ladle breaks the pressure that builds up in the pan from the boiling). Reduce the heat to medium and continue to boil, stirring in the froth from the sides of the pan from time to time.

After 12–15 minutes the frothing will subside. Add the jaggery or sugar, beans and moringa, if using, and boil for another 20 minutes or until the beans are tender if not using the moringa. Add the okra and potato and continue to boil until all the vegetables are cooked. Sprinkle the coriander on top, and leave covered until ready to serve. Serve hot with rice.

VIETNAMESE VEGETABLE AND TOFU CURRY

SPICY WATER SPINACH

BELACAN KANGKUNG

This is perfect side dish for a fiery Malaysian curry or fried noodles.

SERVES 4 (AS A SIDE DISH)

500g water spinach
1 small, dried red chilli
2 garlic cloves, crushed
2 candlenuts or macadamia nuts
6 shallots or 1 small onion, chopped
2 teaspoons belacan (dried shrimp paste)
1 tablespoon dried shrimps, ground
1 tablespoon vegetable oil
1/2 teaspoon palm sugar
salt

Wash the spinach and shake dry. Grind, pound or blend together the chilli, garlic, nuts, shallots, belacan and dried shrimps to make a paste. Heat the oil in a wok or frying pan and fry the paste, stirring, for about 5 minutes or until fragrant.

Add the spinach and toss to coat in the paste. As soon as the leaves start to wilt, add the sugar and salt to taste. Keep tossing until the stems soften and the leaves have wilted.

VEGETABLE AND TOFU CURRY

CARI CHAY

Don't be bound by the vegetables I am suggesting using for this dish. It is a simple recipe so it's easy to play around, use your local produce and show your flair in the combinations you try.

SERVES 4

500g tofu, cut into 2.5cm cubes
oil for deep-frying
3 tablespoons vegetable oil
1 onion, sliced
2 garlic cloves, crushed
1 tablespoon finely chopped fresh ginger
1 tablespoon Vietnamese Curry Powder (see page 228)
400ml coconut milk
juice of 1 lime
1 tablespoon palm sugar
2 tablespoons fish sauce
2 tablespoons annatto extract
(optional)
2 lemongrass stalks, bruised
4–5 kaffir lime leaves, bruised
200g thin asparagus spears, cut into 2.5m pieces
2 aubergines, cut into 2.5cm batons
1/2 cauliflower, cut into florets
2 carrots, cut into 2.5cm batons
1 tomato, cut into wedges
salt
5–6 sprigs of coriander, to garnish

Heat enough oil for deep-frying in a wok. When it is hot (170–180°C), deep-fry the tofu for 2–3 minutes or until light golden. Drain on kitchen paper and set aside.

Heat the oil in a wok and sauté the onion with the garlic, ginger and curry powder for about 30 seconds or until fragrant. Add the coconut milk, lime juice, palm sugar, fish sauce, annatto extract, if using, lemongrass and kaffir lime leaves. Season with salt to taste. Bring to the boil, then reduce the heat to low. Add all the vegetables and simmer for 12–15 minutes or until they are cooked. Serve garnished with coriander sprigs.

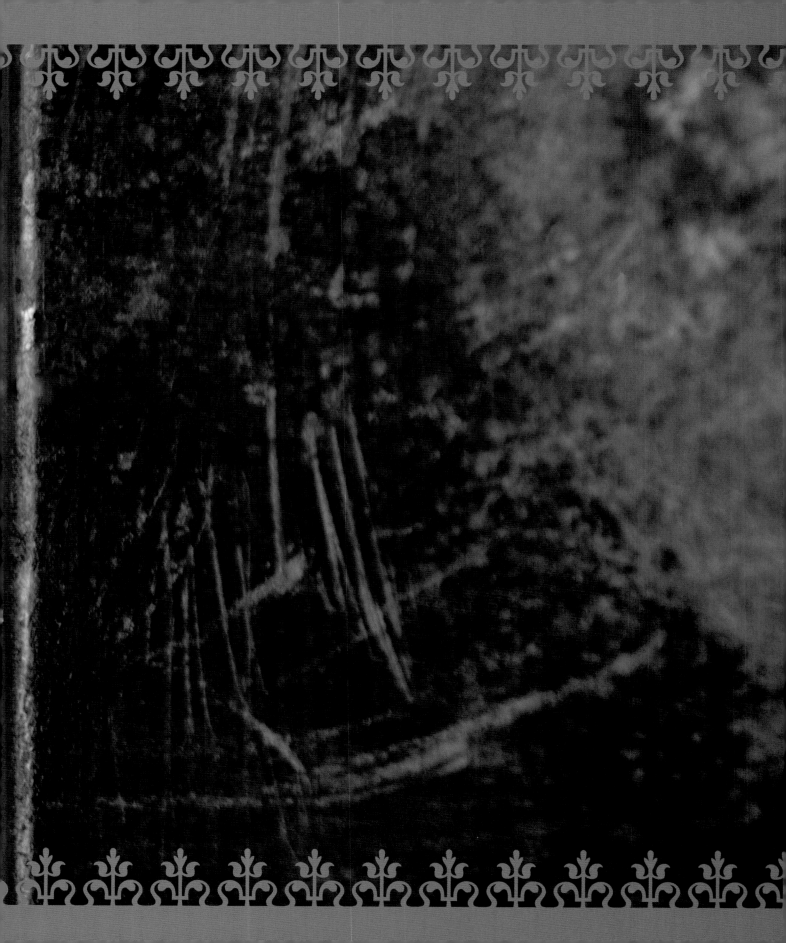

FOUNDATIONS

BAHARAT
(MIDDLE EASTERN SPICE POWDER)

MAKES APPROXIMATELY 400G

100g black peppercorns
50g coriander seeds
50g cassia bark
50g cloves
70g cumin seeds

2 teaspoons green cardamom
seeds (from the pods)
4 nutmegs, freshly grated
100g mild paprika

Put all the ingredients in a blender, spice grinder or coffee grinder and blend to a fine powder. Store in an airtight container and use within 6 months.

BETEL LEAVES

Betel leaf belongs to the *Piperaceae* family, which includes pepper, and indeed the glossy, heart-shaped leaves have a mild peppery taste. Betel leaves are used extensively in Indian and Far Eastern cuisine, often to wrap ingredients, thereby imparting their flavour into the dish.

BURMESE CURRY POWDER

MAKES APPROXIMATELY
20 TABLESPOONS

6 tablespoons coriander seeds
3 tablespoons black
peppercorns
3 tablespoons cumin seeds
2 tablespoons poppy seeds
2 tablespoons green
cardamom pods

4 bay leaves
½ tablespoon fenugreek seeds
¾ tablespoon cloves
1 tablespoons ground
cinnamon
2 tablespoons ground
turmeric

Lightly toast all the spices (except the cinnamon and turmeric) separately in a dry frying pan until fragrant. Tip into a pestle and mortar, spice grinder or coffee grinder, grind to a fine powder, then mix in the ground cinnamon and turmeric. Store in an airtight container and use within 6 months.

CAPE CURRY POWDER
MAKES APPROXIMATELY 200G

100g coriander seeds
3 tablespoons cumin seeds
1 tablespoon fennel seeds
1 tablespoon black mustard
seeds
2 tablespoons fenugreek seeds
3 small piri-piri chillies or 2
large red dried chillies
2 tablespoons black
peppercorns

1 tablespoon cloves
4 tablespoons ground green
cardamom pods or grains
of paradise
4 tablespoons ground
turmeric
1 tablespoon ground ginger
20–30 dried curry leaves,
crushed to a powder

Toast the whole spices separately in a dry frying pan until they become aromatic. Leave to cool, then mix them all together with the powdered spices and tip into a pestle and mortar, spice grinder or coffee grinder. Grind to a fine powder. Store in an airtight container and use within 6 months.

CARDAMOM

There are two types of cardamom – green and black. Both are small pods that contain clusters of small black, fragrant seeds, yet their uses and flavours are very different. Green cardamom is used in savoury and sweet dishes. It has a perfume-like aroma that is quite unique and difficult to describe, but it can add sweet spice – and is often used in sweet Indian tea, for example – or savoury, in meat and rice dishes. Black cardamom is only used in savoury dishes – it has a smoky flavour. Both whole pods and the seeds are used, although whole pods are not supposed to be eaten. For curries and braises, pods are bruised and then sautéed to get most of the flavour out of the pod. Seeds are sold separately by Indian grocers, but you can also take the seeds out of the pods yourself. To make ground cardamom, lightly toast the seeds to harden them, then grind them to a powder.

CARIBBEAN CURRY POWDER
MAKES APPROXIMATELY 100G

1 tablespoon coriander seeds
2 tablespoons cumin seeds
1 tablespoon white poppy seeds
1 tablespoon brown mustard
seeds
1 tablespoon whole cloves

1 tablespoon black
peppercorns
1 tablespoon allspice berries
2 tablespoons ground
turmeric
1 tablespoon ground ginger

Toast the coriander, cumin, poppy and mustard seeds in a dry frying pan. Tip on to a plate and allow to cool. Toast the cloves, peppercorns and allspice berries lightly in the pan. Tip all the toasted and ground spices into a pestle and mortar, spice grinder or coffee grinder and grind to a fine powder. Store in an airtight container and use within 6 months.

CEYLON CURRY POWDER (SRI LANKAN CURRY POWDER)

Sri Lankan preparations are generally a rich, dark colour due to the highly roasted spices. This high roast adds a distinct flavour to the dishes, quite different to any of the other curry powders. This blend is easily available in the UK, but if you would like to make your own here is a simple recipe.

MAKES ABOUT 400G

200g coriander seeds
100g cumin seeds
50g fennel seeds
1 teaspoon fenugreek seeds
a 5cm piece of cinnamon stick
1 teaspoon cloves

1 teaspoon green cardamom seeds
2–3 sprigs of dried curry leaves
2 teaspoons red chilli powder
2 tablespoons ground rice

Toast the coriander, cumin, fennel and fenugreek seeds separately in a dry frying pan over a low heat. Leave to cool, then tip them into a pestle and mortar, spice grinder or coffee grinder with the remaining ingredients and grind to a fine powder. Store in an airtight container and use within 6 months.

CHAAT MASALA

This powdered spice mix typically consists of dried mango powder, cumin, coriander, dried ginger, dried mint, asafoetida, black salt, ordinary salt, and red and black pepper. Used as a salad seasoning, it is served on a small metal plate or in a dried banana leaf bowl at chaat (salad carts) in India. You should be able to find it in Asian food shops.

CHILLI PASTE

Soak dried red chillies in enough water to cover overnight. The next day, drain the chillies, then blend or pound to a fine paste with some of the soaking liquid. This will keep well in a sealed container in the fridge for a few days or you can mix the paste with a little vegetable oil to prolong its life to up to a week.

CHINESE FIVE SPICE POWDER

Chinese five spice powder is used as a fragrant spice mix in Far Eastern countries, most often for duck and other poultry recipes.

MAKES APPROXIMATELY 50G

2 tablespoons Sichuan peppercorns
8 star anise
1 tablespoon fennel seeds

1/2 tablespoon cloves
1 tablespoon ground cinnamon

Toast all the spices, except the cinnamon in a dry frying pan. Tip into a pestle and mortar, spice grinder or coffee grinder with the cinnamon and grind to a fine powder. Sieve. Store in an airtight container and use within 6 months.

CHIRONJI

Chironji or Charoli are bush seeds cultivated in India. The hard shell is cracked to retrieve the soft seeds inside – these are small and slightly flat, with an almond flavour. The seeds can be eaten raw or toasted to intensify their flavour. They are commonly used in sweets, or to thicken sauces and stews.

COCONUT

Some recipes suggest the use of freshly grated coconut. Fresh coconuts are used a great deal on the coast in India, however they are not always that easy to come by in the UK so I've suggested using the same quantity of unsweetened desiccated coconut as an alternative. To extract the flesh from a coconut, push a skewer through one of the three 'eyes' to make a hole and then drain off the liquid (this can be strained and used in drinks). Next crack open the nut – the easiest way is to tap it round its circumference with a hammer, about a third of the way down from the 'eyes'. Break the nut into chunks and cut out the white flesh with a small, sharp knife. Remove the thin brown skin, then grate the flesh. Frozen grated fresh coconut is also now available to buy online and in Asian grocers and this is just as good as grating your own.

COCONUT MILK

Fresh coconut milk is made from the grated flesh of the coconut and should not be confused with the liquid inside the coconut. To prepare coconut milk, soak 500g grated fresh coconut (or frozen, see above) in 300ml lukewarm water for 30 minutes, then whiz in a blender at high speed for a few minutes. Strain the mixture through a sieve lined with muslin. This first extraction should yield about 250ml of 'thick' coconut milk. Repeat the process, with the residue from the first extraction and a further 300ml lukewarm water, to make a 'thin' coconut milk. Canned coconut milk is readily available and makes an acceptable substitute for fresh in most cases.

CRISPY ONIONS

Deep-fried sliced onions are used to add depth of flavour to dishes or as a garnish. Slice onions very finely. Heat some vegetable oil to 180°C in a deep-fat fryer or deep saucepan, add the onions and fry until crisp and brown. Drain on kitchen paper.

DRIED FENUGREEK LEAVES (KASOORI METHI)

Fenugreek leaves taste very different from fenugreek seeds and the two are not interchangeable. Dried fenugreek leaf powder is available from Asian food shops, or you can grind your own dried fenugreek leaves in a pestle and mortar, spice grinder or coffee grinder.

DRIED SHRIMP PASTE

Made from salted, dried and fermented shrimps, this is a pungent flavouring used all over South East Asia. Each country makes its own version (terasi in Indonesia, belacan in Malaysia, kapi or kaapi in Thailand, Laos and Cambodia) but they are very similar, so you can use whichever one you find in Asian shops.

EAST AFRICAN CURRY POWDER (OR PASTE)

Curry powders in East African countries, including Kenya, Malawi, Uganda and Ethiopia, will each be slightly different. To keep things simpler, I've created a powder that I feel represents the essence of the region's curries, rather than using a separate powder for each recipe (although there are certain recipes that do require something a little different to recreate the dish – see Malawi Curry Powder and Meusi Masala, page 225).

MAKES APPROXIMATELY 50G

1 tablespoon green
  cardamom seeds
1 tablespoon ground turmeric
1 teaspoon ground ginger
1 tablespoon ground
  cinnamon
2 tablespoons red chilli
  powder

Mix all the ingredients together. Store in airtight container and use within 6 months.

Instead of ground ginger, fresh ginger is sometimes used. Make a paste by blending 100g fresh ginger and 1 tablespoon of vegetable oil with this mixture. Store in the fridge and use within a week.

GALANGAL

A root from the ginger family that resembles ginger in appearance though not in taste. It has a slightly lighter, more pinkish skin and while it is still a warming aromatic, its flavour is more peppery than ginger. Fresh galangal is used in South East Asian cuisine, particularly in curry pastes, and is now widely available in Asian grocers.

GARAM MASALA

Garam masala is a simple Indian spice mixture that is usually added towards the end of the cooking just before serving. It is used in many dishes and contributes flavour and aroma. In India it would be sprinkled over the dish right at the end, the pot would then be covered with a lid and the garam masala would only be stirred in just before the dish is served. Although garam masala is available to buy, I would strongly advise making your own – the fresh version is infinitely better and if you're going to cook Indian food regularly, it makes such a big difference to the end result.

30g black cardamom seeds	20g black cumin seeds
15g cloves	20g black peppercorns
2.5cm piece of cinnamon stick	a pinch of grated nutmeg (optional)

Briefly roast the ingredients separately in a dry frying pan until they become aromatic. Leave to cool, then grind to a fine powder in a pestle and mortar, spice grinder or coffee grinder. Store the garam masala in an airtight container; it should keep for months.

GARLIC PASTE

Peel a whole bulb of garlic and put the cloves in a blender or mini food processor with 2–3 tablespoons water and 1 tablespoon vegetable oil. Blend to a paste. This can be kept in a tightly covered jar in the fridge for up to a week, or you can freeze it in ice-cube trays (take out a cube when you need it).

GINGER PASTE

Peel 300g fresh ginger and chop it roughly, then blend to a paste with 2 tablespoons water in a blender or mini food processor. Alternatively, grate the ginger very finely and mix with the water. Store in the fridge or freeze as for Garlic Paste above.

GINGER-GARLIC PASTE

Blend equal quantities of peeled garlic and fresh ginger with 10 per cent of their total weight in water, using a blender or mini food processor. Keep in a sealed container in the fridge. If you want to keep this for longer than a few days, add 5 per cent vegetable oil and 2 per cent lemon juice when you blend. Or you can freeze this in ice-cube trays as for Garlic Paste above.

HAWAAYIJ (YEMENI SPICE POWDER)

Hawaayji is the name given to a variety of Yemeni ground spice mixes that are mainly used for soups and stews. This mixture makes a great barbecue rub.

MAKES APPROXIMATELY 60G

2 tablespoons black peppercorns	seeds
1 tablespoon caraway seeds	2 teaspoons ground turmeric
1 teaspoon saffron strands	
1 teaspoon green cardamom	

Grind all the ingredients together in a blender, spice grinder or coffee grinder. Store in an airtight container and use within 6 months.

JAFFNA CURRY POWDER

Ceylon and Jaffna curry powders are the two main blends used in Sri Lankan cuisine. Jaffna is the one used in hot dishes.

MAKES APPROXIMATELY 150G

1 tablespoon uncooked long grain or basmati rice	seeds
2 tablespoons coriander seeds	1/2 teaspoon cloves
2 teaspoons cumin seeds	1/2 teaspoon cardamom seeds
2 teaspoons fennel seeds	1/2 teaspoon black mustard seeds
a 7.5cm piece of cinnamon stick	1 teaspoon black peppercorns
1 1/2 teaspoons fenugreek	3 dried red Kashmiri chillies

Toast all the spices in a dry frying pan until aromatic and golden brown. Leave to cool, then place in a pestle and mortar, spice grinder or coffee grinder and grind to a fine powder. Store in an airtight container and use within 6 months.

JAPANESE CURRY POWDER

Curries were introduced to Japan by the British. Since then the Japanese have used a kind of curry powder that is very specific to Japan; I have tried to re-create something close to it.

MAKES APPROXIMATELY 200G

4 tablespoons ground turmeric

2 tablespoons ground coriander

1 tablespoon ground cumin

1½ teaspoons ground green cardamom

1 tablespoon ground black pepper

1 tablespoon red chilli powder

1 teaspoon ground cloves

1 tablespoon ground fennel

½ teaspoon ground cinnamon

1 tablespoon ground star anise

¼ teaspoon ground nutmeg

1 teaspoon ground allspice

½ teaspoon ground bay leaves

½ teaspoon ground sage

½ teaspoon ground fenugreek

Mix all the ingredients together. Store in an airtight container and use within 6 months.

KORE LAOTIAN (LAOTIAN CURRY PASTE)

MAKES APPROXIMATELY 250G

1 teaspoon cumin seeds, lightly toasted

2 teaspoons coriander seeds, lightly toasted

1 lemongrass stalk, hard outer leaves removed, chopped

1 tablespoon chopped galangal

grated zest and juice of 1 kaffir lime

1 tablespoon finely chopped garlic

1 large shallot, chopped

3 tablespoons chopped coriander root

1 tablespoon chopped fresh turmeric

1 teaspoon ground turmeric

1 tablespoon chopped fresh ginger

4 red Thai or bird's eye chillies

2 teaspoons kaapi (dried shrimp paste)

1 tablespoon medium curry powder

2 tablespoons vegetable oil

Blend or pound all the ingredients together with a small quantity of water to make a smooth paste. It can be kept, tightly covered, in the refrigerator for 3–4 days or frozen in ice cube trays.

KERISIK

This is finely ground toasted coconut. To make it the traditional way, toast unsweetened desiccated coconut in a dry pan until it is brown. When cool, pound in a mortar and pestle or grind in a coffee grinder or spice grinder until very fine.

KROEUNG (CAMBODIAN SPICE PASTE)

This spicy paste is used in many dishes of Cambodian origin. You can use an electric blender to make the paste, but a mortar and pestle gives the most authentic flavour.

MAKES APPROXIMATELY 200G

60ml vegetable oil

5 large lemongrass stalks, outer hard leaves removed, then chopped

2–3 dried red chillies, soaked to rehydrate and deseeded

30g galangal, roughly chopped

50g fresh turmeric, chopped, or ½ teaspoon ground turmeric

6 garlic cloves, finely chopped

2 shallots, chopped

10 kaffir lime leaves, ribs removed

6 green cardamom pods

15–20 black peppercorns

½ teaspoon coriander seeds

½ teaspoon fennel seeds

100ml water

a small bunch of coriander, with stalks and roots

2 teaspoons prahoc or kaapi (dried shrimp paste; optional)

Pound or blend all the ingredients together to make a fine paste. This will keep well in a tightly covered container in the refrigerator for a week, or it can be frozen in ice cube trays.

MALAWI CURRY POWDER

This is one of the hottest curry powder blends from Africa mainly due to its piri-piri chillies. Cinnamon and fennel are the cooling effect spices that balance the flavours.

MAKES APPROXIMATELY 100G

10 dried piri-piri chillies, stems removed
3 tablespoons coriander seeds
1 tablespoon black peppercorns
3 tablespoons black poppy seeds
2 teaspoons black mustard seeds
1 tablespoon cumin seeds
1 teaspoon fennel seeds
1 tablespoon ground turmeric
10 cloves
2 teaspoons ground cinnamon

Lightly toast all the ingredients in a dry frying pan until aromatic. Transfer to a pestle and mortar, spice grinder or coffee grinder and grind to a fine powder. Store in an airtight container and use within 6 months.

MALAYSIAN KURMA POWDER

MAKES APPROXIMATELY 6 TABLESPOONS

2 tablespoons coriander seeds
1 teaspoon cumin seeds
1 teaspoon aniseed
$1/2$ teaspoon black peppercorns
2 cloves
1 star anise
a 5cm piece of cinnamon stick
$1/4$ nutmeg, grated
5 green cardamom pods
1 teaspoon ground turmeric

Toast the all the spices (apart from the turmeric) one at a time in a dry frying pan until fragrant and aromatic. Tip on to a plate and set aside to cool, then grind to a powder in a pestle and mortar, spice grinder or coffee grinder. Transfer to an airtight container and store for up to 1 month.

MALAYSIAN MEAT CURRY POWDER

MAKES APPROXIMATELY 8—10 TABLESPOONS

10 cloves
10 black peppercorns
4 cardamom pods
a 5cm piece of cinnamon stick
4 dried red chillies
4 tablespoons coriander seeds
2 tablespoons cumin seeds
1 teaspoon fennel seeds
1 star anise
1 teaspoon ground turmeric

Lightly toast the whole spices (apart from the turmeric) one at a time in a dry frying pan, then cool. Using a mortar and pestle, spice grinder or coffee grinder, grind the spices to a powder. Mix with the ground turmeric. Strain the powder through a fine sieve. It will keep in an airtight container for 4—8 weeks.

MEUSI MASALA

This is a traditional East African spice blend for curries and stews, often used in Kenya and Tanzania.

MAKES APPROXIMATELY 5—6 TABLESPOONS

2 tablespoons cumin seeds
1 teaspoon cloves
2 blades of mace
$1/2$ tablespoon poppy seeds
1 teaspoon mustard seeds
1 tablespoon coriander seeds
3 dried piri-piri chilies
1 teaspoon ground cinnamon

Toast each spice (apart from the cinnamon) one at a time in a dry pan until fragrant. Tip into a pestle and mortar, spice grinder or coffee grinder, grind to a fine powder, then mix in the ground cinnamon. Store in an airtight container and use within 6 months.

ONION MASALA GRAVY

This is a basic sauce used in North Indian cuisine. It is worth making a batch and storing it. It can be kept in the fridge for a week to 10 days or in the freezer for up to 3 months, well wrapped.

MAKES APPROXIMATELY 300G

3 tablespoons vegetable oil
1 bay leaf
a 2.5cm piece of cinnamon
  bark
2 green cardamom pods
1 teaspoon cumin seeds
2 onions, finely chopped
1 teaspoon Ginger-Garlic

Paste (see page 223)
1/2 teaspoon ground turmeric
1/2 teaspoon ground cumin
1 teaspoon ground coriander
1/2 teaspoon garam masala
1 tablespoon tomato paste,
  mixed with 4 tablespoons
  water

Heat the oil in a pan and sauté the whole spices. Add the chopped onion and sauté over a high heat for 5–7 minutes or until lightly coloured. Add the ginger-garlic paste and sauté over a low heat for 2–3 minutes or until the raw smell of the garlic disappears.

Add the ground spices and sauté for 2–3 minutes. Whizz the sauce in a blender with 225ml water, then add the tomato paste with another 125ml water. Return the sauce to another pan and cook for 15–20 minutes over a low heat. Add more water if it starts to catch on the pan, but the idea is to gently 'fry' the sauce, which will darken in colour to light brown. The final texture should be something like tomato ketchup. While cooking it will gloop occasionally and splatter. It will get extremely hot and can burn or scald, so stir the sauce with caution. Allow to cool, then store in an airtight container in the fridge or freezer.

PALM SUGAR AND JAGGERY

Palm sugar is made from the sap of various palm trees, such as date and coconut, while jaggery is a dark, unrefined sugar from the sugar cane plant. Loosely known as gur, palm sugar and jaggery are largely interchangeable in Indian cooking.

PANCH PHORAN (BENGAL SPICE MIX)

Panch phoran is a Bengali spice mix consisting of equal quantities of five strongly flavoured spices. It's available in Asian shops but mixing your own will be far superior.

MAKES APPROXIMATELY 30G

1 teaspoon fennel seeds
1 teaspoon cumin seeds
1 teaspoon nigella seeds

1 teaspoon black mustard
  seeds
1 teaspoon fenugreek seeds

Mix all the ingredients together. Store in an airtight container and use within 6 months.

PANDAN LEAVES

These bright green, spear-shaped leaves come from the screwpine tree in Asia and are often used to flavour rice or curry dishes. They have a gentle, slightly nutty flavour.

PRAHOC AND TUK PRAHOC

Prahoc is a paste-like condiment made from fish fermented with ground rice and salt, equivalent to the dried shrimp paste used all over South East Asia. Jars of prahoc can be bought from Asian grocers.

Tuk prahoc is a diluted version of prahoc, similar to Thai and Vietnamese fish sauce. To make tuk prahoc, bring 300ml water to the boil in a pan, then reduce to a simmer and add 2 tablespoons of prahoc. Simmer for 10 minutes or until the fish is broken down and the water is cloudy. Strain the liquid through muslin and leave to cool. Store the tuk prahoc in an airtight container in a cool place.

RAS EL HANOUT

Ras el hanout is the most popular Moroccan blend of spices and is used across North Africa. There is no definitive recipe for each blend – it can vary according to shop, company and person. Common ingredients are cardamom, clove, cinnamon, red chilli powder, coriander, cumin, nutmeg, peppercorn and turmeric. Some recipes include over a hundred ingredients, some rarely found in one place in the world, such as ash berries, chufa, grains of paradise, orris root, Monk's pepper, cubebs and dried rose buds. This is one of the recipes I use to make my own version – all the ingredients are readily available.

2 teaspoons ground ginger
2 teaspoons ground cardamom
1 teaspoon ground mace
1 teaspoon ground cinnamon
1 teaspoon ground allspice
1 teaspoon ground coriander
1 teaspoon ground nutmeg
1 teaspoon ground turmeric
1/2 teaspoon ground black pepper
1/2 teaspoon ground white pepper
1/2 teaspoon red chilli powder
1/2 teaspoon ground fennel seeds
1/2 teaspoon ground cloves

Mix all the ingredients together. Store in an airtight container and use within 6 months.

ROASTED CHANA DAL

Chana dal, or yellow split peas, are the most commonly used pulses in India. The whole yellow peas can be roasted until they puff up and split open. The husk is then discarded and the lentils are split and sold as roasted channa dal. These lentils are sold in powdered form in East India, under the name 'sattu', and are used as a filling for breads or for making a refreshing drink on hot summer days.

SAMBAL OLEK
(CONCENTRATED CHILLI PASTE)

200g small red chilies, stalk removed
200ml water
1 teaspoon salt
1 teaspoon sugar
1 tablespoon white wine vinegar
1 tablespoon vegetable oil

Put the chilli and the water in a pan. Bring to a simmer and cook for 15 minutes, covering part of the pan with a lid. Allow to cool slightly, then transfer to a food processor or blender. Add the salt, sugar and vinegar and blend to a fine paste. Cool, then transfer to a sterilised jar. Seal and refrigerate. Use within two weeks.

SEYCHELLES CURRY PASTE

MAKES APPROXIMATELY 5–6 TABLESPOONS

1 tablespoon coriander seeds
1 teaspoon ground cinnamon
3–4 dried red chillies
1 teaspoon allspice berries
1 teaspoon mild paprika or cayenne pepper
1 teaspoon black pepper
1 teaspoon ground turmeric
3 garlic cloves
1 teaspoon grated nutmeg
12–15 curry leaves
1 tablespoon vegetable oil
2 tablespoons lemon juice

Place all the ingredients in a blender with 3–4 tablespoons of water and blend to make a fine paste. Store in an airtight container in the fridge. Use within a week.

SOUTH AFRICAN CURRY POWDER

This curry powder has been developed in South Africa under the influence of Indians and Arabs alike. It is commonly used in most of the South African curries.

MAKES APPROXIMATELY 300G

150g cumin seeds
100g fennel seeds
50g peri-peri chillies
a 5cm piece of cinnamon stick
4 cloves
2–3 tablespoons black peppercorns
1 tablespoon ground turmeric

Toast the whole spices separately in a dry frying pan. Transfer to a plate to cool slightly. Grind in a pestle and mortar, spice grinder or coffee grinder to a fine powder, then mix in the ground turmeric. Store in an airtight container and use within 6 months.

TAMARIND PASTE AND TAMARIND WATER

The long, dark pods of the tropical tamarind tree are used in cooking as a souring agent. They are usually sold dried in compressed blocks. Ready-made tamarind paste is available, but it is often salty and I think it is better to make your own. Break up a 200g pack of dried tamarind and soak in about 400ml hot water for 20 minutes or until softened. Using your fingers, mix the pods with the water, which will thicken to a pulp. Strain through a sieve into a bowl, pressing on the pulp in the sieve to extract as much flavour as possible. The resulting paste can be kept in the fridge for 2–3 weeks or can be frozen.

For a milder flavour, dilute the tamarind paste with water to make tamarind water – use two parts water to one part tamarind paste.

TOASTING AND GRINDING SPICES

Whole spices are often toasted before use to intensify their flavour. Put them in a dry, heavy-based frying pan over a medium heat and toast until they crackle and become aromatic, stirring occasionally or shaking the pan to prevent burning. Once toasted, spices lose their flavour quickly, so always toast just before using. It is good practice to leave your spices to cool before grinding them as the heat generated by grinding them will generate additional heat, which may continue to cook them. To grind spices, pound them in a pestle and mortar for the best flavour, or use a spice grinder, coffee grinder or mini food processor.

TURMERIC RICE

Turmeric rice is made in exactly the same way as boiled rice. You simply add 1/4 teaspoon of ground turmeric to the boiling water before adding the rice (if cooking about 400g rice; increase the turmeric if cooking more). The rice will be yellow in colour and will have a turmeric flavour.

VIETNAMESE CURRY POWDER

Vietnamese curry powder is hugely influenced by Chinese five spice powder (see above), though Vietnam is more spice-savvy than China, hence the Vietnamese have their own spice blends.

MAKES APPROXIMATELY 6–7 TABLESPOONS

4 star anise
2 teaspoons cumin seeds
1 tablespoon coriander seeds
8 cloves
2 bay leaves
3 tablespoons ground turmeric

2 teaspoons ground cinnamon
1 teaspoon ground nutmeg
1 teaspoon garlic powder
1/2 teaspoon red chilli powder
1 teaspoon annatto powder (optional)

Lightly toast the whole spices separately in a dry frying pan. Leave to cool, then tip into a spice grinder or coffee grinder with the powdered spices and grind to a fine powder. Pass through a fine sieve. Store in an airtight container and use within 6 months.

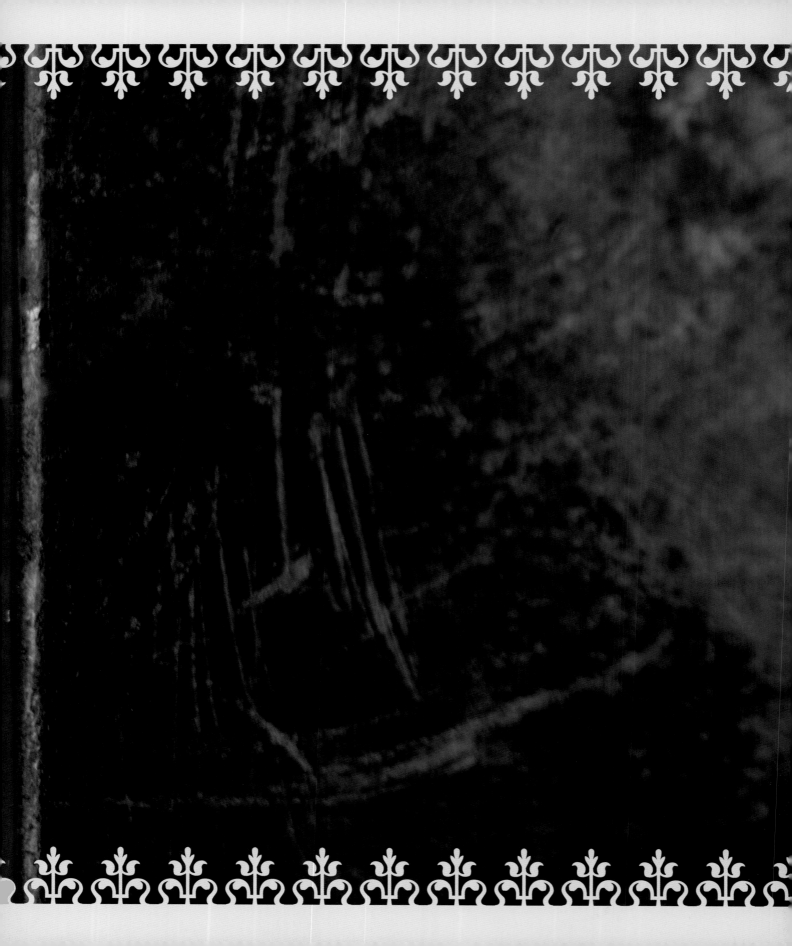

INDEX